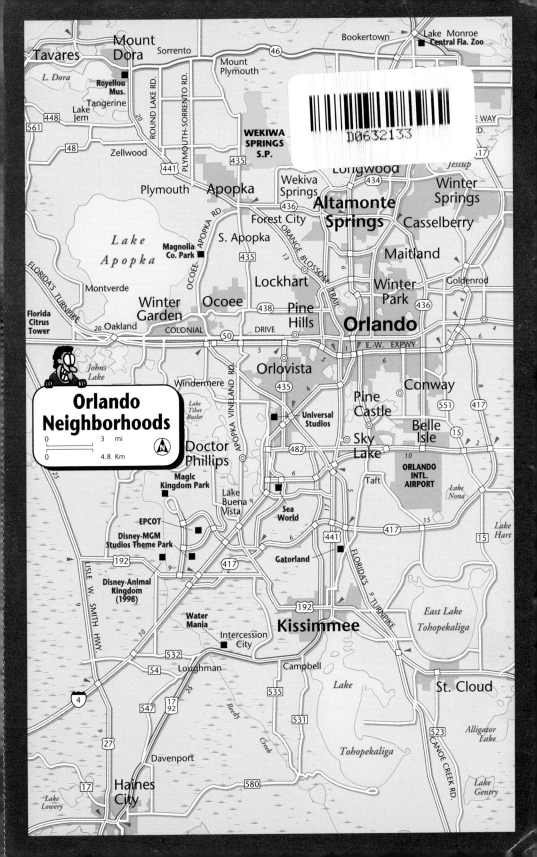

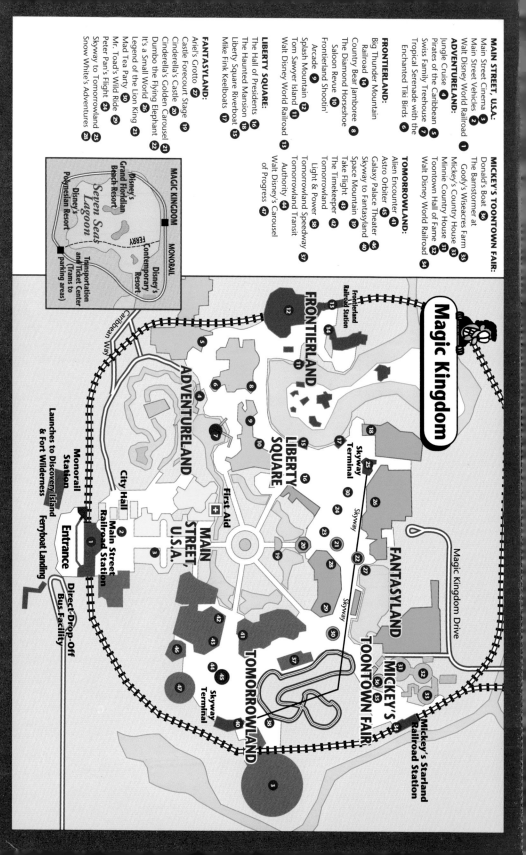

Magic Kingdom

MAGIC KINGDOM

Disney's Grand Floridian Beach Resort

Disney's Contemporary Resort

Seven Seas Lagoon

Disney's Polynesian Resort

MONORAIL

FERRY

Transportation
and Ticket Center
(Trams to
parking areas)

Frontierland
Railroad Station

FRONTIERLAND

ADVENTURELAND

Caribbean Way

LIBERTY SQUARE

Skyway Terminal

Skyway

Skyway

MAIN STREET, U.S.A.

City Hall

First Aid

Main Street Railroad Station

Entrance

Monorail Station

Direct Drop-Off Bus Facility

Launches to Discovery Island & Fort Wilderness

Ferryboat Landing

FANTASYLAND

MICKEY'S TOONTOWN FAIR

Mickey's Starland Railroad Station

Magic Kingdom Drive

TOMORROWLAND

Skyway Terminal

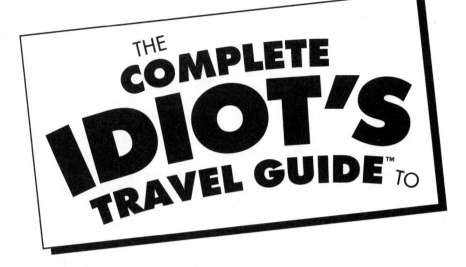

THE COMPLETE IDIOT'S TRAVEL GUIDE™ TO

Walt Disney World & Orlando

by Janet Groene
with Gordon Groene

Macmillan Travel   Alpha Books
Divisions of Macmillan Reference USA
A Simon & Schuster Macmillan Company
1633 Broadway, New York NY 10019-6785

ISBN 0-02-862298-7

ISSN 1096-7591

Editor: John Rosenthal
Production Editor: Lori Cates
Design by: designLab
Page Layout: Daniela Raderstorf
Proofreaders: Kim Cofer & Mary Hunt
Digital Cartography by Peter Bogaty & Ortelius Design
Illustrations by Kevin Spear

Special Sales
Bulk purchases (10+ copies) of Frommer's and selected Macmillan travel guides are available to corporations, organizations, mail-order catalogs, institutions, and charities at special discounts, and can be customized to suit individual needs. For more information write to: Special Sales, Macmillan General Reference, 1633 Broadway, New York, NY 10019-6785.

Manufactured in the United States of America

Contents

Part 4: Orlando's Best Restaurants   101

Part 5: Exploring Walt Disney World & Orlando   139

vii

Maps

About the Authors

 **Janet Groene** and her husband, **Gordon,** roamed full-time aboard their sloop, RV, and twin-engine airplane for 10 years before settling in Central Florida, where they are a full-time travel writing and photography team. They have published hundreds of newspaper and magazine features and more than a dozen books, including *52 Florida Weekends* and *Florida Under Sail* (Country Roads Press) and *Caribbean Guide* (Open Road Publishing). The Groenes won the NMMA Directors Award for boating journalism, and Janet won the Distinguished Achievement in RV Journalism for travel writing about recreation vehicles.

Janet is a member of the Society of American Travel Writers, Gordon is a member of the North American Travel Journalists Association, and both belong to the American Society of Journalists and Authors.

An Invitation to the Reader

In researching this book, we discovered many wonderful places—hotels, restaurants, shops, and more. We're sure you'll find others. Please tell us about them so that we can share the information with your fellow travelers in upcoming editions. If you were disappointed with a recommendation, we'd love to know that, too. Please write to:

Janet Groene & Gordon Groene
*The Complete Idiot's Travel Guide to
  Walt Disney World & Orlando*
Macmillan Travel
1633 Broadway
New York, NY 10019-6785

An Additional Note

Please be advised that travel information is subject to change at any time—and this is especially true of prices. We therefore suggest that you write or call ahead for confirmation when making your travel plans. The authors, editors, and publisher cannot be held responsible for the experiences of readers while traveling. Your safety is important to us, however, so we encourage you to stay alert and be aware of your surroundings. Keep a close eye on cameras, purses, and wallets, all favorite targets of thieves and pickpockets.

The following abbreviations are used for credit cards:

AE	American Express	EURO	Eurocard
CB	Carte Blanche	JCB	Japan Credit Bank
DC	Diners Club	MC	MasterCard
DISC	Discover	V	Visa
ER	enRoute		

Introduction

Hot dog! You're going to Orlando, one of the most popular destinations in the entire world. Even those of us who live here sometimes get lost on streets that seem to sprout up out of the orange groves overnight. We get furious at the traffic, and we are daunted by theme parks that seem to grow more overwhelming with each visit. So let's sort it out together.

You've made the first smart move by buying this book and starting from square one. You need to get into town; find just the right place to stay; and cram as much fun and adventure, and as many memories as possible into every day.

We aren't called the *Complete Idiot's Travel Guide* for nothing. You're not alone in feeling at a loss when faced with a choice of more than 90,000 hotel rooms, five major theme parks, six mammoth water parks, 4,000 restaurants, and enough attractions to fill an encyclopedia. By comparison to Walt Disney World, which covers 40 square miles, Disneyland in California is a postage stamp. And Disney World is only a fraction of Orlando's total picture.

Yet Orlando can give you and your family more dazzle for the vacation dollar than any city on Earth. All it takes is some insider savvy, which we are about to provide.

It's our goal to take you step by step through planning your trip to Orlando, getting around the city, mastering the transportation monster, and wringing the most out of every minute and every dollar you devote to theme parks, restaurant meals, hotels, excursions, admissions, and entertainment.

That's why we're going to narrow down the choices to the very best—not necessarily the most expensive or luxurious, but those that offer the most convenience, fun, or value, whatever your budget and your interests. If it's romance you are seeking, we'll tell you how to get married in a Cinderella setting complete with horse-drawn carriage. If you're bringing tots, we'll tell you about petting zoos and playgrounds. Older children? Orlando has one of the best, most hands-on science museums in the nation. Teens? Senior citizens? We have advice for the most diverse families.

Part 1 answers all those nagging questions you've been asking yourself, such as when to go, how to get there, whether to buy a package, and how much it's all going to cost. It also gives you addresses, phone numbers, and Web sites where you can get more information.

Part 2 is all about hotels. We discuss the various places you can stay around Orlando and Walt Disney World, and we pose questions to help you decide what kind of accommodations you want and what your needs are. A special feature of this book is the use of indexes so that you don't have to read a hundred hotel reviews, but rather just the ones in your preferred neighborhood and price range.

Part 3 is about geography—where things are and how to get around. The various areas of Orlando are described in terms of their convenience to the attractions.

Part 4 is all about food, from hot-dog and burger stands in the parks to sit-down dinners in fine dining rooms. Once again, indexes are provided to help you narrow down your choices.

Part 5 describes the attractions of Orlando. There's a separate chapter on each of the biggest parks, and information about non-theme-park things to see and do while you're here. To help you fit in all that you want to see without getting worn out, we provide some sample itineraries for each park and then lead you through the process of planning an itinerary of your own.

Part 6 belongs to the night. It's all about what to see and do once you've put the kids to bed. We steer you to the hottest bars, clubs, and theaters, as well as some of Orlando's prime cultural attractions.

Extras

This book has several special features that you won't find in other guide-books and that will help you make better use of the information provided and do it faster.

As mentioned above, **indexes** cross-section the information in ways that let you see at a glance what your options are in a particular subcategory—Italian restaurants, downtown hotels, hotels for people with disabilities, and so on.

We've also sectioned off little tidbits of useful information in **sidebars,** which come in several types:

Beating the Lines

These tips will help you spend more of your vacation on the rides and in the shows and less of it waiting in line.

Time-Savers

Here you'll find ways to cut down on downtime, avoid lines and hassles, and streamline the business of traveling.

Tourist Traps

These boxes steer you away from rip-offs, activities that aren't worth it, shady dealings, and pitfalls.

Dollars & Sense

Here you'll find tips on saving money and cutting corners to make your enjoyable trip affordable.

Extra! Extra!

Check these boxes for handy facts, hints, and insider advice.

Bet You Didn't Know

These boxes offer you interesting historical facts or trivia about the city.

Sometimes the best way to fix something in your mind is to write it down, and with that in mind we've provided **worksheets** to help you concretize your thinking and make your decisions. (Underlining or highlighting as you read along isn't a bad idea, either.)

A **kid-friendly icon** is used throughout the book to identify those activities, attractions, and establishments that are especially suited to people traveling with children.

The **Appendix** at the back of the book lists important numbers and addresses covering every aspect of your trip, from reservations to emergencies.

Part 1

Be Prepared: What You Need to Do Before You Go

Planning your upcoming trip to Orlando is half the fun. Just looking ahead to beautiful sunny days spent worrying about nothing more serious than whether to ride the monorail before or after lunch should boost your spirits. So get ready. You've got a lot of fun ahead of you, but a lot of choices to make. None of them is rocket science, but thinking about them in advance will help you get the most out of your vacation, which, no matter how rich or flexible you are, is sure to be limited by time, money, or both. Start as early as possible—months in advance isn't too early. The sooner you take care of the little details, the sooner you can relax and enjoy the fun of counting down the days till you meet Mickey.

You can plan your trip with the help of countless Web sites and toll-free telephone numbers. Like a kid in a candy store, you may feel overwhelmed by the bushels of information available to you. It's our goal to help you pare down those bushels to bouquets, then to neat little nosegays.

Chapter 1

How to Get Started

> ### In This Chapter
>
> ➤ Where to get information before you leave home
>
> ➤ When should you go?
>
> ➤ Tips for travelers with special needs

Devil-may-care types might just blunder into town and take what comes, but you'll make better use of your time and money if you start as early as possible to shop for hotel rates, airfares, rental-car reservations, and, most importantly, packages combining all of the above.

If you're an organizational freak, pick a spare corner of a bookshelf, countertop, or drawer and make it your battle station for attacking Orlando. Then arm yourself with a notebook, highlighters, Post-its, and a shoe box or folder to hold loose materials like maps and brochures as they arrive. Or if you prefer, just stick everything inside the covers of this book (we already have nearly all the maps, hotel and restaurant reviews, and travel advice you could possibly want), and leave it someplace conspicuous to remind yourself of the fun you're going to have.

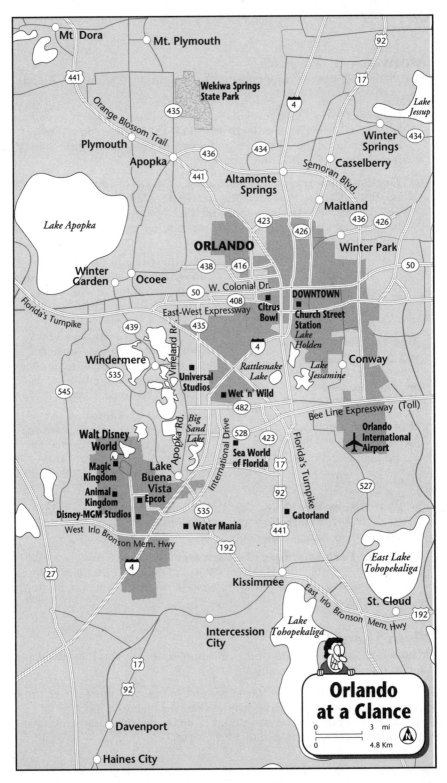

Information, Please

More than a half-dozen visitor bureaus provide information on the Orlando area.

➤ **Central Florida Convention & Visitors Bureau,** 600 N. Broadway, Suite 300, Bartow, FL 33830 (☎ **941/534-4375**): Here you can get information on the attractions and accommodations along the I-40 corridor between Orlando and Tampa.

➤ **Florida Department of Commerce,** Division of Tourism, Visitor Inquiries, 126 Van Buren St., Tallahassee, FL 32399-2000 (☎ **904/ 487-1462**): Request a state map and the *Florida Vacation Planner.* If you have special interests such as camping, birding, or biking, ask for additional brochures on these topics.

Bet You Didn't Know

The Orlando Sentinel, the region's major daily newspaper, can be accessed on the Web at www.orlandosentinel. com. It's an excellent source of information about upcoming special events and shows.

➤ **Orlando/Orange County Convention & Visitors Bureau,** 8723 International Dr., Suite 101, Orlando, FL 32891 (☎ **407/ 363-5871;** www.goflorida.com/ orlando): Ask for maps, brochures, visitors guides, and the "Magicard" discount booklet, which is good for deals on admissions, meals, rental cars, and accommodations.

➤ **Kissimmee–St. Cloud Convention & Visitors Bureau,** 1925 E. Irlo Bronson Memorial Hwy. (U.S. 192), Kissimmee, FL 34744 (☎ **800/327-9159** or 407/847-5000; www.floridakiss.com).

➤ **Walt Disney World Co.,** Box 10000, Lake Buena Vista, FL 32830-1000 (☎ **407/934-7639;** www.disneyworld.com): Request the *Walt Disney World Vacations* brochure.

➤ **Winter Park Chamber of Commerce,** 150 E. New York Ave. (P.O. Box 280), Winter Park, FL 32790 (☎ **407/644-8281**): Handles information requests about the trendy, historic Winter Park area, 5 miles north of Orlando.

When Should I Go?

Orlando is obscenely hot and steamy in summer. So why do all those people stand in line and sweat in August?

Because they've got kids. Any time kids aren't in school—summer, Christmas vacation, spring break, or any holiday weekend—Orlando is mobbed. At these times, you can bank on two things more certain than death and taxes: higher hotel prices and longer lines at the parks.

Beating the Lines

Many savvy parents take their kids out of school a few days before or after holidays and vacations, to visit the Orlando area before or after the most crowded times. Some schools allow it, especially if your trip will include a visit to an educational attraction on which the child can write a report, such as the Orlando Science Center or Ocala National Forest.

But Orlando can also fill to the brim at less predictable times. Big conventions and sporting events (some as far away as Daytona Beach, like the Daytona 500) make hotel rooms scarce and pricey. Sometimes going a week earlier or later can make all the difference in the price you pay. Ask the hotel for prices on different dates, and be flexible if you can.

Slack times (well, relatively speaking) at the theme parks include the period just after Thanksgiving until mid-December, when the parks glitter with holiday activities and decorations. You have all the hoopla of the holidays without the crowds. The parks are also less crowded during the 6 weeks before and after spring breaks. Mondays tend to be more crowded than later days in the week because most people on package tours arrive then.

Central Florida Average Temperatures

	Jan	Feb	Mar	Apr	May	June	July	Aug	Sept	Oct	Nov	Dec
High °F	71.7	72.9	78.3	83.6	88.3	90.6	91.7	91.6	89.7	84.4	78.2	73.1
°C	22.0	22.7	25.7	28.7	31.3	32.5	33.2	33.1	32.0	29.1	25.7	22.8
Low °F	49.3	50.0	55.3	60.3	66.2	71.2	73.0	73.4	72.5	65.4	56.8	50.9
°C	9.6	10.0	12.5	15.7	19.0	21.8	22.7	23.0	22.5	18.6	13.8	10.5

From the middle of June to the middle of September, weather forecasts vary hardly at all. Highs are in the 90s accompanied by cloying humidity and afternoon thundershowers that leave the theme parks washed, sparkly, and cool. After sundown, it's usually comfortable, unless the rains come too early and the sun comes out again before evening, creating another steam bath.

Spring and fall weather is best, with long dry spells and infrequent rains. Winter weather in Orlando (mid-September through mid-June) is just about perfect. Most days are shirtsleeve-warm, except during cold fronts, which usually give several days' notice before plunging the mercury to the 20s or 30s. It isn't long before warm, dry, sunshine is back again, but that's not much comfort if your vacation happens to coincide with a cold snap. Annual rainfall is 51 inches, and it rains on an average of 116 days each year.

Tourist Traps

Stock up on featherweight rain ponchos or folding umbrellas at a discount store, and carry them with you at all times. If you have to buy one during a downpour at a tourist attraction, you'll get soaked on the price.

Orlando Calendar of Events

Believe it or not, this is only a sampling of the biggies—there are even more special events and festivals all year long. But these are the ones you may want to attend—or the times to avoid the crowds.

January

➤ **CompUSA Florida Citrus Bowl.** A major college football game, held in downtown Orlando. Tickets go on sale in late October or early November. Call ☎ **407/423-2476** for information, 407/839-3900 for tickets.

February

➤ **The Silver Spurs Rodeo.** Check out real cowboys in contests of calf roping, bull and bronco riding, barrel racing, and more—it's a glimpse of the area's personality, pre-Disney. It's held at the Silver Spurs Arena, 1875 E. Irlo Bronson Memorial Hwy. (U.S. 192) in Kissimmee, on the third weekend in February. Call ☎ **407/847-5000** for details.

March

➤ **Kissimmee Bluegrass Festival.** Major bluegrass and gospel entertainers from all over the country perform at this 4-day event, beginning the first weekend of March at the Silver Spurs Arena, 1875 E. Irlo Bronson Memorial Hwy. Tickets are $12 to $20; multiday packages are available. Call ☎ **800/473-7773** for details.

Bet You Didn't Know

Shamu, the killer whale at Sea World, eats more than 65,000 pounds of fish per year.

➤ **The Central Florida Fair.** During 11 days in early March (some years beginning late February), the fair, held at the Central Florida Fairgrounds, 4603 W. Colonial Dr., features rides, entertainers, 4-H and livestock exhibits, a petting zoo, and food booths. Call ☎ **407/295-3247** for details.

➤ **Bay Hill Invitational.** Hosted by Arnold Palmer, this PGA Tour event is held in mid-March at the Bay Hill Club, 9000 Bay Hill Blvd. Call ☎ **407/876-2888** for details.

➤ **The Spring Flower Festival.** From March to May at Cypress Gardens, there are stunning displays of colorful plants, flowers, and imaginative topiaries. You have to pay admission to the park to get into the festival. Call ☎ **941/324-2111** for details.

April

➤ **Fringe Festival.** More than 100 diverse acts from around the world participate in this eclectic event, held for 10 days at various stages in downtown Orlando. Call ☎ **407/648-1333** for details.

➤ **Easter.** There's an interdenominational sunrise service at the Atlantis Theatre at Sea World, 7007 Sea World Dr. It is hosted by a well-known person each year, such as Elizabeth Dole. Admission is free. Call ☎ **407/351-3600** for details. Easter Sunday is celebrated in Walt Disney World with an old-fashioned Easter Parade and early opening/ late closing throughout the season. Call ☎ **407/824-4321** for details.

May

➤ **Epcot International Flower and Garden Festival.** A month-long event with theme gardens, topiary characters, special floral displays, speakers, and seminars.

June

➤ **Gay Weekend.** The first weekend in June draws tens of thousands of gay and lesbian travelers to Central Florida. In 1997, Universal City Travel offered a "Gay Weekend" tour package including tickets to Universal Studios, Sea World, and Church Street Station. This has all grown out of "Gay Day," which has been held unofficially at Walt Disney World for about 5 years, drawing upward of 40,000 folks. Special events throughout the weekend cater to gay and lesbian travelers throughout Central Florida. Universal City Travel offers special packages (☎ **800/224-3838** for information). Also, get information on the Web at www.gayday.com.

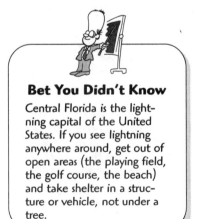

Bet You Didn't Know

Central Florida is the lightning capital of the United States. If you see lightning anywhere around, get out of open areas (the playing field, the golf course, the beach) and take shelter in a structure or vehicle, not under a tree.

➤ **Walt Disney World All-American College Orchestra and College Band.** The best collegiate musical talent in the country performs at Epcot and the Magic Kingdom throughout the summer. Call ☎ 407/824-4321 for details.

July

➤ **Independence Day.** Walt Disney World's Star-Spangled Spectacular brings bands, singers, dancers, and unbelievable fireworks displays to all the Disney parks, which stay open late. Call ☎ 407/824-4321 for details. Sea World also features a dazzling laser/fireworks spectacular; call ☎ 407/351-3600 for details.

➤ **The Silver Spurs Rodeo.** This event returns to Kissimmee every year over the July 4th weekend (see "February," above, for more information).

September

➤ **Night of Joy.** One weekend in September, the Magic Kingdom hosts a festival of contemporary Christian music featuring top artists. This is a very popular event; obtain tickets early. Admission to the concert is about $25 to $30 per night. Exclusive use of Magic Kingdom attractions is included. Call ☎ 407/824-4321 for details about the concert.

October

➤ **Halloween Horror Nights.** Universal Studios Florida transforms its studios and attractions for several weeks before Halloween—with haunted attractions, live bands, a psychopath's maze, special shows, and hundreds of ghouls and goblins roaming the studio streets. The studio essentially closes at dusk, reopening in a new macabre form an hour later. Special admission is charged. Call ☎ 407/363-8000 for details.

Bet You Didn't Know

There are enough mouse ears sold every year in the Disney parks to cover the head of every man, woman, and child in Pittsburgh.

➤ **Walt Disney World Oldsmobile Golf Classic.** Top PGA tour players compete for a $1 million purse at WDW golf courses; daily ticket prices range from $8 to $15. The event is preceded by the world's largest golf tournament, the admission-free Oldsmobile Scramble. Call ☎ 407/824-4321 for details.

November

➤ **Mum Festival.** November's month-long flower festival at Cypress Gardens features millions of colorful blooming mums. Call ☎ 941/324-2111 for details.

➤ **The Walt Disney World Festival of the Masters.** One of the largest art shows in the South takes place at Disney's Village Marketplace for 3 days, including the second weekend in November. The exhibition features top artists, photographers, and craftspeople. Free admission. Call ☎ **407/824-4321** for details.

➤ **Walt Disney World Doll and Teddy Bear Convention.** The top doll and teddy-bear designers from around the world travel to WDW for this major November event. Call ☎ **407/824-4321** for details.

➤ **Jolly Holidays Dinner Shows.** From late November to mid-December, these all-you-can-eat events are offered at the Contemporary Resort's Fantasia Ballroom. A cast of more than 100 Disney characters, singers, and dancers performs in an old-fashioned Christmas extravaganza. Call ☎ **407/W-DISNEY** for details and ticket prices.

➤ **Poinsettia Festival.** A spectacular floral showcase of more than 40,000 red, white, and pink poinsettia blooms (including topiary reindeer) highlights this flower festival from late November to mid-January at Cypress Gardens. Call ☎ **941/324-2111** for details.

Bet You Didn't Know

Since Walt Disney World opened in 1971, the total miles logged by monorail trains in the area is equal to about 25 trips to the moon.

December

➤ **Christmas at Walt Disney World.** During the Walt Disney World Christmas Festivities, Main Street is lavishly decked out with lights and holly, and visitors are greeted by carolers. An 80-foot tree is illuminated by thousands of colored lights. Epcot and MGM Studios also offer special embellishments and entertainments throughout the holiday season, as do all Disney resorts. Some holiday highlights include **Mickey's Very Merry Christmas Party,** an after-dark event with admission of about $25. This takes place weekends at the Magic Kingdom with a traditional Christmas parade and a breathtaking fireworks display; the admission price includes free cookies and cocoa and a souvenir photo. The best part? Short lines to the rides. **The Candlelight Procession** at Epcot features hundreds of candle-holding carolers, a celebrity narrator telling the Christmas story, and a 450-voice choir. Call ☎ **407/824-4321** for details about all of the above, 407/W-DISNEY to inquire about hotel/events packages. **The Osborne Family Christmas Lights** at Disney-MGM is a dazzling display of millions of twinkling lights.

➤ **Christmas at Sea World.** Sea World features a special Shamu show and a luau show called Christmas in Hawaii. The 400-foot sky tower is lit like a Christmas tree nightly. Call ☎ **407/351-3600** for details.

➤ **Walt Disney World New Year's Eve Celebration.** For 1 night, the Magic Kingdom is open until 2am for a massive fireworks exhibition. Other New Year's festivities in the WDW parks include a big bash at Pleasure Island featuring music headliners, a special Hoop-Dee-Doo Musical Revue show, and guest performances by well-known musical groups at Disney-MGM Studios and Epcot. Call ☎ **407/824-4321** for details.

➤ **The Citrus Bowl Parade.** On an annually selected date in late December, the parade features lavish floats and high-school bands for a nationally televised parade. Reserved seats in the bleachers are $12. Call ☎ **407/423-2476** for details.

➤ **CompUSA Florida Citrus Bowl New Year's.** The official New Year's Eve celebration of the CompUSA Florida Citrus Bowl takes place at Sea World. Events include headliner concerts, a laser and fireworks spectacular, a countdown to midnight, and special shows throughout the park. Admission is charged. Call ☎ **407/423-2476** for details.

We Are Family: Traveling with Your Kids

Orlando loves children and makes every effort to deliver a vacation that the kids will never forget (and hope some day to repeat). The children's programs at Orlando's hotels put those in other cities to shame, offering goody bags, children's activities, kiddy pools and playgrounds, and special room furnishings, including beds that look like rocket ships or bear caves. Even business hotels here are kid-savvy.

Time-Savers

Disney-MGM Studios and Universal Studios offer parent-swap programs in which parents take turns watching each others' kids while the other parents ride. Disney parks, Universal Studios, and Sea World all have play areas within the attractions for parents and kids to take a break.

In many hotels, kids also sleep and/or eat free and can get tucked in at night by a costumed character. All the theme parks and major malls have strollers for rent, and almost any hotel can find a reliable baby-sitter for you. The Orlando Science Museum is one of the best in the Southeast, offering hands-on play for children of all ages. Every restaurant has lower-priced kids' menus, and some will even let kids eat free.

Travel Tips for the Senior Set

According to 1996 figures (the latest available), empty nesters spent $161.10 average per person daily during an Orlando vacation, compared to $131.20 per person daily for the family visitor. And *that's* after the senior discounts they receive at many hotels, restaurants, and attractions. It's obvious that Orlando's charms are not limited to the younger generation. So it helps to carry a photo ID to prove you're a senior.

In addition, most of the major domestic airlines, including American, United, Continental, US Airways, and TWA, offer discount programs for senior travelers—be sure to ask whenever you book a flight.

The **American Association of Retired Persons** (AARP) offers discounts for members and spouses of any age. Many hotels, car-rental agencies, and restaurants in the Orlando area offer AARP discounts. Always ask. To join, contact **AARP,** 601 E St. NW, Washington, DC 20049 (☎ **202/434-AARP**).

Dollars & Sense

Walt Disney World parks don't offer senior discounts (they seem to have no problem luring the young at heart at regular prices), but almost all the other attractions do. Age limits vary, with some starting as young as age 50. Savings are usually 10%, sometimes more. The most generous discount is that at Cypress Gardens, which gives seniors $5 off the $29.50 admission (a 17% discount).

Mature Outlook, P.O. Box 9390, Des Moines, IA 50306-9519 (☎ **800/ 336-6330;** fax 847/286-5024) offers discounts on car rentals and hotel stays at many Holiday Inns, Howard Johnsons, and Best Westerns. The $20 annual membership fee also gets you $100 in Sears coupons and a bimonthly magazine. Membership is open to all Sears customers 18 and over, but the organization's primary focus is on the 50-and-over market.

The Mature Traveler, a monthly 12-page newsletter on senior citizen travel, is available by subscription ($30 a year) from GEM Publishing Group, Box 50400, Reno, NV 89513-0400. GEM also publishes *The Book of Deals,* a collection of more than 1,000 senior discounts on airlines, lodging, tours, and attractions around the country; it's available for $9.95 by calling ☎ **800/460-6676.** Another helpful publication is *101 Tips for the Mature Traveler,* available from Grand Circle Travel, 347 Congress St., Suite 3A, Boston, MA 02210 (☎ **800/221-2610** or 617/350-7500; fax 617/350-6206).

Grand Circle Travel is also one of the literally hundreds of travel agencies specializing in vacations for seniors. But beware: Many of them are of the tour-bus variety, with free trips thrown in for those who organize groups of 20 or more. Seniors seeking more independent travel should probably consult a regular travel agent. **SAGA International Holidays,** 222 Berkeley St., Boston, MA 02116 (☎ **800/343-0273**), offers inclusive tours and cruises for those 50 and older.

Access Orlando:
Advice for Travelers with Disabilities

A disability shouldn't stop anybody from traveling to the Orlando area. And today, there are more options and resources for disabled travelers than ever before. *A World of Options,* a 658-page book of resources for disabled travelers, covers everything from biking trips to scuba outfitters. It costs $45 and is available from **Mobility International USA,** P.O. Box 10767, Eugene, OR 97440 (☎ **541/343-1284,** voice and TDD; www.miusa.org). For more personal assistance, call the **Travel Information Service** at ☎ **215/ 456-9603,** or 215/456-9602 for TTY.

Many of the major car-rental companies now offer hand-controlled cars for disabled drivers. Avis can provide such a vehicle at any of its locations in the United States with 48-hour advance notice; Hertz requires between 24 and 72 hours of advance reservation at most of its locations.

Extra! Extra!

Wheelchair Wagon Express, Box 700637, St. Cloud, FL 43770 (☎ **407/ 957-2044;** fax 407/ 957-2043), provides transportation for people in wheelchairs. For barrier-free vacation packages in Orlando, check out the Web site www.barrier-free-vacations.com. It can book you in a hotel room that has a roll-in shower.

You can rent wheelchair vans by calling **Wheelers Inc.** (☎ **407/826-0616**) or **Vantage Mini Vans** (☎ **407/ 521-8002**). **Wheelchair Getaways** (☎ **800/873-4973;** www.blvd.com/ wg.htm) rents specialized vans with wheelchair lifts and other features for the disabled in more than 100 cities across the United States.

All public buses in Orlando are wheelchair accessible. The buses serve Universal Studios, Sea World, the shopping areas, and downtown Orlando. Disney offers special shuttle buses to and from their hotels that can accommodate wheelchairs.

Travelers with disabilities may also want to consider joining a tour that caters specifically to them. One of the best operators is **Flying Wheels Travel,** 143 W. Bridge (P.O. Box 382), Owatonna, MN 55060 (☎ **800/525-6790**). This company offers various escorted tours and cruises, as well as private tours in minivans with lifts. Another good company is **FEDCAP Rehabilitation Services,** 211 W. 14th St., New York, NY 10011. Call ☎ **212/727-4200** or fax 212/721-4374 for information about membership and summer tours.

By Florida law, every hotel and motel must have at least one wheelchair-accessible room, and a few, including **Best Western Buena Vista Suites** (☎ 407/239-8588), **Embassy Suites** (☎ 407/239-1144), and **Sleep Inn** (☎ 407/396-1600), have wheel-in showers. If you're looking for rock-bottom rates, **Hostelling International Orlando/Kissimmee Resort** is wheelchair accessible. It has a pool, a lake, air-conditioning, and en suite bathrooms. Rates are $14 per person. Contact **Hostelling International,** 733 15th St. NW #840, Washington, DC 20005 (☎ 202/783-6161; fax 202/783-6171; Web site www.taponline.com). Make your special needs known when making reservations.

Accessibility at the Parks

Most attractions at the various theme parks, especially newer ones, are designed to be accessible to a wide variety of people. People with wheelchairs and their parties are often given preferential treatment so that they can avoid long lines. Of course, they also get the parking spaces closest to the entrance.

Walt Disney World is extremely accommodating to disabled guests. They even publish a *Guidebook for Guests with Disabilities.* To obtain a copy, call ☎ **407/824-4321.** Some examples of Disney services:

➤ Almost all Disney resorts have rooms for those with disabilities.

➤ Braille directories are located inside the Magic Kingdom in front of the Main Street train station and in a gazebo in front of the Crystal Palace restaurant.

➤ Complimentary guided-tour audiocassette tapes and recorders are available at Guest Services to assist visually impaired guests.

➤ Personal translator units are available to amplify the audio at selected Epcot attractions (inquire at Earth Station).

Universal Studios also publishes a *Disabled Guest Guidebook,* rents wheelchairs, and provides information about Telecommunications Devices for the Deaf (TDD). Universal also provides audio descriptions on cassette for visually impaired guests and has sign-language guides and scripts for all its shows (advanced notice is required; call ☎ **407/363-8000** for details).

Most of the attractions at **Sea World** are easily accessible to those in wheelchairs. Sea World provides a Braille guide for the visually impaired. It also provides a very brief synopsis of shows for the hearing impaired. For information, call ☎ **407/351-2600.**

Out & About: Advice for Gay & Lesbian Travelers

The Gay Weekend started by Walt Disney World some years ago, always held the first weekend in June, has spread to other theme parks and attractions and now brings more than 40,000 visitors to the area. It has its own Web site at **www.gayday.com**.

The local gay newspaper is ***The Triangle,*** which you'll find on newsstands or by calling ☎ **407/425-4527** or 407/849-0099.

For additional information, contact **Gay & Lesbian Community Services,** 714 E. Colonial Dr., Orlando, FL 32084 (☎ **407/THE-GAYS**).

Accommodations that cater to gays and lesbians include the **Parliament House Motor Inn,** 410 N. Orange Blossom Trail (☎ **407/425-7571**), which is boisterous around the clock and maybe a little on the seedy side, and the more sedate **A Veranda Bed and Breakfast,** 115 N. Summerlin Ave. (☎ **800/420-6822** or 407/849-0321). This downtown cluster of cottages offers five units, each with its own entrance, cable TV, and telephone with answering machine.

Money Matters

We wish we could tell you that a trip to Orlando can be done on a wing and a prayer, but the puppet masters of the world's most-visited tourist destination are geniuses at separating tourists from their wallets. They know that this is your trip of a lifetime, and they bank on the fact that your kids will be begging for a Mickey Mouse T-shirt, or that you and your new spouse will decide to end your honeymoon at Victoria and Albert's with a $110 fixed-price dinner.

So let's discuss portable funds, keeping them safe, and squeezing every nickel until the buffalo yells "uncle."

Should I Carry Traveler's Checks or the Green Stuff?

Traveler's checks are something of an anachronism from the days when people used to write personal checks all the time instead of going to the ATM. In those days, travelers could not be sure of finding a place that would cash a check for them on vacation. Because they could be replaced if lost or stolen, traveler's checks were a sound alternative to filling your wallet with cash at the beginning of a trip.

Bet You Didn't Know

Orlando has more than 82,000 hotel rooms and is still growing. By the turn of the century, Universal Studios alone will add 13,000 rooms.

These days, traveler's checks are less necessary because most cities have 24-hour ATMs linked to a national network that most likely includes your bank at home. **Cirrus** (☎ **800/424-7787** or 800/4CIRRUS) and **Plus** (☎ **800/843-7587**) are the two most popular networks; check the back of your ATM card to see which network your bank belongs to. The 800-numbers will give you specific locations of ATMs where you can withdraw money while on vacation. You should withdraw only as much cash as you need every couple of days so that you don't feel insecure carrying around a huge wad of cash.

Tourist Traps

Note, however, that many banks have begun to impose a fee ranging from 50¢ to $3 every time you use the ATM in a different city. Your own bank may also charge you a fee for using ATMs from other banks. Also keep in mind that some cards have a *daily* withdrawal limit regardless of your balance. Don't let your cash reserves get too low.

Still, if you feel you need the security of traveler's checks and don't mind the hassle of showing identification every time you want to cash a check, you can get them at almost any bank. **American Express** offers checks in denominations of $10, $20, $50, $100, $500, and $1,000. You'll pay a service charge ranging from 1% to 4%, though AAA members can obtain checks without a fee at most AAA offices. You can also get American Express traveler's checks over the phone by calling ☎ **800/221-7282;** American Express gold and platinum cardholders who call this number are exempt from the 1% fee.

Visa also offers traveler's checks, available at Citibank locations across the country and at several other banks. The service charge ranges between 1.5% and 2%; checks come in denominations of $20, $50, $100, $500, and $1,000. **MasterCard** also offers traveler's checks. Call ☎ **800/223-9920** for a location near you.

ATMs to the Left of Me, ATMs to the Right of Me
In Central Florida you're never far from an ATM machine. ATMs belonging to major networks can be found at every major mall in greater Orlando, at banks, on Main Street and in Tomorrowland in the Magic Kingdom, in the

Disney Crossroads Shopping Center, at the WDW All-Star Sports Resort, at Disney-MGM Studios, at Epcot, at Pleasure Island, at Sea World, and at Universal Studios, as well as at most of the area's Circle K and 7-11 convenience stores. There's a real bank, a **Sun Trust,** on Main Street in the Magic Kingdom and at 1675 Buena Vista Dr. across from Disney Village. Both branches are open weekdays 9am to 4pm, Thursdays until 6pm.

Plastic

Credit cards are invaluable when traveling. They are a safe way to carry money and provide a convenient record of all your travel expenses when you arrive home.

Disney parks, resorts, shops, and restaurants (though not the fast-food outlets) all accept American Express, MasterCard, and Visa.

In addition, Disney hotel guests get a charge card that can be used to charge everything within Walt Disney World to the hotel room. There is also a Disney credit card, available through any Disney store, that can be used at any Disney store, catalog, restaurant, or vacation property.

You can also get **cash advances** off your credit cards at any bank (though you'll start paying interest on the advance the moment you receive the cash, and you won't receive frequent-flyer miles on an airline credit card). At most banks, you don't even need to go to a teller; you can get a cash advance at the ATM if you know your PIN number. If you've forgotten your PIN number or didn't even know you had one, call the phone number on the back of your credit card and ask the bank to send it to you. It usually takes 5 to 7 business days, though some banks will do it over the phone if you tell them your mother's maiden name or pass some other security clearance.

Tourist Traps

Disney Dollars, currency imprinted with Disney characters instead of presidents, come in denominations of $1, $5, and $10. They are redeemable like cash anywhere throughout the Disney universe, but they're not worth any more than regular dollars and they're not worth the hassle. They just mean waiting in two more lines: once when you buy them and once when you cash them in.

Stop, Thief!
(What to Do If Your Money Gets Stolen)

Orlando's wholesome, friendly image persuades many travelers to let their guard down, often with disastrous results. Crimes against tourists are one of Central Florida's biggest problems, so don't become a statistic. Take the same precautions you would take at home. For those of you who live on Walton's

Mountain, that means use ATMs only in well-lighted areas, shield your numbers from prying eyes, and don't put anything in the trash that has your account number or other personal information on it.

Bet You Didn't Know

Plenty of coins are dropped in Disney fountains as visitors stop to make a wish. To literally squeeze every dime out of its operations, Disney has devised an elaborate mechanical system to get that change out of the fountains and back into the tills of its restaurants and stores—dried, sorted, and rolled—sometimes by the end of the day.

Almost every credit-card company has an emergency 800-number you can call if your wallet or purse is stolen. They may be able to wire you a cash advance off your credit card immediately, and in many places, they can get you an emergency credit card in a day or two. The issuing bank's 800-number is usually on the back of the credit card. (That doesn't help you much if the card was stolen, so just call 800-information—that's **800/555-1212**—to find out the number.) **Citicorp Visa**'s U.S. emergency number is ☎ **800/ 645-6556. American Express** cardholders and traveler's check holders should call ☎ **800/221-7282** for all money emergencies. **MasterCard** holders should call ☎ **800/307-7309.**

Dollars & Sense

Set a spending limit. Kids should know they have a set amount to spend on souvenirs and toys. So should Mom and Dad.

If you opt to carry traveler's checks, be sure to keep a record of their serial numbers so that you can handle just such an emergency.

Odds are that if your wallet is gone, you've seen the last of it, and the police aren't likely to recover it for you. However, after you realize that it's gone and you cancel your credit cards, it is still worth a call to inform the police. You may need the police report number for credit-card or insurance purposes later.

So, What's This Trip Gonna Cost?

That's a complicated question, but the answer is, probably, more than you originally thought. The average family spends enough money in a day at Walt Disney World to make a Third-World nation envious. Even if you stay at modestly priced hotels, skip the most expensive restaurants, drink nothing but water all day, and refrain from buying a life-size Shamu doll that has to be shipped home in a moving van, a trip to Orlando can add up quickly. Admission prices and parking at the theme parks alone for a family of four can set you back close to $200 per day.

But before you start to panic, remember, there are lots of ways to save money, and we're here to share them with you throughout this book. Look especially for sidebars called "Dollars & Sense" for some smart consumer tips.

And we can make some educated guesses about your final vacation bill depending on the hotel you choose. So when you plan your vacation budget (see the worksheet at the end of this chapter), start with your hotel room. All the other pieces will fall into place much more easily.

Dollars & Sense

Entertainment Publications, Inc., offers a book of deep discounts for Orlando hotels, restaurants, airfares, and attractions. The book, which sells for $34.95, will pay for itself during your first few days in Florida. Call ☎ **800/374-4464** to order it.

Lodging

Your choice of hotel will determine many other costs, including:

➤ Whether you need a rental car always, sometimes, or not at all;

➤ Whether you must eat all meals in restaurants or can prepare simple breakfasts and lunches in your room;

➤ How much you pay in tips and taxes, which are charged as a percentage of the room rate;

➤ Whether you'll pay extra for children's activities.

Tips on Tipping

Generally tip 15% for restaurant service and cab rides; more if the service merits it. At the end of your stay, don't forget to tip the hotel housekeeper $1 to $2 each day for cleaning up your messes, making your beds, and keeping you supplied with fresh towels. Leave more than that if she has had to make extra beds, supply a crib, clean up after a pizza party, or vacuum up after your shedding dog.

A dollar should do for a hotel staffer who delivers the extra pillows or hair dryer you requested. If the doorman has been helpful, give him a few dollars when you arrive or leave, plus $1 when he hails a cab for you.

A dollar a bag is fair for luggage handlers, but if one person unloads your bag from the car and another carries it to your room, you don't need to tip both of them. Valet parking attendants get $1 to $2 for retrieving the car, though you may also be charged a hefty valet parking fee by the hotel. Theme park employees, except for restaurant servers or private tour guides, are not tipped.

Tourist Traps

Orlando, a former swamp, doesn't have mountains or oceans, so don't pay extra for a hotel room with a so-called view. Most hotels and all of WDW are so perfectly manicured that almost every room looks out on a beautiful scene.

All this assumes that gratuities are not already part of your package. If you pay a service charge on your hotel bill, that's supposed to cover all other tips to the bell staff and housekeeping. Always check hotel and restaurant bills to see whether an automatic service charge has been added. There's no point in tipping twice.

Transportation

Obviously, getting there is going to cost you either airfare or gas money. Whether you're flying or driving, refer to chapter 3 for more details on how to save serious dough. Since Orlando is such a major destination, many airlines offer competitive rates and frequent sales.

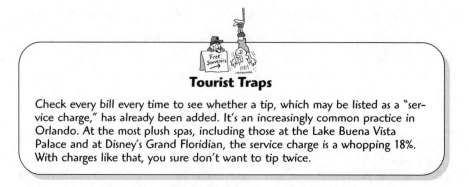

Tourist Traps

Check every bill every time to see whether a tip, which may be listed as a "service charge," has already been added. It's an increasingly common practice in Orlando. At the most plush spas, including those at the Lake Buena Vista Palace and at Disney's Grand Floridian, the service charge is a whopping 18%. With charges like that, you sure don't want to tip twice.

Chapters 4 and 8 deal with rental cars, shuttle service, and other modes of transportation in Orlando. If you're renting a car, you can probably get a rate of $25 to $35 per day for a basic economy car.

But weigh the pros and cons of staying at a Disney resort. They usually have higher rates, but if you're going to concentrate your time in the Disney theme parks, you may not need a rental car at all, since free transportation to the parks is included.

What Things Cost in Orlando/Walt Disney World

Taxi from airport to WDW hotels, party of four	$40
Shuttle fare, airport to WDW, per adult	$14 one way; $25 round-trip
Bus fare from the airport to downtown	75¢
Cheapest room, cheapest season, WDW Grand Floridian Beach Resort	$284
Double room at Doubletree Resort & Conference Center	$99
Cheapest room, cheapest season, WDW All-Star Resort	$69
Campsite with full hookup at Fort Wilderness Resort	$43–$59
Bed and breakfast for two, Comfort Inn Maingate, low season	$37
Room that sleeps up to four, off season, Days Inn Maingate West	$29
Toll I-75 to I-4 or the Bee Line	$2.50
Burger, fries, and soda at fast-food restaurants in theme parks	$5–$7.50
Burger, fries and soda at fast-food restaurants outside theme parks	$2–$5
Chicken noodle soup at Race Rock Orlando	$4.50
Early-bird dinner, Kobé Japanese restaurants	$8.95
Popcorn in WDW parks	$2 single, $3.75 double, $4 triple
Five-day Park-Hopper Pass to WDW	$189 adults; $151 ages 3–9
Family pass, whole family, whole year, Orlando Science Center	$60
Dinner, drinks, and a show at Sleuths Mystery Dinner Show	$34.95 adults; $22.95 children ages 3–11
Evening admission, Pleasure Island	$17.95 (adults only)
Camp Holiday, Holiday Inn Main Gate East	$2/hour first child; $1/hour each additional child
Mouseketeer Club child care, WDW	$4/hour, 4-hour maximum Contemporary Resort
Evening child-care center WDW Polynesian Resort	$8/hour, 3-hour minimum

What If I'm Worried I Can't Afford It?

Stop worrying! You supply the common sense and we'll supply the insider tips that will help you shave the cost of your Orlando vacation. Here's a list of strategies to keep in mind:

➤ **Buy a package.** This doesn't mean an escorted tour, just a package of airfare and accommodations purchased together. When you're traveling to the Orlando area, packages are a must. You can book airfare, hotel, ground transportation, and even some sightseeing just by making one call to a travel agent or packager for a lot less than if you tried to put the trip together yourself. See chapter 3 for details on the leading package tour operators that will get you to Orlando.

Dollars & Sense

The **Magic Kingdom Club Gold Card** program ($45 per person annually and free for many government employees) brings discounts on WDW lodgings and tick-ets. Call ☎ **714/490-3200** or write Magic Kingdom Club, P.O. Box 3850, Anaheim, CA 92803.

➤ **Go in the off-season.** If you can travel at nonpeak times (September through November, or April through June, for example), you'll find hotel prices that are as much as half off the prices offered during peak months.

➤ **Travel on off days of the week.** Airfares vary depending on the day of the week. Staying over on a Saturday night can cut your airfare by more than half. If you can travel on a Tuesday, Wednesday, or Thursday, you may find cheaper flights to your destination. When you inquire about airfares, ask whether you can obtain a cheaper rate by flying on a different day.

➤ **Always ask for corporate, weekend, or other discount rates.** Membership in AAA, frequent-flyer plans, trade unions, AARP, or other groups may qualify you for discounted rates on car rentals, plane tick-ets, hotel rooms, even meals. Ask about everything; you could be pleas-antly surprised.

➤ **Ask whether your kids can stay in your room with you free.** A room with two double beds usually doesn't cost any more than one with a queen-size bed. And many hotels won't charge you the addition-al person rate if the additional person is pint-sized and related to you. Even if you have to pay $10 or $15 for a rollaway bed, you'll save hun-dreds by not taking two rooms.

➤ **Reserve a hotel room with a kitchen and do your own cook-ing.** It's not much of a vacation for the family chef or dishwasher, but you'll save a lot of money by not eating in restaurants three times a day. Even if you make only breakfast and an occasional bag lunch in the kitchen, you'll still save in the long run. And you'll never be shocked by a hefty room-service bill.

➤ **If you have a multiday pass to a theme park, in-and-out privileges are permitted.** Go back to your hotel for a picnic lunch and a swim or nap. You'll eat economically, miss the midday sun, and be fueled for a gala dinner and evening at the park.

➤ **Stock up on drinks yourself.** If your room doesn't have a refrigerator, buy a disposable foam cooler in a discount store, and keep juices, milk, and sodas on ice in your room and car. A small orange juice at a hotel sells for about $3.50; a bedtime glass of milk from room service can cost $5 or more. Ice is free in most hotels.

➤ **Pace yourself so you're not tempted to splurge.** Your money goes fastest when you are too hungry, too thirsty, or too tired to care. Start the day with a big breakfast, which will cost less at a fast-food restaurant than at your hotel, and less at your hotel than inside a theme park. Stop often at drinking fountains. Cold sodas in the attractions are sinfully overpriced. Leave the parks before you're too exhausted to use free transportation, which requires waiting and standing in line. Taxi fares are outrageous.

Dollars & Sense

Sales tax is not charged on supermarket food, but 6% to 7% tax is added to restaurant and take-out meals. So if you can prepare some of your meals in your suite or condo, you save doubly.

➤ **Brown-bag it to parks, the beach, and attractions that provide shady picnic areas.** Note, however, that the theme parks, ballparks, and some other attractions are wise to this scheme and won't let you bring in your own food or drinks.

➤ **Skip the fast food.** Deli sections in Orlando-area supermarkets sell ready-to-eat meals ranging from sandwiches and salads to full hot meals for much less than you'd pay at fast-food chains.

➤ **Try expensive restaurants at lunch, not dinner.** And don't forget to check out early-bird specials.

➤ **Pick up every free tourist magazine you see.** They all contain coupons for savings on restaurants and tickets.

➤ **You don't have to spend every day at a theme park.** Discover your hotel's pool, sundeck, playground, gardens, workout facilities, get-togethers, and other freebies.

➤ **Don't send clothes to the hotel laundry.** The bills will be out of sight. The hotel may have a coin-op machine for guest use.

➤ **Who needs souvenirs?** They're usually overpriced and you don't have room in your luggage anyway. If you're on a budget, here's a place to tighten up.

Budget Worksheet: You Can Afford This Trip	
Expense	Amount
Airfare (× no. of people traveling)	
Car rental (if applicable)	
Lodging (× no. of nights)	
Parking (× no. of nights)	
Breakfast may be included in your room rate (× no. of nights)	
Lunch (× no. of nights)	
Dinner (× no. of nights)	
Baby-sitting and resort's kiddy programs	
Attractions (admission charges to museums, theme parks, tours, theaters, nightclubs, etc.)	
Transportation (cabs, theme-park shuttle, buses, etc.)	
Souvenirs (T-shirts, postcards, that antique you just gotta have)	
Tips (think 15% of your meal total plus $1 a bag every time a bellhop moves your luggage)	
Don't forget the cost of getting to and from the airport in your home town, plus long-term parking (× no. of nights)	
Grand Total	

How Will I Get There?

Getting there may not really be half the fun, but it doesn't have to be a hassle, either. Orlando is so totally geared for tourists that it's designed to get you started on your vacation quickly and efficiently. The Orlando airport is clean, modern, and bright, and it is served by most major airlines. Its highways connect to the interstate routes in all directions, putting you right in the heart of everything from the moment your plane lands.

Travel Agent: Friend or Foe?

A good travel agent is like a good mechanic or a good plumber: hard to find, but invaluable once you've found the right person. And the best way to find a good travel agent is the same way you find a good plumber or mechanic or doctor—word of mouth.

Any travel agent can help you find a bargain airfare, hotel, or rental car. A good travel agent will stop you from ruining your vacation by trying to save a few dollars. The best travel agents can tell you how much time you should budget in a destination, find you a cheap flight that doesn't require you to change planes in Atlanta and Chicago, get you a better hotel room for about the same price, arrange for a competitively priced rental car, and even give recommendations on restaurants.

Travel agents work on commission. The good news is that *you* don't pay the commission; the airlines, accommodations, and tour companies do. The bad news is that unscrupulous travel agents will try to persuade you to book the vacations that snap them the most money in commissions.

Bet You Didn't Know

In a recent year, guests at Universal Studios consumed 1,101,245 burgers and 131 miles of hot dogs.

To make sure you get the most out of your travel agent, do a little homework. Read about your destination (you've already made a sound decision by buying this book) and pick out some accommodations and attractions you think you like. If necessary, get a more comprehensive travel guide like Frommer's or the Unofficial Guide. If you have access to the Internet, check prices on the Web yourself in advance (see "Happy Landings: Winning the Airfare Wars," later in this chapter, for more information on how to do that) so that you can do a little prodding.

Then take your guidebook and Web information to the travel agent and ask him or her to make the arrangements for you. Because travel agents have access to more resources than even the most complete Web travel site, they should be able to get you a better price than you could get by yourself. And they can issue your tickets and vouchers right there. If they can't get you into the hotel of your choice, they can recommend an alternative, and you can look for an objective review in your guidebook right then and there. It's always more effective to be a well-informed consumer.

Dollars & Sense

Travel agents receive a commission from WDW, and they are a better source of information than WDW itself because (1) WDW doesn't have a toll-free number and (2) WDW agents answer your questions but do not volunteer any money-saving tips. Shop around among airlines, too. Delta, the big player in WDW packages, has just cut its travel-agent commission from 10% to 8%, but we don't yet know how this will affect travel agents' enthusiasm for booking with Delta.

In the past two years, some airlines and resorts have begun limiting or eliminating travel-agent commissions altogether. The immediate result has been that travel agents don't bother booking these services unless the customer specifically requests them. But some travel-industry analysts predict that if other airlines and accommodations throughout the industry follow suit, travel agents may have to start charging customers for their services. When that day arrives, the best agents should prove even harder to find.

After you've read all the information below on package tours, you can let your travel agent book the same airline package (at no added cost to you) plus add-ons such as airport transfers and side trips.

The Pros & Cons of Package Tours

Package tours are not the same thing as escorted tours. They are simply a way of buying your airfare and accommodations at the same time. And for popular destinations like Orlando, they are really the smart way to go, because they save you a ton of money. In many cases, a package that includes airfare, hotel, and transportation to and from the airport will cost you less than just the hotel alone if you booked it yourself.

That's because packages are sold in bulk to tour operators, who resell them to the public. It's kind of like buying your vacation at Sam's Club, except that it's the tour operator who buys the 1,000-count box of garbage bags and resells them 10 at a time at a cost that undercuts what you'd pay at your average neighborhood supermarket.

Packages vary as much as garbage bags, too. Some packages offer a better class of hotels than others. Some offer the same hotels for lower prices. Some offer flights on scheduled airlines, whereas others book charters. In some packages, your choices of accommodations and travel days may be limited. Some packages let you choose between escorted vacations and independent vacations; others will allow you to add on excursions or escorted day trips (also at prices lower than if you booked them yourself). And it really pays to compare, because different packages may include accommodations at the same hotel for different prices.

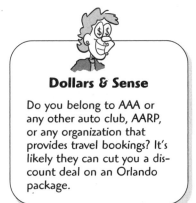

Dollars & Sense

Do you belong to AAA or any other auto club, AARP, or any organization that provides travel bookings? It's likely they can cut you a discount deal on an Orlando package.

Pick a Peck of Pickled Packagers

The best place to start looking is the travel section of your local Sunday newspaper. Also check the ads in the back of national travel magazines like *Travel & Leisure* and *Condé Nast Traveler*. **Liberty Travel** (many locations; check your local directory since there's not a central 800-number) is one of the biggest packagers in the Northeast, and it usually boasts a full-page ad in Sunday papers. You won't get much in the way of service, but you will get a good deal. **American Express Vacations** (☎ 800/241-1700) is another option.

Disney itself offers a dizzying array of package choices that can include air-fare, accommodations on or off Disney property, theme park passes, a rental car, meals, a Disney Cruise Line cruise, courses at the Disney Institute, and/or a stay at Disney's beach resorts in Vero Beach or Hilton Head. And unlike the main Disney number, the number to call for a **Disney vacation package** is free: ☎ **800/828-0228.** Some packages are tied into a season and others are themed to a special vacation such as golf, a honeymoon, or a spa makeover.

Bet You Didn't Know

Star of more than 120 cartoons and movies, Mickey Mouse made his film debut in 1928's *Steamboat Willie.* His significant other, Minnie (no relation), also appeared in the film. Mickey's dad almost named him Mortimer, but his mom (Mrs. Disney) persuaded her husband that Mortimer was too pompous a name for a mouse and suggested Mickey.

It's hard to beat a Disney Vacation Company package for an all-Disney vacation, especially if you get other discounts such as the Magic Kingdom Club or are a Disney shareholder. For those who want to see more than Walt Disney World, and most people do, comparisons are definitely in order. A really motivated travel agent could put together a package of Disney and non-Disney accommodations and attractions for less than what Disney charges.

So should you book with Walt Disney World Vacation Company? In a nutshell:

➤ Nobody knows Walt Disney World's pleasures and treasures better.

➤ Your WDW vacation can be seamless, including a cruise or beach stay.

➤ Accommodations in almost all price ranges are available.

but...

➤ WDW resort guests all get the same perks, whether you buy Disney's package or somebody else's.

➤ You have to prod the agents for money-saving tips, such as going a day earlier or later than your stated dates.

➤ Some package features, such as a welcome cocktail, have little or no dollar value.

Another good resource is the airlines themselves, which often package their flights with accommodations. When you pick the airline, you can choose one that has frequent service to your hometown and the one on which you accumulate frequent flyer miles. Among the airline packages, your options include **American Airlines FlyAway Vacations** (☎ **800/321-2121**), **Delta Dream Vacations** (☎ **800/872-7786**), and **US Airways Vacations** (☎ **800/455-0123**).

Dollars & Sense

There are some fudge factors affecting package prices. The same package at the same hotel can differ in price if a different-class room is included, or if one package tour operator buys in greater bulk from that particular hotel and gets a deeper discount. Package prices are also affected greatly by the days you fly. US Airways's rates are cheapest for departures Sunday through Wednesday, returning any day but a weekend.

The Orlando market is cutthroat-competitive, so don't overlook a package just because it has features you won't use. Our cousins in New York found that they could fly to Orlando, pick up their rental car, but discard their 4 hotel nights (they were staying with us) yet still pay less than if they had booked their airfare and car rental separately. Here are some sample prices we were quoted for early December 1997.

Delta Dream Vacations (☎ 800/872-7786), the big fish in the Orlando pond, quoted a 4-night WDW vacation for two adults and two children (ages 8 and 10) that includes accommodations in Disney's Dixie Landings, airfare from New York, transfers, taxes, and a 4-day Park Hopper Pass for $2,257. At **American Express** (☎ 800/241-1700), we were quoted $2,145 for the same family of four out of New York, staying 4 nights at the Courtyard by Marriott in Walt Disney World Plaza, including 4-day Park Hopper Passes and airport transfers. The hotel runs a free shuttle to WDW. A very liberal trip-cancellation policy is available from American Express for an additional $30 per person.

US Airways Vacations (☎ 800/455-0123) quoted $2,313 for a quad room at Disney's Dixie Landings for 4 nights, airfare from New York, airport transfers, and unlimited passes to all WDW parks. The **Disney Institute** (☎ 800/4-WONDER) offered a 3-night package for $499 per person based on double occupancy. Included are accommodations in a bungalow, admission to one park for 1 day, evening entertainment, a choice of daily Institute programs, baggage handling, and gratuities.

Happy Landings: Winning the Airfare Wars

Airfares are capitalism at its purest. Passengers within the same cabin on an airplane rarely pay the same fare. Rather, they pay what the market will bear.

Business travelers who need the flexibility to purchase their tickets at the last minute or change their itinerary at a moment's notice, or who want to get home before the weekend, pay the premium rate, known as the full fare.

Passengers who can book their ticket long in advance, who don't mind staying over Saturday night, or who are willing to travel on a Tuesday, Wednesday, or Thursday pay the least, usually a fraction of the full fare. On most flights, even the shortest hops, the full fare is close to $1,000 or more, but a 7-day or 14-day advance purchase ticket is closer to $200 to $300. Obviously, it pays to plan ahead.

Bet You Didn't Know

Most airlines will put a no-strings "courtesy hold" on your reservations for 24 hours (some airlines will hold your reservation for up to 7 days). It locks in your rate while giving you time to shop around.

The airlines also periodically hold sales, in which they lower the prices on their most popular routes. These fares have advance-purchase requirements and date-of-travel restrictions, but you can't beat the price: usually no more than $400 for a cross-country flight. Keep your eyes open for these sales as you are planning your vacation; then pounce on them. The sales tend to take place in seasons of low travel volume. You'll almost never see a sale around the peak summer vacation months of July and August, or around Thanksgiving or Christmas, when people have to fly, regardless of what the fare is.

Consolidators, also known as bucket shops, are a good place to check for the lowest fares. Their prices are much better than the fares you could get yourself, and are often even lower than what your travel agent can get you. You see their ads in the small boxes at the bottom of the page in your Sunday travel section. Some of the most reliable consolidators include **1-800-FLY-4-LESS** and **1-800-FLY-CHEAP.** Another good choice, **Council Travel** (☎ **800/226-8624**), caters especially to young travelers, but their bargain-basement prices are available to people of all ages.

Dollars & Sense

Do you own any stock in Walt Disney World? If so, special discounts are available to you. Call **Shareholder Relations** at ☎ **818/505-7040** during Pacific Time business hours.

Surfing the Net to Fly the Skies

Another way to find the cheapest fare is by using the Internet to do your searching for you. After all, that's what computers do best—search through millions of pieces of data and return information in rank order. The number of virtual travel agents on the Internet has increased exponentially in recent years. Agencies now compete the way locksmiths do in the Yellow Pages for the first alphabetical listing. At this writing, 007Travel, 1st Choice Travel, and 1Travel.com all preceded A Plus Travel in an alphabetical listing of online travel agents.

There are too many companies now to mention, but a few of the better-respected ones are **Travelocity** (www.travelocity.com), **Microsoft Expedia** (www.expedia.com), and **Yahoo!'s Flifo Global** (http://travel.yahoo.com/travel/).

Each company has its own little quirks—Travelocity, for example, requires you to register with them—but they all provide variations of the same service. Just enter the dates you want to fly and the cities you want to visit, and the computer looks for the lowest fares.

The Yahoo! site has a feature called "Fare Beater," which will check flights on other airlines or at different times or dates in hopes of finding an even cheaper fare. Expedia's site will e-mail you the best airfare deal once a week if you so choose. Travelocity uses the SABRE computer reservations system that most travel agents use, and it has a "Last Minute Deals" database that advertises really cheap fares for those who can get away at a moment's notice.

Bet You Didn't Know

Goofy first appeared along with Mickey Mouse in a 1932 cartoon called *Mickey's Revue*. Though his original name was Dippy Dawg, which later evolved into Dippy the Goof, and finally, Goofy, there has been, for years, an ongoing controversy as to exactly what kind of animal he is. The claim of Disney representatives that he is supposed to be a human being has never been substantiated.

Great last-minute deals are also available directly from the airlines themselves through a free e-mail service called **E-savers.** Each week, the airline sends you a list of discounted flights, usually leaving the upcoming Friday or Saturday and returning the following Monday or Tuesday. You can sign up for all the major airlines at once by logging on to **Epicurious Travel (http://travel.epicurious.com/travel/c_planning/02_airfares/email/signup.html)**, or you can go to each individual airline's Web site:

American Airlines: www.americanair.com

Continental Airlines: www.flycontinental.com

TWA: www.twa.com

Northwest Airlines: www.nwa.com

US Airways: www.usairways.com

Does It Matter Which Airport I Fly Into?
Orlando International Airport (MCO) is the major player, but it's not the only game in town. Some large charter flights go into **Sanford**

Orlando International Airport, which lies 20 minutes north of downtown and about 35 minutes north of the attractions area, farther away from all things Disney than Orlando International. If you come on one of the packages that uses this airport, ground transportation will be included.

As long as you're price shopping, see whether you can get to **Tampa (TPA)** cheaper than to MCO. With today's seesaw prices, discounts, and deals, it's always possible. Tampa is less than 2 hours southwest of the attractions area and 30 minutes east of the Gulf beaches. A Tampa package that combines airfare, a rental car, and beach accommodations before or after your Orlando visit can be a bonanza.

Extra! Extra!

If you have special dietary needs, be sure to order a special meal. Most airlines offer vegetarian meals, macrobiotic meals, kosher meals, meals for the lactose intolerant, and several other meals in a large variety of categories. Ask when you make your reservation whether the airline can accommodate your dietary restrictions. Some people without any special dietary needs order special meals anyway because they are made to order, unlike the mass-produced dinners served to the rest of the passengers.

The Comfort Zone: How to Make Your Flight More Pleasant

The seats in the front row of each airplane cabin, called the **bulkhead seats,** usually have the most leg room. They have some drawbacks, however. Because there's no seat in front of you, there's no place to put your carry-on luggage, except in the overhead bin. The front row also may not be the best place to see the in-flight movie. And lately, airlines have started putting passengers with young children in the bulkhead row so the kids can sleep on the floor. This is terrific if you have kids, but a nightmare if you have a headache.

Beating the Lines

Delta has stopped allowing families with children to board first on Orlando flights. It's fairer to the other passengers, and really better for the kids because they aren't cooped up any longer than necessary.

Emergency-exit row seats also have extra legroom. They are assigned at the airport, usually on a first-come, first-served basis. Ask when you check in whether you can be seated in one of these rows. In the unlikely event of an emergency, you'll be expected to open the emergency exit door and help direct traffic.

Wear comfortable clothes. The days of getting dressed up in a coat and tie to ride an airplane went out with Nehru jackets and poodle skirts. And dress in layers; the supposedly controlled climate in airplane cabins is anything but predictable. You'll be glad to have a sweater or jacket that you can put on or take off as the temperature onboard dictates.

Bring some toiletries aboard on long flights. Airplane cabins are notoriously dry places. Take a travel-size bottle of moisturizer or lotion to refresh your face and hands at the end of the flight. If you're taking an overnight flight (aka the red-eye), don't forget to pack a toothbrush to combat that feeling upon waking that you've been sucking on your seat cushion for 6 hours. If you wear contact lenses, take them out before you get onboard and wear glasses instead. Or at least bring eye drops.

Beating the Lines

Ask for a seat toward the front of the plane. The minute the captain turns off the "Fasten Seat Belts" sign after landing, people jump up out of their seats as though Ken Griffey, Jr., had just hit a home run. They then stand in the aisles and wait for 5 to 10 minutes while the ground crew puts the gangway in place. The closer to the front of the plane you are, the less hurry-up-and-waiting you'll have to do. Why do you think they put first class in the front?

Jet lag is not usually a problem for flights within the United States, but some people are affected by 3-hour time-zone changes. The best advice is to get acclimated to local time as quickly as possible. Stay up as long as you can the first day, and then try to wake up at a normal time the second day. Drink plenty of water both days, as well as on the plane, to avoid dehydration.

And **if you're flying with kids,** don't forget chewing gum for ear-pressure problems with swallowing, a deck of cards or favorite toys to keep them entertained, extra bottles or pacifiers, diapers, and so on.

Even if *you're* not flying with kids, keep in mind that many people on Orlando flights *are* bringing the little monsters. Inbound, they'll be swinging from the overheads with excitement about going to see Mickey Mouse. Outbound, they fill all the luggage racks with souvenirs and stuffed toys before you can stow your briefcase.

Worksheet: Fare Game—Choosing an Airline

Arranging and booking flights is a complicated business—that's why a whole industry has grown up to handle it for you. If you're searching around for a deal, though, it helps to leave a trail of breadcrumbs through the maze so you can easily find your way to your destination and back. You can use this worksheet to do just that.

There's a chance that you won't be able to get a direct flight, especially if you're looking to save money, so we've included space for you to map out any connections you'll have to make. If a connection is involved in the fares you're quoted, make sure to ask how much of a layover you'll have between flights, 'cause nobody likes hanging around the airport for 8 or 10 hours. Be sure to mark the layover times in the appropriate spot on the worksheet, so you can compare them easily when you go back over everything to make your decision.

Just to make it all just that much easier, we've included a sample worksheet at the end of the chapter to get you started. Check it out, then get down to business. Good luck.

Other Ways to Get There

Driving to Orlando is a good choice unless (1) distances are so great that it eats up too much of your vacation or (2) you don't have an air-conditioned car. Without A/C, you and your family will dread driving around the area.

The city lies just off the Florida Turnpike, which links up at Wildwood with I-75. That's the interstate that runs from the Midwest to southwest Florida. The city is also on I-4, which runs between Daytona Beach and Tampa. At Daytona, it joins I-95, the north-south interstate that runs the length of the eastern seaboard.

Orlando can also be reached on **Amtrak,** which stops downtown at 1400 Sligh Ave. (between Columbia and Miller), and at 111 Dakin St., at Thurman Street, in Kissimmee. The downtown train station is 2 blocks from a LYNX bus station, where buses run once an hour to the International Drive area. From here, you'll still need a taxi to get to Walt Disney World hotels, a ride costing about $28. If you debark at the Kissimmee station, you'll need a taxi costing about $28 to get to WDW hotels.

The **Auto-Train** (☎ **800/USA-RAIL**) is a unique service that allows you to bring your car from Lorton VA, which is 2 hours from Philadelphia and 4 hours from New York, to Sanford, which is 23 miles northeast of Orlando. Ride in a passenger seat or a sleeping car for the overnight trip.

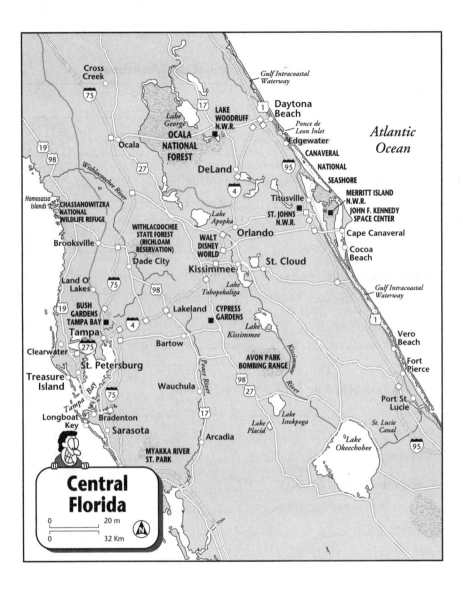

Central Florida

Cross Creek

Gulf Intracoastal Waterway

Lake George

Lake Woodruff N.W.R.

Daytona Beach

Ponce de Leon Inlet

Ocala National Forest

Ocala

Edgewater

Atlantic Ocean

DeLand

Canaveral National Seashore

Merritt Island N.W.R.

Homosassa Islands Chassahowitzka National Wildlife Refuge

Withlacoochee River

Lake Apopka

Titusville

St. Johns N.W.R.

John F. Kennedy Space Center

Brooksville

Withlacoochee State Forest (Richloam Reservation)

Walt Disney World

Orlando

Cape Canaveral

Cocoa Beach

Dade City

Kissimmee

St. Cloud

Land O' Lakes

Lake Tohopekaliga

Gulf Intracoastal Waterway

Bush Gardens Tampa Bay

Lakeland

Cypress Gardens

Tampa

Bartow

Lake Kissimmee

Vero Beach

Clearwater

St. Petersburg

Avon Park Bombing Range

Fort Pierce

Treasure Island

Peace River

Wauchula

Kissimmee River

Port St. Lucie

Tampa Bay

Longboat Key

Bradenton

Sarasota

Arcadia

Lake Placid

Lake Istokpoga

St. Lucie Canal

Lake Okeechobee

Myakka River St. Park

Central Florida

0   20 m

0   32 Km

1 Schedule & Flight Information Worksheets

Travel Agency: _____ **Phone #:** _____

Agent's Name: _____ **Quoted Fare:** _____

Departure Schedule & Flight Information

Airline: _____ Airport: _____

Flight #: _____ Date: _____ Time: _____ am/pm

Arrives in _____ Time: _____ am/pm

Connecting Flight (if any)

Amount of time between flights: _____ hours/mins.

Airline: _____ Flight #: _____ Time: _____ am/pm

Arrives in _____ Time: _____ am/pm

Return Trip Schedule & Flight Information

Airline: _____ Airport: _____

Flight #: _____ Date: _____ Time: _____ am/pm

Arrives in _____ Time: _____ am/pm

Connecting Flight (if any)

Amount of time between flights: _____ hours/mins.

Airline: _____ Flight #: _____ Time: _____ am/pm

Arrives in _____ Time: _____ am/pm

2 Schedule & Flight Information Worksheets

Travel Agency: _____ **Phone #:** _____

Agent's Name: _____ **Quoted Fare:** _____

Departure Schedule & Flight Information

Airline: _____ Airport: _____

Flight #: _____ Date: _____ Time: _____am/pm

Arrives in _____ Time: _____ am/pm

Connecting Flight (if any)

Amount of time between flights: _____ hours/mins.

Airline:_____ Flight #:_____ Time: _____am/pm

Arrives in _____ Time: _____ am/pm

Return Trip Schedule & Flight Information

Airline:_____ Airport: _____

Flight #: _____ Date: _____ Time: _____am/pm

Arrives in _____ Time: _____ am/pm

Connecting Flight (if any)

Amount of time between flights: _____ hours/mins.

Airline:_____ Flight #:_____ Time: _____am/pm

Arrives in _____ Time: _____ am/pm

3   Schedule & Flight Information Worksheets

Travel Agency: _____ **Phone #:** _____

Agent's Name: _____ **Quoted Fare:** _____

Departure Schedule & Flight Information

Airline: _____ Airport: _____

Flight #: _____ Date: _____ Time: _____am/pm

Arrives in _____ Time: _____ am/pm

Connecting Flight (if any)

Amount of time between flights: _____ hours/mins.

Airline:_____ Flight #:_____ Time: _____am/pm

Arrives in _____ Time: _____ am/pm

Return Trip Schedule & Flight Information

Airline:_____ Airport: _____

Flight #: _____ Date: _____ Time: _____am/pm

Arrives in _____ Time: _____ am/pm

Connecting Flight (if any)

Amount of time between flights: _____ hours/mins.

Airline:_____ Flight #:_____ Time: _____am/pm

Arrives in _____ Time: _____ am/pm

4   Schedule & Flight Information Worksheets

Travel Agency: _____ **Phone #:** _____

Agent's Name: _____ **Quoted Fare:** _____

Departure Schedule & Flight Information

Airline: _____ Airport: _____

Flight #: _____ Date: _____ Time: _____am/pm

Arrives in _____ Time: _____ am/pm

Connecting Flight (if any)

Amount of time between flights: _____ hours/mins.

Airline:_____ Flight #:_____ Time: _____am/pm

Arrives in _____ Time: _____ am/pm

Return Trip Schedule & Flight Information

Airline:_____ Airport: _____

Flight #: _____ Date: _____ Time: _____am/pm

Arrives in _____ Time: _____ am/pm

Connecting Flight (if any)

Amount of time between flights: _____ hours/mins.

Airline:_____ Flight #:_____ Time: _____am/pm

Arrives in _____ Time: _____ am/pm

Chapter 4

Tying Up the Loose Ends

> **In This Chapter**
>
> ➤ The ins and outs of renting a car
>
> ➤ Travel insurance tips
>
> ➤ What to do in case of illness
>
> ➤ Two on the aisle: making reservations and getting tickets ahead of time
>
> ➤ Packing up

OK, you're almost there. Now all you have to do is find a place to stay (we'll deal with that question separately in chapters 5 and 6), plan your itinerary, make the reservations, put the dog in the kennel, pack your bags, and do 50 other last-minute things. Organizing these "details" ahead of time will save you precious vacation hours waiting in line, trying to get tickets, calling around town, and buying the underwear you forgot to bring. So in this chapter, we'll help you make sure that you've got everything covered, right down to remembering comfortable walking shoes. And maybe you still have a few questions before you take the plunge and choose your hotel and book your flights. Like "Do I Need a Car?" "What If I Get Sick?" "What Should I Take?"

Well, you asked, so here goes.

Do I Need to Rent a Car in Orlando?

Maybe you can't imagine life anywhere in America without a car. But before you go plunking down a lot of money for a rental, think about it. Do you really need one? When making your decision, remember that parking is an additional expense at most theme parks, sporting events, the Bob Carr Performing Arts Center, the convention center, and some hotels and restaurants.

If you're really going to do nothing else but visit Walt Disney World, you can do nicely without a car. Everything is here: theme parks, restaurants, night-clubs, entertainment of all kinds, golf, tennis, boating, water parks, nature watching, and swimming pools galore. All transportation within WDW is free—the monorail, buses, and ferries—though you should be aware that it can sometimes take hours, and several transfers, to get where you need to go. A car is useful sometimes in getting around faster, and it can also get you out of the high-priced World to find moderately priced restaurants and shopping in the real world. Still, our recommendation is to forego the car while at WDW, then move to other lodgings and rent a car for the non-WDW portion of your trip.

Staying outside WDW without a car is pretty difficult, but it can be done, especially along International Drive and at any resort hotel that has every-thing you need for dining and recreation. Hotels run shuttles to the theme parks; other shuttles run among International Drive's attractions and to downtown.

If your vacation orbit will include trips into the beach and to shopping malls and supermarkets, you've just gotta have wheels. This isn't a city where you want to depend on taxis, which are expensive, or the bus system, which is good but serves routes more useful to local commuters than to tourists.

Be a Smart Shopper

If you decide to rent a car, remember that car-rental rates vary even more than airline fares. The price depends on the size of the car, the length of time you keep it, where and when you pick it up and drop it off, where you take it, and a host of other factors.

Time-Savers

There are Internet resources that can make comparison-shopping easier. For example, Yahoo!'s partnership with Flifo Global travel agency allows you to look up rental prices for any size car at more than a dozen rental companies in hundreds of cities. Just enter the size car you want, the rental and return dates, and the city where you want to rent, and the server returns a price. It will even make your reservation for you. Point your browser to http://travel.yahoo.com/travel/ and then choose "Reserve car" from the options listed.

Asking a few key questions could save you hundreds of dollars. For example, weekend rates may be lower than weekday rates. Ask whether the rate is the same for pickup Friday morning as it is Thursday night. If you're keeping the car 5 or more days, a weekly rate may be cheaper than the daily rate. Some companies may assess a drop-off charge if you do not return the car to the same renting location; others, notably National, do not. Ask whether the rate is cheaper if you pick up the car at the airport or a location in town.

If you see an advertised price in your local newspaper, be sure to ask for that specific rate; otherwise, you may be charged the standard (higher) rate. Don't forget to mention membership in AAA, AARP, frequent-flyer programs, and trade unions. These usually entitle you to discounts ranging from 5% to 30%. Ask your travel agent to check any and all of these rates.

And most car rentals are worth at least 500 miles on your frequent-flyer account!

On top of the standard rental prices, other optional charges apply to most car rentals. The Collision Damage Waiver (CDW), which requires you to pay for damage to the car in a collision, is illegal in some states but is covered by many credit-card companies. Check with your credit-card company before you go so that you can avoid paying this hefty fee (as much as $10 a day).

The car-rental companies also offer additional liability insurance (in case you harm others in an accident), personal accident insurance (in case you harm yourself or your passengers), and personal effects insurance (in case your luggage is stolen from your car). If you have insurance on your car at home, you are probably covered for most of these unlikelihoods. If your own insurance doesn't cover you for rentals, or if you don't have auto insurance, you should consider the additional coverages (the car-rental companies are liable for certain base amounts, depending on the state). But weigh the likelihood of getting into an accident or losing your luggage against the cost of these coverages (as much as $20 a day combined), which can significantly add to the price of your rental.

Tourist Traps

Some rental-car companies offer refueling packages, in which you pay for an entire tank of gas up front. The price is usually fairly competitive with local gas prices, but you don't get credit for any gas remaining in the tank. If you reject this option, you pay only for the gas you use, but you have to return it with a full tank or face charges of $3 to $4 a gallon for any shortfall. If a stop at a gas station on the way to the airport will make you miss your plane, then by all means take advantage of the fuel purchase option. Otherwise, skip it.

Car-Rental Comparison Worksheet

Company	Type of Car	No. of Days	Rate
Avis (☎ 800/331-1212)			
Budget (☎ 800/527-0700)			
Dollar (☎ 800/800-8000)			
Hertz (☎ 800/654-3131)			
National (☎ 800/227-7368)			
Thrifty (☎ 800/367-2277)			
Other			
Other			
Other			

What About Travel Insurance?

There are three kinds of travel insurance: trip-cancellation insurance, medical, and lost luggage. Trip-cancellation insurance is a good idea if you have paid a large portion of your vacation expenses up front and would lose out if your trip was canceled—say, if you bought a package (and you shouldn't buy this type of insurance from the packager). It's also critical if you or someone in your immediate family gets sick or dies and you can't go.

But the other two types of insurance don't make sense for most travelers. Your existing health insurance should cover you if you get sick while on vacation (but check to make sure that you are fully covered

Dollars & Sense

The airlines are responsible for $1,250 on domestic flights if they lose your luggage; if you plan to carry anything more valuable than that, keep it in your carry-on bag.

when away from home). And your homeowner's insurance should cover stolen luggage if you have off-premises theft. Check your existing policies before you buy any additional coverage.

Some credit cards (American Express and certain gold and platinum Visa and MasterCards, for example) offer automatic flight insurance against death or dismemberment in case of an airplane crash.

If you still feel you need more insurance, try one of the companies listed below. But don't pay for more insurance than you need. For example, if you need only trip-cancellation insurance, don't purchase coverage for lost or stolen property. Trip-cancellation insurance costs approximately 6% to 8% of the total value of your vacation.

Among the reputable issuers of travel insurance are:

➤ **Access America,** 6600 W. Broad St., Richmond, VA 23230 (☎ **800/284-8300**)

➤ **Mutual of Omaha,** Mutual of Omaha Plaza, Omaha, NE 68175 (☎ **800/228-9792**)

➤ **Travel Guard International,** 1145 Clark St., Stevens Point, WI 54481 (☎ **800/826-1300**)

➤ **Travel Insured International, Inc.,** P.O. Box 280568, East Hartford, CT 06128 (☎ **800/243-3174**)

What If I Get Sick Away from Home?

Bring all your medications with you, as well as a prescription in case you need a refill. Orlando pharmacists can network with your home pharmacist by telephone, but a written Rx will save time and expense. If you have health insurance, carry your identification card in your wallet. Bring an extra pair of contact lenses in case you lose one. And don't forget small supplies of over-the-counter medications for common travelers' ailments.

If you suffer from a chronic illness, talk to your doctor before taking the trip. For such conditions as epilepsy, diabetes, or a heart condition, wear a **Medic Alert Identification Tag,** which will immediately alert any doctor to your condition and give him or her access to your medical records through Medic Alert's 24-hour hot line. Membership is $35, plus a $15 annual fee. Contact the Medic Alert Foundation, P.O. Box 1009, Turlock, CA 95381-1009 (☎ **800/825-3785**).

If you worry about getting sick away from home, purchase medical insurance (see the section on travel insurance above). It will cover you more completely than your existing health insurance.

If you do get sick, ask the concierge or front desk at your hotel to recommend a local doctor—most hotels have a doctor and dentist on call—or steer you to the nearest emergency room or walk-in clinic.

Extra! Extra!

We hope you don't need any medical care on your trip, but just in case.... For non-emergencies, try **Orlando Regional Walk-in Medical Care** (☎ 407/841-5111); **Housemed/Mediclinic** (☎ 407/396-1195); **Mainstreet Physicians** (☎ 407/238-1009); or **Buena Vista Walk-In Center** (☎ 407/239-7777). The 24-hour **Walgreen's** at 534 Hunt Club Blvd. (☎ 407/869-5220) has a drive-through pharmacy. You can call in your prescription, then pick it up without having to leave your car.

If a child or pet swallows a Florida plant that you fear is unsafe, call **Poison Control** at ☎ **800/282-3171.** Among the more common poisonous flowers found in the Orlando area are oleander, lantana, and trumpet vine.

Two on the Aisle: Making Reservations and Getting Tickets Ahead of Time

Compared to New York and San Francisco, where restaurant tables at the best places are snapped up weeks in advance, Orlando is easy. In most instances, you can wait until you get to Florida to make dining reservations. Your hotel's concierge will be glad to help.

At Walt Disney World, a system called **Priority Seating** is used. With it, you make a reservation that ensures that you'll get the next available table after your arrival at the restaurant. It's not like reservations, in which an empty table is held for you, but it's far better than just showing up and waiting your turn. Still, waits could range from moments to more than an hour. We explain exactly how it works in chapter 9.

Bet You Didn't Know

Universal Studios (☎ **407/224-7638**) offers free seating for special events that are being filmed or televised. Even locals sometimes get the word about these late in the game. Your best bet is to write well in advance, listing the dates you'll be in town. Ask what tickets are available. Write Universal Studios, 1000 Universal Studios Plaza, Orlando, FL 32819. **Walt Disney World,** including Pleasure Island and Downtown Disney, is constantly hosting film shoots, world-class sports events, and special shows (☎ **407/824-4321** or Web site www.disneyworld.com).

Evening shows can be booked as far in advance as you wish; **restaurants and character meals** can be booked up to 60 days in advance by calling ☎ **407/WDW-DINE.** Note in our restaurant listings that a few restaurants in WDW and elsewhere require reservations at all times.

Ticketmaster is the key player in ticketing for most events in Orlando. If you know of a blockbuster event that will be playing while you're in Orlando, check first with your hometown Ticketmaster outlets to see whether they sell tickets for it. If you live as close as Miami or Atlanta, they probably do. Otherwise, call Ticketmaster at ☎ **407/839-3900** or hit their Web site, www.ticketmaster.com. Ticketmaster accepts American Express, MasterCard, and Visa and takes calls from 9am to 9pm Monday to Friday and 9am to 7pm Saturday and Sunday.

Dozens of rock, rap, jazz, pop, country, blues, and folk stars are in town in any given week, and they are featured in a page called New Tix in the ***Orlando Sentinel's* Calendar section,** published every Friday. Pick it up while you're here, or find it at Web site www.orlandosentinel.com.

For tickets to events at the **Daytona International Speedway,** which is only a couple of hours from Orlando, call ☎ **904/253-7223.**

Silver Springs, an hour north of Orlando, has become the Nashville of Central Florida, with appearances by artists like the Gatlin Brothers, Johnny Cash, Tanya Tucker, and Randy Travis. Call ☎ **800/234-7458.** Seating is almost unlimited and is not reserved, but you can avoid standing in long lines by buying park admission tickets in advance. Concerts are included, so arrive early and spend the day seeing Florida's oldest tourist attraction.

Heigh-Ho, Heigh-Ho, Let's Get This Show on the Road! Time to Pack!

Start your packing by taking everything you think you'll need and laying it out on the bed. Then get rid of half of it. Remember, suitcase straps can be particularly painful to sunburned shoulders.

Bet You Didn't Know

As a rule, you're allowed two pieces of carry-on luggage, both of which must fit in the overhead compartment or the seat in front of you. But note that some airlines are beginning to limit this to only one carry-on—so ask when you book your flight! And then show your carry-on bag when you first check in to avoid problems at the gate or on board. All airlines are getting more strict about not letting passengers exceed the size limit.

Some essentials:

➤ An unlined windbreaker plus a sweatshirt can provide enough warmth for almost any temperatures that an Orlando winter can dish out. Dress in layers. For dressier occasions during the cold months, bring a dress shirt, sweater, and blazer, and wear one, two, or all three as needed for warmth. And even when it's broiling out, you may want to bring along layers to compensate for overzealous air conditioning.

➤ Because most diners have spent the day in the theme park, even the fanciest restaurants inside the parks aren't dressy. Dress for comfort and a lot of walking.

➤ Sun cover-ups are essential. Even on cool, cloudy days, you can get a painful sunburn at this latitude. Bring a hat and sunglasses. Use plenty of sunblock, preferably a waterproof type that won't sweat or swim away.

➤ If you bring two bathing suits, you'll always have a dry one ready to slip into. Beach shoes are a plus if you'll be going to the Atlantic or the Gulf, where sands can have patches of shell rubble.

➤ Bring at least two pairs of shoes and plenty of socks so that you can start each day with fresh, dry footwear. Standing in line at theme parks on hot days is harder on the feet than marine boot camp. Feet swell in Orlando's humid weather, so veteran theme-park fans bring along an extra pair of socks and change their footwear around midday.

When packing, start with the biggest, hardest items (usually shoes), then fit smaller items in and around them. Pack breakable items in between several layers of clothes, or keep them in your carry-on bag. Put things that could leak, like shampoos and suntan lotions, in Zip-lock bags. Lock your suitcase with a small padlock (available at most luggage stores, if your bag doesn't already have one), and put an identification tag on the outside.

In your carry-on bag, you'll want a book if you want to read, any breakable items you don't want to put in your suitcase, maybe your personal headphone stereo, a snack in case you don't like the airline food, any vital documents you don't want to lose in your luggage (like your return tickets, passport, and wallet), and some empty space for the sweater or jacket you might need in flight or in the air-conditioned terminal.

Don't Forget Your Toothbrush! A Packing Checklist

☐ Socks (bring two pairs for each day during the hottest months)

☐ Underwear

☐ Shoes (don't forget a good pair of walking shoes for the parks)

☐ Pants and/or skirts

☐ Shirts or blouses

☐ Sweaters and/or jackets

☐ Umbrella and/or poncho (essential for Orlando's late-afternoon thunderstorms)

☐ A belt

☐ Shorts

☐ Bathing suits (and maybe a beach towel; better resorts provide them free)

☐ Workout clothes if you'll be using your hotel's gym

☐ Toiletries (don't forget a razor, toothbrush, comb, deodorant, makeup, contact lens solution, hair dryer, extra pair of glasses, sewing kit)

☐ Camera (don't forget the film; it can be very expensive when you're traveling)

☐ Medications (pack these in a carry-on so that you'll have them even if you lose your luggage)

Part 2

Finding the Hotel That's Right for You

First things first. You've gotta have a place to stay, and the place you choose will determine a lot about the rest of your vacation: whether you need to rent a car, how your itineraries will be set up, and how much you'll be spending.

One thing's for sure: You won't have a shortage of choices. There are about a zillion resorts, hotels, motels, and condos in central Florida. And they all seem to have a gimmick. Where, you might ask, are you supposed to begin? And how are you supposed to tell the tasteful from the tacky?

Well, we'll take it from here. In chapter 5, we'll start by giving you some strategies and money-saving tips and filling you in on the decisions you have to make about choosing a location. Then in chapter 6, you'll find reviews of what we consider to be the very best options out there. We've even thrown in an easy-to-use worksheet so that you can zero in on the one you want.

Ready? Let's get to it.

Pillow Talk: The Lowdown on Orlando's Hotel Scene

Let's start out by telling you about a couple of pluses you can take for grant-ed. Almost every hotel here has been built or renovated in the past 25 years, so the facilities are likely to be up-to-date. And they all try to make every kid feel like Mickey's personal invited guest.

So, really, your major choices boil down to location and price. And although you'll pay more for the best locations, you may find it worth the conve-nience. The closer your hotel is to the things you want to do and see, the less time you'll spend penned in by a traffic jam or walking the death march from Parking Area ZZZ to the theme park entrance. Seeking to be penny-wise could truly be pound-foolish if the cost in aggravation is higher than the dol-lar savings.

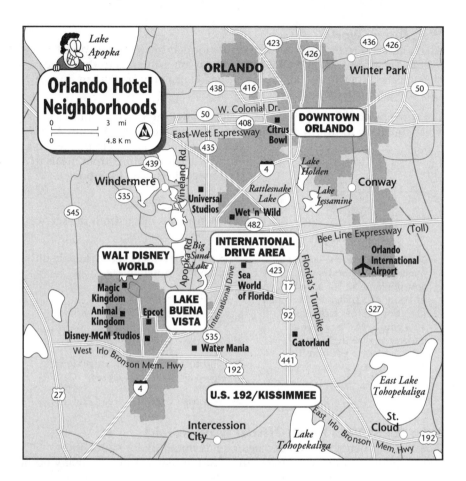

Location, Location, Location

So you thought you could save a pile of dough by getting as far from WDW as possible? Wrong!

People are flocking to Central Florida for lots of different reasons that have nothing to do with theme parks: weddings, honeymoons, business and investing, conferences, spring break, class trips, conventions, and visiting the gazillion grandmas and grandpas who have retired to this area. And if you plan on a maximum Mickey vacation, you may actually save money by staying within WDW because you won't have to rent a car. See "Should I Bunk with Mickey?" later in this chapter.

Here are some pros and cons for each of the major hotel neighborhoods in the Orlando area.

Walt Disney World

The hotels and resorts in this category are located smack dab in Walt Disney World. These are for you if all you care about are daily trips to the Disney theme parks. They're also all on the Disney Transportation System, so you can skip renting a car and save money on that front.

But convenience has its price. The cheapest hotels here cost about twice what you'd pay in nearby Kissimmee for the same accommodations. And if you don't rent a car, you're trapped in a World where everything from meals to spa services is equally high-priced.

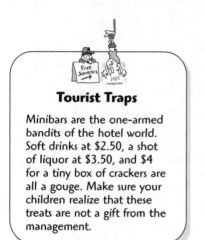

Tourist Traps

Minibars are the one-armed bandits of the hotel world. Soft drinks at $2.50, a shot of liquor at $3.50, and $4 for a tiny box of crackers are all a gouge. Make sure your children realize that these treats are not a gift from the management.

In a nutshell:

➤ It's seamless magic from the service to the landscaping.

➤ Some WDW perks are available only to WDW hotel guests.

➤ Security is tops.

But...

➤ You pay a premium price.

➤ The total immersion in pixie dust may get old after a few days.

➤ You won't see the "real" Florida.

Lake Buena Vista Area (Official WDW Hotels)

Think of this neighborhood as a bedroom community for Walt Disney World, close to Disney Crossroads and Pleasure Island. You'll get many of the same perks enjoyed by people staying inside WDW (some of these are "official" Disney hotels even though they're not owned by Disney or on Disney land) without being constantly amid the hubbub, and you'll have free transportation to and from the WDW theme parks (though you're not on the WDW transportation system).

In a nutshell:

➤ The area is so new and meticulously maintained that it fairly sparkles.

➤ There's a wider range of choices for hotels and restaurants in every price category.

➤ You're conveniently close to WDW without being inside it 24 hours a day.

But...

➤ This is still a high-rent district.

➤ It's difficult to manage without a car.

U.S. 192/Kissimmee

This once-sleepy city is actually closer to Walt Disney World than Orlando is. The highway is lined with hotels, attractions, and restaurants, many of them priced for us average underpaid Joes. Yet the city also offers historic neighborhoods and nice folks who were born and grew up here.

In a nutshell:

➤ You can't beat the price for a room.

➤ Restaurants and other services are priced to match.

➤ Many hotels offer shuttle service to the theme parks.

But...

➤ You'll need a car.

➤ Your vacation clock ticks on while you're sitting in traffic.

➤ Fast-food joints and gas stations aren't a pretty sight.

Tourist Traps

Don't make a telephone call from your hotel room without fully understanding hotel policy; ask when you check in. Some hotels offer free local and toll-free calls, but others may charge $1 or more each time you pick up the phone, even if you are using your calling card or charging the call to your home phone.

Say you dial an 800-number to access your phone-card service. The party you're calling doesn't answer, or the line is busy. Yet the hotel charges you $1.75 each time the 800-number answers. The fact that you didn't reach your party is irrelevant. As far as the hotel was concerned, your call was completed when the 800-number answered.

Charging a long-distance call to your room is even worse. The hotel charges top dollar plus fees and surcharges.

Many pay phones in Central Florida now cost 35¢ or more, but they're still a bargain compared to local calls placed from your room at 50¢ to 75¢ or more.

International Drive Area

This is the nerve center of Orlando's attractions area. It's convenient to all the theme parks, including Sea World and Universal Studios. There's some schlock, but at these real-estate prices, only the best restaurants, hotels, and attractions can survive.

In a nutshell:

➤ It's convenient to theme parks, shopping, the airport, and I-4.

➤ This classy area captures the upbeat theme-park mood without hitting you over the head with a sledgehammer.

➤ You don't need a car since there's a shuttle among hotels and eateries and many hotels offer shuttles to theme parks.

But...

➤ Big events at the Convention Center overrun everything with congestion.

➤ Crooks love this area because tourists let down their guard. Keep your wits about you.

Downtown

Believe it or not, Orlando was a city before that mouse moved in. Downtown is an increasingly vibrant neighborhood, with countless bars, restaurants, coffeehouses, and a night-time theme park for adults, Church Street Station.

In a nutshell:

➤ It's convenient to museums, sporting events, and cultural performances.

➤ Orlando is called the City Beautiful because of its pretty lakes, parks, and green spaces.

➤ There are more full-service hotels catering to the business traveler and devoid of over-the-top themes.

But...

➤ Pockets of sleaze and crime are problems.

➤ It's difficult to manage without a car.

➤ Much of downtown doesn't have the look of shiny newness found in the attractions area.

The Price Is Right

The **rack rate** is the maximum rate that a hotel charges for a room. It's the rate you'd get if you walked in off the street and asked for a room for the night. It's also the rate you may find posted on the back of your hotel room door.

But *you don't have to pay it.* Hardly anybody does. Simply ask whether there's a discount or better rate, and our guess is you'll be pleasantly surprised.

Usually, room rates depend on many factors, not the least of which is how you make your reservation. A travel agent may be able to negotiate a better price with certain hotels than you could get by yourself because the hotel gives the agent a special discount.

Reserving a room through the hotel's 800-number may also result in a lower rate than if you called the hotel directly. On the other hand, the central reservations number may not know about discount rates at specific locations. For example, local franchises may offer a special group rate for a wedding or family reunion, but they may neglect to tell the central booking line. Your best bet is to call both the local number and the 800-number and see which one gives you a better deal.

Dollars & Sense

Be sure to mention membership in AAA, AARP, frequent-flyer programs, and any other corporate rewards program when you make your reservation. You never know when it might be worth a few dollars off your room rate.

Room rates also change with the season and as occupancy rates rise and fall. If a hotel is close to full, it is less likely to extend discount rates; if it's close to empty, it may be willing to negotiate. Some resorts offer mid-week specials; some downtown hotels offer cheaper weekend rates.

Room prices are subject to change without notice, so even the rates quoted in this book may be different from the actual rate you receive when you make your reservation.

About Our Price Categories

Orlando is an inexpensive city compared to New York or San Francisco. Sure, you can spend $1,500 a night for a suite in one of the better hotels; but there are tons of bargains to be had, and you generally get good value for your money here. We have used these breakdowns:

$$$$$ = $250 and up

$$$$ = $200 to $250

$$$ = $100 to $200

$$ = $50 to $100

$ = under $50

What Do You Get for Your Money?

It starts with location. You pay a premium for staying in Walt Disney World, but you may save the difference because you don't have to rent a car and pay the daily parking fee in the theme parks. (See "Should I Bunk with Mickey?" later in this chapter.) Rooms with "water views" aren't worth the extra money, since the water is just a small lake. But rooms overlooking the nightly fireworks that several of the theme parks produce may be worth the extra outlay if it means you can watch them from the privacy of your own balcony.

Hotels without restaurants are cheaper, but only if you have a car or if the hotel is within walking distance of affordable restaurants. It's also a plus if the hotel is on a free shuttle or trolley line. Ask too whether an airport shuttle is available.

Most hotels are priced for two people, so if you're a single or a family, extra homework is in order. Some hotel tariffs are the same for one to four people in a room. Many other hotels charge extra per person for more than two, although young children may sleep free in their parents' room.

Dollars & Sense

A kitchenette may cost only a few dollars extra per day, but it can buy you big savings if you make your own breakfasts, lunches, and snacks.

Also keep in mind that at the priciest hotels, everything is expensive: restaurants, room service, telephone calls, children's programs, and even that glass of cold beer you order at the pool bar. This snowballs when you add a 15% tip and the 6% to 7% sales tax. Don't pop for the most expensive hotel unless you have a champagne budget for everything else, too.

Finding Bargains

Just when you think you have high season and low season figured out, you find out that Orlando hotels are full because of some convention or event you never heard of. Generally, though, the area's hotel rates rise and fall according to school vacations, which in turn determine when most families are free to travel.

Heaviest times are summer, Easter and spring break, Christmas week, and holiday weekends. But there's a lot of wiggle room, because school holidays vary from state to state, and even country to country (don't forget that children from Europe and South America all want to meet Mickey Mouse, too).

At most WDW hotels, there are three different rate seasons, which vary slightly from year to year. Roughly, they are as listed here:

Low season (a.k.a. Value Pricing)	January 1 to February 6 and August 24 to December 17
Regular rates	February 7 to March 20 and April 3 to August 23
High season (a.k.a. Holiday Pricing)	March 21 to April 2 and December 18 to 31

Note that at deluxe resorts like Disney's BoardWalk Inn, Disney's BoardWalk Villas, Disney's Old Key West, and the Villas at the Disney Institute, Value Pricing season begins 6 weeks earlier (roughly July 7).

Non-Disney hotels tend to mirror these rate seasons, but you never know when a downtown convention or a special event in a nearby city (like the Daytona 500) can play havoc with hotel rates and availability.

If you're quoted what seems like a really high rate, be flexible and try another set of dates. You may be shocked at what a difference a few days can make.

Taxes & Service Charges

There is a state sales tax of 6% on all hotel rooms, restaurant meals, and bar drinks. In addition, Orange County (Orlando, Winter Park, Maitland) levies a 5% bed tax on hotel rooms, bringing the total tax to 11%. In Osceola County (Kissimmee–St. Cloud), the bed tax is 6%, thus doubling the tax on a hotel room.

What Kind of Place Is Right for You?

No matter where you stay in Orlando, especially in the attractions area, it's likely that whimsy and mouse ears will play a big role. Even the regal Peabody, one of the finest hotels in the South, has real ducks swimming in its lobby fountain just for the fun of it. Just as gaming motifs rule in Las Vegas and Atlantic City, Orlando's hotels never stray far from the magic.

But there's more variety here than you might have guessed. Orlando has a number of B&Bs, two hostels, campgrounds, cabins, fish camps, condos, time shares, and chain hotels and motels that don't cater to theme-park travelers. The sources we list in chapter 1 will be glad to supply lists of offbeat lodgings that are not covered here.

This book, however, assumes that you're coming for a typical Orlando vacation. The hotels we recommend are listed to give you the widest possible variety of price ranges and locations close to the attractions area.

Bet You Didn't Know

Disney employees appearing in costume as the Kingdom's most famous cartoon characters, such as Mickey and Minnie, are not allowed to speak as they meet park visitors. That's because your child would immediately know that the voice was wrong.

Should I Bunk with Mickey?

Within Walt Disney World itself are 15 Disney-owned hotels and 9 privately owned accommodations designated as "official" hotels. They come in every price range (including a campground) and have significant benefits over staying outside the World. If Disney is high on your list of vacation priorities (or your kids' lists of priorities), it might make sense to stay in the Mouse's house.

Here's why:

➤ You get unlimited free transportation (which would cost $6 to $12 per person per day at many hotels) to and from all Disney parks as well as to a variety of other Disney attractions.

➤ You're guaranteed admission to all the parks, even when all the parking lots are full.

➤ If you rent a car, you can park it free in any WDW lot.

➤ You can arrange for Disney characters to show up for meals with your kids at several hotel restaurants.

➤ You get preferred tee times at any of the five Disney golf courses.

➤ At the higher-end resorts, villas, and campgrounds (except the Dolphin), you get charge privileges throughout the World.

➤ And here's a real biggie: They let you into all three parks before everybody else on certain days of the week, so you can enjoy the facilities in relative freedom from crowds.

The best place to start for a Disney hotel is the **Central Reservations Operations,** P.O. Box 10000, Lake Buena Vista, FL 32830-1000 (☎ **407/ W-DISNEY** [that's 934-7639]), which is open Monday through Friday from 8am to 10pm, Saturday and Sunday from 9am to 6pm. They can recommend a hotel that will fit your plans and budget.

Family Ties: Hotel Strategies for Families Traveling with Kids

Bet You Didn't Know

Walt Disney built Disneyland in Anaheim, California, in 1955, and it quickly became one of the most popular tourist attractions in the country. However, though he conceived of Disney World and initiated its plan, he never lived to see his Florida parks open; the Magic Kingdom opened its gate in 1971, 6 years after Walt passed away.

Kids Most Orlando hotels adore children and fall all over themselves to create a vacation that will keep the kids begging to come back. We've marked the most kid-friendly hotels with a special icon. Even so, you can expect almost any Orlando hotel to give your kids the red-carpet treatment.

The most common room configuration contains two double beds, which can be crowded for a family of four. "Kids sleep free in your room" means in existing bedding; a crib or roll-away bed may cost extra, so ask explicitly.

If you want a little more privacy or separate beds for older children, think about getting a suite. At many of the all-suite hotels, for the price of a double room, you get a double (or queen or king) bedroom, one bath, a living room with sofa bed, and televisions and telephones in each room. However, in most one-bedroom suites, guests sleeping on the sofa bed can't get to the bathroom without walking through the bedroom. Ask when you reserve whether this is the case.

Usually, a two-bedroom villa or suite has a master bedroom with its own bathroom and a second bathroom that is shared by the second bedroom and the people who are sleeping on the sofa bed in the living room.

Some other tips: Compare costs for supervised children's play programs. Are they just day care, or do they offer evening hours so that Mom and Dad can have a night out? Do kids eat free? At discounted rates? Is a special children's menu available? Is the dining room child-friendly? Is room service available for times when the kids are fussy and you just want a simple meal in privacy? Are there plenty of low-priced noshes available at affordable prices? (Show me the food court.) How about a refrigerator where you can keep juices, milk, and sodas so that you're not spending a fortune just for drinks? Is there a kiddy pool or a play-ground where the kids can burn off excess energy?

Older offspring aren't forgotten in Orlando, where hotels commonly offer VCRs, video rental, in-room video games or an on-site video arcade, bicycle rental, and other treats for hard-to-please teens and preteens.

Tourist Traps

It's likely that you'll be approached at a tourist attraction, park, or beach by a time-share salesperson who offers an attractive premium (such as free tickets to a theme park) if you'll listen to a spiel. Decide what your time is worth, because they'll take a good chunk of it.

What If I Didn't Plan Ahead?

If you arrive without a reservation during high season, you're probably out of luck. But you might find something in the area with the help of the **Official Visitor Center,** 8723 International Dr., Suite 101, Orlando, FL 32819 (☎ 507/363-5872), which is open 8am to 8pm every day except Christmas, offering discount ticket sales, free brochures, information in many different languages, and free assistance in finding last-minute lodgings. From I-4, exit onto Sand Lake Road, go east to International Drive, turn right and go about half a mile, and look for the Official Visitor Center on your right.

Exceedingly helpful, too, is the **Kissimmee-St. Cloud Convention & Visitors Bureau** (☎ 800/333-KISS or 407/847-5000). Call them from the airport if you need a room.

Getting the Best Room

Somebody has to get the best room in the house. It might as well be you.

Always ask for a corner room. They're usually larger, quieter, and closer to the elevator; they often have more windows and light than standard rooms; and they don't always cost any more.

When you make your reservation, ask whether the hotel is renovating; if it is, request a room away from the renovation work. Many hotels now offer nonsmoking rooms; by all means ask for one if smoke bothers you. Inquire, too, about the location of the restaurants, bars, and discos in the hotel—these could all be a source of irritating noise. In any case, check out your room before you unpack. Then ask for another room if you don't like the one assigned to you.

A Word About Smoking

Florida law permits smoking only in certain places. As a result, many public areas, including the airport, are now entirely smoke free. Most hotels offer no-smoking rooms or floors; be sure to request your choice when you book.

Chapter 6

Hotels A to Z

In This Chapter

➤ Quick indexes of hotels by location and price

➤ A review of our favorite area hotels

➤ A worksheet to help you make your choice

OK, this is it. It's time to choose your place to snooze.

We've started this chapter with some handy lists that break down our favorite hotels by neighborhood and price, then reviewed them, giving you all the information you'll need to make your decision.

But do you really want to read reviews of every hotel in Orlando? Of course not. Only a really twisted person (or a writer of travel guides) would want to do that. You want somebody else to go look at every hotel, pick out the best ones, and then arrange them according to location and price range. Well, now you can thank us, because we've already done that, and we've narrowed down the list to the very best choices. We've been selective so that you don't have to waste tons of time reading reviews of places we're not enthusiastic about.

The reviews are arranged alphabetically so that they're easier to refer to, and each hotel's location appears right under its name—check the locations against the maps to give yourself a better idea of where the hotels are in relation to what you want to see.

As far as price goes, we've noted rack rates in the listings and also preceded each entry with a dollar-sign icon to make quick reference easier. The more $$$ signs under the name, the more you pay. But note that these are general guidelines, used primarily for comparison. In some seasons, packages, or discount deals, you can stay in **$$$$** hotels for **$$** rates. You can also find **$$$$** rooms and suites in some **$** and **$$** hotels. Rates are per room, based on double occupancy. It runs like this:

$$$$$ = $250 and up

$$$$ = $200 to $250

$$$ = $100 to $200

$$ = $50 to $100

$ = under $50

Parking is free pretty much everywhere, so we haven't wasted your time by noting that over and over on every listing.

Kids We've also added a "kid-friendly" icon to those hotels that are especially good for families, though just about all of these places make a special effort to welcome your kids. We've also included special features throughout called "Extra! Extra!" that will direct you to the best hotels for those of you with special considerations in mind.

Hint: As you read through the reviews, you'll want to keep track of the ones that appeal to you. We've included a chart at the end of this chapter where you can rank your preferences, but to make matters easier on yourself now, why don't you just put a little check mark next to the ones you like? Remember how your teachers used to tell you not to write in your books? Now's the time to rebel. Scrawl away.

Quick Picks: Orlando's Hotels at a Glance
Hotel Index by Location

Walt Disney World

Disney's All-Star Music Resort ($$)

Disney's All-Star Sports Resort ($$)

Disney's Beach Club Resort ($$$$)

Disney's BoardWalk ($$$$)

Disney's Caribbean Beach Resort ($$$)

Disney's Contemporary Resort ($$$$)

Disney's Dixie Landings Resort ($$$)

Disney's Fort Wilderness Resort and Campground ($–$$$$)

Disney's Grand Floridian Beach Resort ($$$$)

Disney's Old Key West Resort ($$$$)

Disney's Polynesian Resort ($$$$$)

Disney's Port Orleans Resort ($$$)

Disney's Wilderness Lodge ($$$–$$$$)

Disney's Yacht Club Resort ($$$$)

Walt Disney World Dolphin ($$$$)

Walt Disney World Swan ($$$$$)

Lake Buena Vista (includes Official Disney Hotels)

Buena Vista Palace ($$$–$$$$)

Doubletree Guest Suites Resort ($$$)

Grosvenor Resort ($$–$$$)

Hilton at Walt Disney World Village ($$$–$$$$)

U.S. 192/Kissimmee

Colonial Hotel Lodge ($–$$)

Comfort Inn Maingate ($)

Days Inn Eastgate ($)

Econo Lodge Maingate East ($)

Holiday Inn Hotel & Suites Main Gate East ($$)

Howard Johnson Inn–Maingate East ($$)

Larson's Lodge Main Gate ($)

Ramada Inn ($)

Ramada Ltd. ($)

International Drive Area

Country Hearth Inn ($)

Orlando Marriott ($$)

Peabody Orlando ($$$$)

Summerfield Suites ($$–$$$)

Downtown

Harley of Orlando ($$)

Near the Airport

Renaissance Orlando Hotel–Airport ($$)

Hotel Index by Price Category

$$$$$ ($250 and up)

Disney's Polynesian Resort (Walt Disney World)

Walt Disney World Swan (Walt Disney World)

$$$$ ($200 to $250)

Buena Vista Palace (International Drive Area/ Official Disney Hotel)

Disney's Beach Club Resort (Walt Disney World)

Disney's BoardWalk (Walt Disney World)

Disney's Contemporary Resort (Walt Disney World)

Disney's Grand Floridian Beach Resort (Walt Disney World)

Disney's Old Key West Resort (Walt Disney World)

Disney's Wilderness Lodge (Walt Disney World)

Disney's Yacht Club Resort (Walt Disney World)

Hilton at Walt Disney World Village (International Drive Area/Official Disney Hotel)

Peabody Orlando (International Drive Area)

Walt Disney World Dolphin (Walt Disney World)

$$$ ($100 to $200)

Buena Vista Palace (Lake Buena Vista/Official Disney Hotel)

Disney's Caribbean Beach Resort (Walt Disney World)

Disney's Dixie Landings Resort (Walt Disney World)

Disney's Port Orleans Resort (Walt Disney World)

63

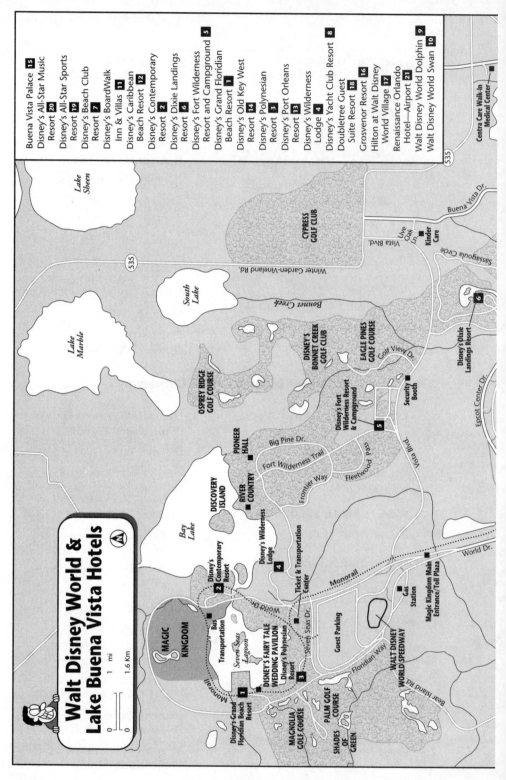

Walt Disney World & Lake Buena Vista Hotels

0 ___ 1 mi
0 ___ 1.6 Km

Buena Vista Palace **15**
Disney's All-Star Music Resort **20**
Disney's All-Star Sports Resort **19**
Disney's Beach Club Resort **7**
Disney's BoardWalk Inn & Villas **11**
Disney's Caribbean Beach Resort **12**
Disney's Contemporary Resort **2**
Disney's Dixie Landings Resort **6**
Disney's Fort Wilderness Resort and Campground **5**
Disney's Grand Floridian Beach Resort **1**
Disney's Old Key West Resort **14**
Disney's Polynesian Resort **3**
Disney's Port Orleans Resort **13**
Disney's Wilderness Lodge **4**
Disney's Yacht Club Resort **8**
Doubletree Guest Suite Resort **18**
Grosvenor Resort **16**
Hilton at Walt Disney World Village **17**
Renaissance Orlando Hotel—Airport **21**
Walt Disney World Dolphin **9**
Walt Disney World Swan **10**

Lake Sheen

Lake Marble

Lake Marble

South Lake

Bonnet Creek

Winter Garden-Vineland Rd.

535

535

CYPRESS GOLF CLUB

Live Oak Ln

Vista Blvd.

Kinder Care

Buena Vista Dr.

Sassagoula Circle

Centra Care Walk-In Medical Center ■

OSPREY RIDGE GOLF COURSE

DISNEY'S BONNET CREEK GOLF CLUB

EAGLE PINES GOLF COURSE

Golf View Dr.

Disney's Dixie Landings Resort **6**

Epcot Center Dr.

PIONEER HALL

Big Pine Dr.

Fort Wilderness Trail

Frontier Way

Disney's Fort Wilderness Resort & Campground **5**

Fleetwood Pass

Security Booth

RIVER COUNTRY

DISCOVERY ISLAND

Bay Lake

Disney's Wilderness Lodge **4**

Ticket & Transportation Center

Monorail

World Dr.

Disney's Contemporary Resort **2**

World Dr.

Bus Transportation

MAGIC KINGDOM

Seven Seas Lagoon

DISNEY'S FAIRY TALE WEDDING PAVILION

Disney's Polynesian Resort **3**

Seven Seas Dr.

Guest Parking

Gas Station

Magic Kingdom Main Entrance/Toll Plaza

WALT DISNEY WORLD SPEEDWAY

Floridian Way

Bear Island Rd.

Disney's Grand Floridian Beach Resort **1**

MAGNOLIA GOLF COURSE

PALM GOLF COURSE

SHADES OF GREEN

64

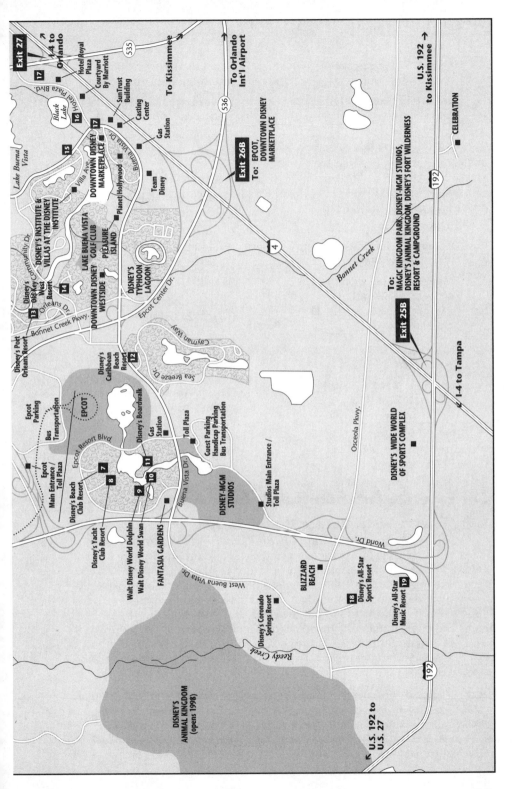

Disney's Wilderness Lodge
(Walt Disney World)

Doubletree Guest Suites Resort
(Lake Buena Vista/Official
Disney Hotel)

Summerfield Suites
(International Drive Area)

$$ ($50 to $100)

Colonial Lodge Hotel (U.S.
192/Kissimmee)

Disney's All-Star Music Resort
(Walt Disney World)

Disney's All-Star Sports Resort
(Walt Disney World)

Grosvenor Inn (Lake Buena
Vista/Official Disney Hotel)

Harley of Orlando
(Downtown)

Holiday Inn Hotel & Suites
Main Gate East (U.S.
192/Kissimmee)

Howard Johnson
Inn–Maingate East (U.S.
192/Kissimmee)

Orlando Marriott
(International Drive Area)

Renaissance Orlando Hotel–
Airport (near the Airport)

Summerfield Suites
(International Drive Area)

$ (under $50)

Comfort Inn Maingate (U.S.
192/Kissimmee)

Country Hearth Inn
(International Drive Area)

Econo Lodge Maingate East
(U.S. 192/Kissimmee)

Larson's Lodge Main Gate
(U.S. 192/Kissimmee)

$–$$$$

Disney's Fort Wilderness
Resort and Campground (Walt
Disney World). Campsites are
in the $ category; for $$$$
you can get a "cabin" that
sleeps up to six and has a full
kitchen and bath.

Our Favorite Orlando Hotels from A to Z

Kids Buena Vista Palace Resort & Spa
$$$–$$$$. Lake Buena Vista/Official WDW Hotel.

The lakefront setting and spacious grounds lend a resort atmosphere to what is also a first-class hotel for businesspeople, honeymooners, and spa-seekers. It's great if you want to see the attractions but also want a place to get away from it all at day's end. On the edges of Walt Disney World, but not immersed in its merriment around the clock, this posh hotel has 1,014 rooms and offers restaurants (including the famous Arthur's 27), lounges, pools, gardens, and sundecks. Disney-character breakfasts are served in the cafe. The Kids Stuff program and The Spa are outstanding. Shuttles to theme parks are free.

1900 Lake Buena Vista Dr., just north of Hotel Plaza Blvd. ☎ ***800/327-2990*** *or 407/827-2727. Fax 407/827-6034. www.bvp-resort.com.* **Parking:** *Free self-parking; valet parking $7 nightly.* **Rack rates:** *$145–$250 standard double; $245–$290 Crown Level; up to $455 for a 2-bedroom suite. Packages available including spa service or WDW admissions. AE, CB, DC, DISC, MC, V.*

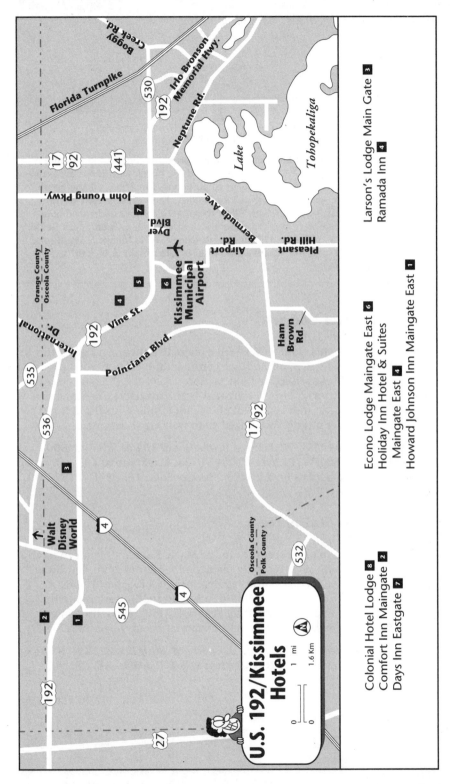

U.S. 192/Kissimmee Hotels

Colonial Hotel Lodge **8**
Comfort Inn Maingate **2**
Days Inn Eastgate **7**

Econo Lodge Maingate East **6**
Holiday Inn Hotel & Suites
Maingate East **4**
Howard Johnson Inn Maingate East **1**

Larson's Lodge Main Gate **3**
Ramada Inn **4**

Extra! Extra!

If you're traveling with kids... well, Orlando is probably the most kid-friendly destination on the planet. We've singled out those hotels with the most exceptional children's programs, but it's hard to go wrong. Just about all the hotels and motels in the area will go all out for families. The **hotels in Walt Disney World** are in a class by themselves. All of them are ideal for children. In addition to the Disney hotels, our top picks are the **Doubletree Guest Suites Resort** (Lake Buena Vista; $$$), the **Hilton at Walt Disney World Village** (Lake Buena Vista; $$$–$$$$), and the **Holiday Inn Hotel & Suites Main Gate East** (U.S. 192/Kissimmee; $$).

Colonial Hotel Lodge
$–$$. U.S. 192/Kissimmee.

When you can get this close to WDW for prices like these, and get extras like two junior Olympic-size pools and free continental breakfast, you've found a whale of a deal. Guest Services sells attraction tickets at a discount; the shuttle to the parks costs $12; airport transport is also available. Apartments have full eat-in kitchens, so they're a great choice for families. An IHOP is next door, but for fancier dining you'll need good walking shoes or a car.

1815 W. Vine St., on U.S. 192, between Bermuda and Thacker aves. ☎ **800/325-4348** *or 407/8847-6121. Fax 407/847-0728.* **Rack rates:** *$23–$50 for up to 4 people in a standard room; $50–$90 2-bedroom apt. AE, CB, DC, DISC, MC, V.*

Comfort Inn Maingate
$. U.S. 192/Kissimmee.

Only a mile from the main entrance to the Magic Kingdom, you can have a clean, comfortable (though typically plain vanilla) motel room, but little extras such as the coffeemaker and refrigerator add a touch of home. A Waffle House is across the street. Opt for a garden room overlooking the gazebo for a surprisingly pretty setting at rock-bottom rates. Discounted WDW tickets are available; round-trip transportation to the parks is $7.

7571 W. Irlo Bronson Memorial Hwy. (U.S. 192). ☎ **800/221-2222** *or 407/396-7500. Fax 407/396-7497.* **Rack rates:** *$38–$70 double. AE, CB, DC, DISC, JCB, MC, V.*

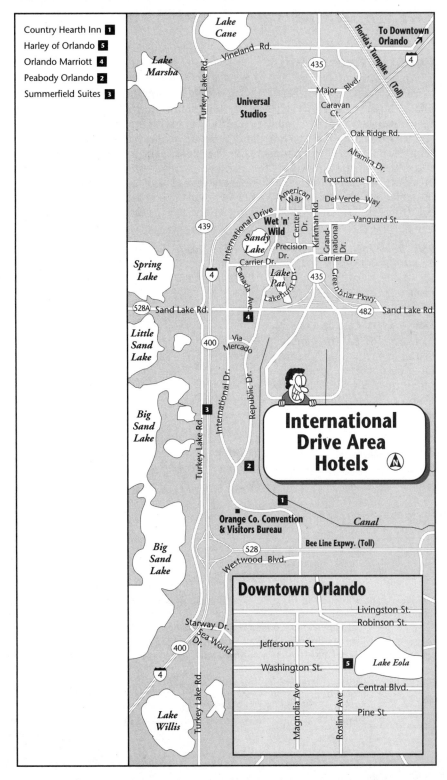

Country Hearth Inn **1**
Harley of Orlando **5**
Orlando Marriott **4**
Peabody Orlando **2**
Summerfield Suites **3**

International Drive Area Hotels

Downtown Orlando

Country Hearth Inn
$. International Drive.

I-Drive is the high-rent district, but here's an amazing deal. It's a homey, hospitable hotel in the heart of the attractions action, just across the street from the convention center. Combine country decor with a pool, room refrigerators, ceiling fans, and a private patio or balcony, and you've got a winner for skinflint travelers. Deluxe rooms have sofa beds, hair dryers, microwaves, and coffeemakers. The weekly wine and cheese parties, the free continental breakfast, and features such as room service and free HBO put this in the Best Buy category. Discounted WDW tickets are available; a shuttle to WDW parks is $10. The restaurant is modestly priced; the Front Porch lounge serves at happy-hour prices from 5:30 to 7pm.

9861 International Dr., between the Bee Line Expressway and Sand Lake Rd.
☎ ***800/447-1890*** *or 407/352-0008. Fax 407/352-5449.* **Rack rates:**
$59–$139 double. Extra person $10. Children under age 18 stay free in parents' room. AE, CB, DC, DISC, MC, V.

Days Inn Eastgate
$. U.S. 192/Kissimmee.

You're in the heart of theme-park country here. Balconies overlook the swimming pool. On the grounds are a picnic area and a children's play area. A cafe is open for breakfast; other restaurants are a short drive away. Discount tickets to attractions are available; a shuttle to the WDW parks is $7 round trip.

5245 W. Irlo Bronson Memorial Hwy. (U.S. 192), between Poinciana and Polynesian Isle blvds., Kissimmee. ☎ ***800/423-3864*** *or 407/396-7700. Fax 407/396-0293.* **Rack rates:** *$40–$79 for up to 4 people. Higher rates during special events. AE, CB, DC, DISC, JCB, MC, V.*

Extra! Extra!

If you want a kitchen so that you can do some of your own cooking, check out the following:

➤ Colonial Motor Lodge (U.S. 192/Kissimmee; $)
➤ Disney's BoardWalk (Walt Disney World; $$$$)
➤ Disney's Fort Wilderness Resort and Campground (Walt Disney World; $$$$)
➤ Doubletree Guest Suites Resort (Lake Buena Vista; $$$)
➤ Howard Johnson Inn–Maingate East (U.S. 192/Kissimmee; $$)
➤ Larson's Lodge Main Gate (U.S. 192/Kissimmee; $)
➤ Summerfield Suites (International Drive; $$–$$$)

Kids **Disney's All-Star Music Resort**
$$. Walt Disney World.

This is a good value. In this thoroughly music-themed resort, you'll find lots of young people (including entire school bands), sardine-size rooms (about 260 square feet), and round-the-clock good times. The kids, including teenagers, will love the ambiance here. Who cares if you don't have 24-hour room service? Rooms, though small, are comfortable; rates are rock-bottom; and the swimming pools are supersize. Dine in the food court, play the video arcade, or walk the nearby pine woods. Even though children under age 18 stay in your room free, we'd suggest getting two rooms unless you've shrunk the kids.

1801 W. Buena Vista Dr., at World Dr. and Osceola Pkwy. ☎ ***407/W-DISNEY** or 407/939-6000. Fax 407/354-1866. www.disneyworld.com. **Rack rates:** $69–$89 double. Children under age 18 stay free in parents' room; extra adults pay $8 nightly. AE, MC, V.*

Kids **Disney's All-Star Sports Resort**
$$. Walt Disney World.

Substitute a sports theme and this place is practically a clone of the All-Star Music Resort. The sports motif is so captivating and complete that your little pitcher will love it. Again, though, two rooms are better than one for a family of four or more, which begins to negate the price advantage. One of the big swimming pools has a baseball theme; the other has a surfer motif. Room service is available for pizza only, but there are lots of meal choices available in the food court.

1701 W. Buena Vista Dr., at World Dr. and Osceola Pkwy. ☎ ***407/W-DISNEY** or 407/939-5000. Fax 407/354-1866. www.disneyworld.com. **Rack rates:** $69–$89 double. Children under age 18 stay free in parents' room; extra adults pay $8 nightly. AE, MC, V.*

Kids **Disney's Beach Club Resort**
$$$$. Walt Disney World.

Picture yourself in a swank, turn-of-the-century New England resort next to the local yacht club. The 25-acre lake, which serves as the pool, seems as big as the Atlantic (sans sharks); the gardens are a picture. Spacious rooms have two queen-size beds or a king and a double. You'll also have an in-room safe, a ceiling fan, an extra phone in the bath, and decor brightly done in blonde wood and pastels. Ask for a room with a balcony overlooking the water. You can order from 24-hour room service, dine in Ariel's, have a clambake in the Cape May Café, or book a Disney-character breakfast.

1800 Epcot Resorts Blvd., off Buena Vista Dr. ☎ ***407/W-DISNEY** or 407/ 934-8000. www.disneyworld.com. **Rack rates:** $260–$330 double, depending on the view and the season. Children under age 17 stay free in parents' room. AE, MC, V.*

Extra! Extra!

If you're disabled, we suggest you start out by calling **Barrier Free Vacations** (☎ 800/749-5635; www.barrier-freevacations.com). They can arrange a WDW vacation that includes accommodations with roll-in shower, WDW tickets, and airport transfers in a wheelchair-accessible vehicle. Note, too, that **all Walt Disney World Hotels,** transportation, and entertainments are wheelchair accessible. (But note that guests in wheelchairs can't board the monorail at the Contemporary Resort. Stay at the Polynesian or Grand Floridian for monorail access or elsewhere for access to buses.) In addition to any of the Disney hotels, we recommend the **Buena Vista Palace Resort & Spa** (International Drive; $$$–$$$$) and the **Holiday Inn Hotel & Suites Main Gate East** (U.S. 192/Kissimmee; $$).

Disney's BoardWalk
$$$$. Walt Disney World.

Atlantic City in its heyday was no match for this complex with its "seaside" entertainments, plush accommodations, and real, wooden boardwalk. Rich furnishings and roomy rooms, which sleep up to five, add up to homelike comforts in a nostalgic setting. The villas, which sleep up to 12, have kitchens and washer-dryers. Some even have whirlpools. The ambiance may be homey, but the service and amenities are downtown all the way: concierge, 24-hour room service, free newspaper, boat transport to MGM and Epcot, swimming pools, tennis, whirlpool, croquet, jogging path, playground, supervised child care, and free valet parking. Rooms overlooking the boardwalk have the best views, but they can be noisy.

*2101 N. Epcot Resorts Blvd., off Buena Vista Dr. ☎ 407/W-DISNEY or 407/939-5100. www.disneyworld.com. **Rack rates:** $260–$615 double, depending on the season and view. Villas come in studios or 1- or 2-bedroom units, ranging from $260 to $480. Children under age 18 stay free in parents' room. AE, MC, V.*

Disney's Caribbean Beach Resort
$$$. Walt Disney World.

Imagine you're in Jamaica, Martinique, or Aruba. Each of the five two-story complexes forms an island "village," deliciously themed to a splashy, tropical setting. With 2,112 rooms, this is a hotel of Las Vegas proportions. The villages rim a lake where you can watch the ducks or jog the path that surrounds it. The swimming pool looks like an ancient fort. Rooms are bright and comfortably furnished in the pineapple theme that stands for "welcome" in the West Indies. Walk to Parrot Cay, where there are picnic tables and a nature trail. Dine at a choice of moderately priced stalls in the food court, or on American favorites in the Captain's Tavern.

900 Cayman Way, off Buena Vista Dr. ☎ *407/W-DISNEY or 407/934-3400. Fax 407/354-1866. www.disneyworld.com.* **Rack rates:** *$114–$149 double. Extra adult $12. AE, MC, V.*

Kids Disney's Contemporary Resort
$$$$. Walt Disney World.

An enormous pyramid large enough to swallow the monorail, this original WDW hotel still holds a lot of magic for loyal guests, even if it doesn't seem as "contemporary" as it once did. The pool area, newly redone, is a miniature water park. The decor is *moderne;* oversize rooms are adequate for a family of four or five in two queen-size beds and a child's daybed. One of the best things about staying here is that you can hop on the monorail and come back to the hotel for lunch, a nap, or a swim, and still be back in the Magic Kingdom in time for the afternoon parade and additional fun. The 15th-floor California Grill has great food and great views. Or dine in the Concourse Steakhouse or Contemporary Café. You can also book a character breakfast here for the kids.

4600 N. World Dr. ☎ *407/W-DISNEY or 407/824-1000. Fax 407/354-1866. www.disneyworld.com.* **Rack rates:** *$230–$315 double. Children under age 17 sleep free in parents' room. AE, MC, V.*

Extra! Extra!

If you're looking for a romantic getaway or the perfect spot for a honeymoon, consider a spa package at the **Buena Vista Palace Resort & Spa** (Lake Buena Vista; $$$–$$$$), where you can also have a romantic dinner at Arthur's 27. At **Disney's Grand Floridian Beach Resort** (Walt Disney World; $$$$), you can book a king-size room, enjoy some decadent spa treatments, and have a candlelit dinner one night in the fabulously romantic (though wickedly expensive) Victoria and Albert's. The **Peabody Orlando** (International Drive; $$$$) provides all the pampering a couple needs for a romantic recharge. Surprise your partner by ordering a VIP turndown. (It's not just mints on the pillow, but something fabulous like chocolate-covered strawberries, milk and cookies, or two tiny bottles of a special liqueur.) For lovebirds on a more modest budget, the **Harley of Orlando** (Downtown; $$) provides a nostalgic flight to the 1940s. Ask about special weekend packages.

Kids Disney's Dixie Landings Resort
$$$. Walt Disney World.

With two double beds in each room, these units offer ample room for a family of three or four, and the modest prices attract families by the boatload. It's a boisterous place, with a Cajun theme that calls for waterfalls, rustic furnishings, and a fishin' hole where you can angle for catfish. Dine American or Cajun at various restaurants, or order pizza from room service. Swim in a choice of six pools, or shop in Fulton's General Store. Boats go from here to Pleasure Island, Port Orleans, and the Village Marketplace.

1251 Dixie Dr., off Bonnet Creek Pkwy. ☎ *407/W-DISNEY or 407/934-6000. Fax 407/934-5777. www.disneyworld.com.* **Rack rates:** *$114–$149 for up to 4 in a room. AE, MC, V.*

Kids Disney's Fort Wilderness Resort and Campground
$–$$$$. Walt Disney World.

This may be one of the priciest campgrounds in the world, but you get a lot of bang for your buck. Even the lowliest tent campers have all the pools and playgrounds of a first-rate resort at their doorstep, and the location is one of WDW's best for getting to the theme parks and water parks. Bring your own camper or rent an on-site RV that sleeps six and has a full kitchen. Visit the theme parks; then come back to dine in Trails End or Crockett's Tavern, or fire up your own barbecue. Go horseback riding or swimming; visit the petting farm; fish; or play baseball, tennis, or golf. Some campsites accept pets. From the beach, you can see the nightly water pageant in summer. The Hoop-Dee-Doo Musical Revue plays nightly in Pioneer Hall.

3520 Fort Wilderness Trail. ☎ *407/W-DISNEY or 407/824-3000. Fax 407/ 354-1866. www.disneyworld.com.* **Rack rates:** *$43–$64 for campsites with full hookup; $185–$230 for trailers, known in Disney-speak as "Wilderness Homes." Add $2 per person for more than 2 adults in a campsite, and $5 per person for more than 2 adults in a Wilderness Home. AE, MC, V.*

Kids Disney's Grand Floridian Beach Resort
$$$$$. Walt Disney World.

The grand summer mansions of Newport and Jekyll Island inspired the Victorian splendor that characterizes this opulent, 40-acre resort on the

Dollars & Sense

According to the latest available figures, hotel rates are highest in March, when they average just over $80, and lowest in August, when they average about $67. Year-round, the average daily rate is about $75.

shores of the Seven Seas Lagoon. The decor is filled with the elegance of yester-year, and the spacious grounds are a photographer's paradise. Return to a more gracious past in a room richly furnished with chintz, mahogany, and a four-poster bed. Balconies overlook picture-book gardens and lakes. Here you can sail on a 200-acre lagoon, play croquet, or swim in the big pool with its poolside cabanas. Order from 24-hour room service, or dine in a half dozen restaurants; don't miss afternoon tea in the Garden View Lounge. Take WDW transportation to the theme parks; a trolley takes you around the resort.

4401 Floridian Way. ☎ *407/W-DISNEY or 407/824-3000. Fax 407/354-1866. www.disneyworld.com.* **Rack rates:** *$184–$530 double, depending on the view and season. Extra adult $15. AE, MC, V.*

Kids Disney's Old Key West Resort
$$$$. Walt Disney World.
Time-share isn't always a nice word in Orlando, but Disney does it right. When the owners of these units aren't in residence, the accommodations are made available to hotel guests. The homelike furnishings—big-screen TVs, VCRs, TVs in the bedrooms, extra phones, and much more—make this a good choice for a longer stay. Unpack, provision the pantry, and make yourself at home in a studio or a villa with one, two, or three bedrooms. Enjoy the sandy playground, swimming pools, tennis courts, video arcade, whirlpool, health club, or boating. In the rec center, two free Disney movies play nightly.

1510 N. Cove Rd., off Community Dr. ☎ *407/W-DISNEY or 407/827-7700. Fax 407/354-1866. www.disneyworld.com.* **Rack rates:** *From $209 for a studio in low season to $860 for a 3-bedroom Grand Villa during the holidays. AE, MC, V.*

Kids Disney's Polynesian Resort
$$$$$. Walt Disney World.
It wasn't easy to re-create the lushness of Hawaii in Central Florida, with its occasional droughts and freezes, but Disney magic did the trick, transporting guests to the South Pacific. Combine the convenience of monorail access to the parks with the privacy of spread-out accommodations that seem far more off the beaten track than they really are. Relax in a hammock on the white-sand beach, book a character breakfast, water-ski, jog the 1.5-mile trail, fish, or hop on the monorail or boat to the Magic Kingdom. Among the restaurants and lounges is a 24-hour ice-cream parlor.

1600 Seven Seas Dr. ☎ *407/W-DISNEY or 407/824-4000. www.disneyworld. com.* **Rack rates:** *$260 standard double; $415–$430 concierge-level double. AE, MC, V.*

Kids Disney's Port Orleans Resort
$$$. Walt Disney World.
Think of it as the French Quarter without the sleaze. Dixieland and good times greet you in this resort, with its courtyard fountains, New Orleans–style wrought-iron balconies, and colorful shutters. There's a big pool with an oversized water slide. There's also a whirlpool, a kiddy pool, and gardens galore. Rent a bike, play in the video arcade, jog the riverfront path, and enjoy New Orleans–style dining. Along with Dixie Landings, this one is on the "Sassagoula River."

2201 Orleans Dr., off Bonnet Creek Pkwy. ☎ *407/W-DISNEY or 407/934-5000. Fax 407/934-5353. www.disneyworld.com.* **Rack rates:** *$114–$149 double. AE, MC, V.*

Disney's Wilderness Lodge
$$$–$$$$. Walt Disney World.

Walk into the awesome lobby and you're in Yellowstone, complete with thermal springs, grand lodgepole woods, and a massive stone fireplace.

Extra! Extra!

If you want the best tennis and golf facilities, look no further than **Disney's Contemporary Resort** (Walt Disney World; $$$$) or **Disney's Wilderness Lodge** (Walt Disney World; $$$–$$$$).

Guests don't exactly have to rough it in this rustic, Teddy Roosevelt–era "log" building done in Native-American motifs. Swim from the resort's sandy beach, soak in the spa, rent a bike, sail, or jog the 2-mile trail. Dining is in the romantic Artist Point or in the Western-style Whispering Canyon Cafe. Children can join the Cub's Den for supervised activities.

901 Timberline Dr., on the southwest shore of Bay Lake, east of the Magic Kingdom. ☎ *407/W-DISNEY or 407/824-3200. Fax 407/354-1866. www.disneyworld.com.* **Rack rates:** *$184–$245 double. AE, MC, V.*

Kids Disney's Yacht Club Resort
$$$$. Walt Disney World.

Surround yourself with fellow commodores, and imagine you're living the good life on Martha's Vineyard or Nantucket. The nautical theme is tastefully elegant; real yachties will love the hardwoods, shiny brasses, and staff in 1880s swim costumes. The resort also boasts grassy lawns and an eye-popping swimming pool. There's a working fireplace in the lobby bar and several restaurants, including a pubby lounge, a cafe, and a plush steak house. Rooms are done in a nautical motif; French doors open onto the balcony. Room service is 24 hours; the resort has the same facilities as Disney's Beach Club Resort (above).

1700 Epcot Resorts Blvd. ☎ *407/W-DISNEY or 407/934-7000. Fax 407/354-1866. www.disneyworld.com.* **Rack rates:** *$260–$335 double; $380–$430 concierge-level double. Rates vary according to season and view. AE, MC, V.*

Kids Doubletree Guest Suites Resort
$$$. Lake Buena Vista/Official WDW Hotel.

Families will appreciate the kid-glove treatment that pint-sized guests receive here. Kids have their own check-in desk, pool, activities, theater, and menus. You get enough of a kitchen to whip up light meals, and you're in a central location for theme parks and Orlando's best shopping. Luxury-seekers will be wowed by the seven-story atrium lobby and the many little extras, such as a TV in the bathroom. Suites have wet bars, refrigerators, coffeemakers, and microwave ovens, and provisions are sold on-site. Take the free shuttle to the theme parks, or stay "home" to enjoy the big pool, whirlpool, and kiddy pool with fountain. Play tennis or volleyball, use the fitness room, rent a boat, jog, or shop.

2305 Hotel Plaza Blvd., just west of Apopka–Vineland Rd./FL 535. ☎ ***800/ 222-8733*** *or 407/934-1700. Fax 407/934-1101.* ***Rack rates:*** *$139–$235 for up to 6 in a 1-bedroom suite; to $475 for 2-bedroom suite. Children under age 18 stay free in parents' room. AE, CB, DC, DISC, JCB, MC, V.*

Econo Lodge Maingate East
$. U.S. 192/Kissimmee.

One of the most secluded motels along Kissimmee's strip is this cluster of low-rise units set well back from the roar of the busy highway. Breakfast and lunch are available; snacks are sold at the pool bar. Rooms have balconies, and there's a pool, a kiddy pool, volleyball, shuffleboard, picnic tables, barbecue grills, and coin-op guest laundry facilities. Scheduled shuttles serve the theme parks and airport. When you're having breakfast under the oak trees around the pool, it's a country vacation; when you hop on the free shuttle to Walt Disney World, it's uptown all the way.

4311 W. Irlo Bronson Memorial Hwy. (U.S. 192), between Hoagland Blvd. and FL 535, Kissimmee. ☎ ***800/ENJOY-FL*** *or 407/ 396-7100. Fax 407/239-2636.* ***Rack rates:*** *$29–$79 for up to 4 people. AE, CB, DC, DISC, JCB, MC, V.*

Extra! Extra!

If you want a gorgeous swimming pool, lots of places have what you're looking for, but not all pools are created equal. All the Disney hotels have gorgeous pools, but our favorite is at Disney's Caribbean Beach Resort (Walt Disney World; $$$), which re-creates a Caribbean fort with cannons and stone walls. It also has a fun water slide so that you can make a big, splashy entrance.

Grosvenor Resort
$$–$$$. Lake Buena Vista/Official WDW Hotel.

If you prefer traditional styling, plenty of stay-at-home entertainments (including a dinner theater and a VCR in your room), and a moderate price in a central location, find it here. A stately Colonial look and a forest of palms welcome guests to a homey resort that has a Sherlock Holmes museum, Disney characters, and a Saturday-night mystery theater. Each room has a coffeemaker, a safe, room service, a minibar (stocked on request), and a VCR. The resort offers tennis, swimming, a whirlpool, a playground, and lawn games. Dine in Baskerville's, Moriarty's Pub, or the 24-hour food court. Discount theme-park tickets and a complimentary shuttle are available.

1850 Hotel Plaza Blvd., just east of Buena Vista Dr. ☎ ***800/624-4109*** *or 407/828-4444. Fax 407/828-8192.* ***Parking:*** *Free self-parking; valet parking $6 nightly.* ***Rack rates:*** *$99–$175 double. AE, CB, DC, DISC, JCB, MC, V.*

Harley of Orlando
$$. Downtown.

If you want to be away from the theme parks, the mellow old Harley, in Orlando's recently revived downtown area, is for you. You can walk to downtown clubs and restaurants, or drive to the Centroplex for performances, games, and conventions in just a couple of minutes. Ask for a room with a balcony overlooking Lake Eola Park, with its pretty fountains and vast greenways. Rooms are smallish and somber, but the tradeoff involves a pool, a sundeck, free newspapers on weekdays, and a handy location. You can do your dining and drinking on-site or at Church Street Station, which is a short walk away. The free Lymmo, a downtown shuttle, also stops here.

151 E. Washington St. ☎ *800/321-2323 or 407/841-3220. Fax 407/849-1839.* **Rack rates:** *$95–$150 double. AE, MC, V.*

Extra! Extra!

If you're into nightlife, the **Harley of Orlando** (Downtown; $$) is close to downtown nightclubs, Church Street Station, and performances at the Bob Carr Auditorium and Orlando Arena. The closest hotels to WDW nightlife at Pleasure Island and Downtown Disney are the **Buena Vista Palace Resort & Spa** (Lake Buena Vista; $$$–$$$$), **Disney's Dixie Landings Resort** (Walt Disney World; $$$), **Disney's Old Key West Resort** (Walt Disney World; $$$$), **Disney's Port Orleans Resort** (Walt Disney World; $$$), and the **Grosvenor Resort** (Lake Buena Vista; $$–$$$).

Kids Hilton at Walt Disney World Village
$$–$$$. Lake Buena Vista/Official WDW Hotel.

Hilton promises a touch of posh pampering to help you recover from the relentless theme-park brouhaha. When you lose yourself in the 23 acres, with their two big lakes, the World seems miles away. Count on Hilton to provide everything the family or business traveler could ask for: phones with voice mail and modem jack, coffeemaker, plenty of dining choices from simple to splurge, two swimming pools plus a kiddy pool, a health club with a sauna, tennis courts, rental boats, a beauty/barber shop, and a supervised child-care center.

1751 Hotel Plaza Blvd., just east of Buena Vista Dr. ☎ *800/782-4414 or 407/827-3890. Fax 407/827-3890. www.hilton.com.* **Parking:** *Free self-parking; valet parking $8 nightly.* **Rack rates:** *$150–$260 double; Tower rooms $40 more. Children of any age stay free in parents' room. Ask about packages and weekend rates. AE, CB, DC, DISC, JCB, MC, V.*

Holiday Inn Hotel & Suites Main Gate East
$$. U.S. 192/Kissimmee.

There are several branches of Holiday Inn around Orlando, but this is one of the best because of its sprawling grounds, kid-friendly and pet-friendly rooms, and location (only 3 miles from the Magic Kingdom). We like the nice mix of mouse-theme merriment and no-nonsense hospitality. All the rooms are child-safe and feature refrigerators, microwaves, and VCRs. Specially designed Kidsuites™ have a playhouse that sleeps up to three. Suites have hair dryers, microwaves, refrigerators, VCRs, CD players, irons, and ironing boards. Some have whirlpool tubs. Shuttles to WDW are free. Transport to other theme parks and attractions is available.

5678 Irlo Bronson Memorial Hwy. (U.S. 192), Kissimmee. ☎ *800/FON-KIDS or 407/396-4488. Fax 407/396-1296. www.familyfunhotel.com.* **Rack rates:** *$75–$105 double; Kidsuites $25–$30 extra. AE, CB, DC, DISC, JCB, MC, V.*

Howard Johnson Inn–Maingate East
$$. U.S. 192/Kissimmee.

Howard Johnson isn't known for its hoity-toity touches, but this particular branch works hard at keeping its rating as one of Howard's top motels. You'll be only 3 miles from the Magic Kingdom in the heart of Kissimmee's strip. You'll find a swimming pool, whirlpool, kiddy pool, video arcade, and coin-op laundry, as well as a free shuttle to the Disney parks. Family suites have full kitchens and living rooms with sofa beds. Efficiencies have sink, refrigerator, and two-burner cooktop. A pool bar serves snacks. An IHOP and a huge water park are next door; lots of other restaurants are a short drive away. Call the special toll-free guest services number (☎ **800/TOUR-FLA**) to arrange tickets and all sorts of reservations to create your own custom package.

2009 W. Vine St. (U.S. 192 at Thacker Ave.), Kissimmee. ☎ *800/288-4678 or 407/396-1748. Fax 407/649-8642. www.Hojo.com.* **Rack rates:** *$60–$80 for up to 4 people; $90–$100 family suite. Children under age 19 stay free in parents' room. AE, CB, DC, DISC, JCB, MC, V.*

Extra! Extra!

If you want a spa vacation, the **Buena Vista Palace Resort & Spa** (Lake Buena Vista; $$$–$$$$) has a European-style spa with a long menu of spa and salon services. In Walt Disney World itself, **Disney's Grand Floridian Beach Resort** (Walt Disney World; $$$$) has the most lavish spa. The **Walt Disney World Swan** (Walt Disney World; $$$$$) has a full-service Body by Jake, aerobics, personal trainers, classes, and a full range of the latest machines.

Larson's Lodge Main Gate
$. U.S. 192/Kissimmee.
It's the next best thing to staying in Walt Disney World. This is a motel with its own water park (WaterMania) and a Shoney's on-site. You could spend whole days here without moving the car. The shuttle to WDW is $8 round-trip; discount admission tickets are available. Efficiencies have microwave ovens and refrigerators. On-site are a whirlpool, a barbecue, picnic tables, a heated pool, and shops; you can play tennis free nearby. The lobby offers free coffee and newspapers in the morning. Pets are welcome.

6075 W. Irlo Bronson Memorial Hwy. (U.S. 192), just east of I-4. ☎ **800/327-9074** *or 407/396-6100. Fax 407/396-6965.* **Rack rates:** *$39–$79 double; $15 more for a room with kitchenette. Children under age 19 stay free in parents' room. AE, CB, DC, DISC, MC, V.*

Orlando Marriott
$$. International Drive.
If you need to take some time off from the theme parks, the Marriott is your relaxation station par excellence. You're minutes away from most of the attractions, yet the classy, parklike setting will make you feel that you're in a secluded resort. Roam 48 sunny acres, swim in three pools, play tennis, or jog. Villa suites are available with full kitchens. Free trams offer 24-hour service around the grounds; you can ride round-trip to WDW for $8. Dine in the hotel's restaurants, or there are lots of choices nearby. Discounted attractions tickets are available.

8001 International Dr., at Sand Lake Rd. ☎ **800/421-8001** *or 407/351-2420. Fax 407/345-5611.* **Rack rates:** *$79–$139 double; $110–$300 suite. AE, CB, DC, DISC, JCB, MC, V*

Peabody Orlando
$$$$. International Drive.
A favorite of business travelers and visiting celebrities, the Peabody is famous for the ducks in its lobby fountain. A prestige business address, proximity to the theme parks, and a location within walking distance of the Convention Center make this a fine choice for those who want the best. Rooms have two phones, cable TV with a laser movie disc player, a small TV in the bathroom, and 24-hour room service. Unlimited shuttles to theme parks are $6 a day. There's also an Olympic-length swimming pool, a 7-mile jogging path, and a high-tech fitness center; guests also enjoy golf privileges nearby. Your dining options range from a formal restaurant to the B-Line Diner.

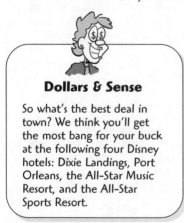

Dollars & Sense

So what's the best deal in town? We think you'll get the most bang for your buck at the following four Disney hotels: Dixie Landings, Port Orleans, the All-Star Music Resort, and the All-Star Sports Resort.

9801 International Dr., between the Bee Line Expressway and Sand Lake Rd.
☎ *800/PEABODY or 407/352-4000. Fax 407/351-0073.* **Parking:** *Free self-parking; valet parking $7 nightly.* **Rack rates:** *$240–$300 double; up to $1,350 suite. Ask about packages and senior discounts. AE, CB, DC, DISC, JCB, MC, V.*

Ramada Inn
$. U.S. 192/Kissimmee.
You'd never look twice at this standard, budget-beige motel—but check out the prices and the location! For $6 over the standard double rate, you can get an efficiency with stovetop, sink, and refrigerator (but no pots or tableware). Outdoors there are a picnic area, a playground, and a pool. Restaurants abound nearby. The Ramada Ltd., a block away, has similar rates. Both offer a shuttle to WDW for $9; both accept pets for $6 extra per night.

4559 W. Irlo Bronson Memorial Hwy. (U.S. 192), between Siesta Logo Dr. and Bass Rd. (also called Old Vineland Rd.). ☎ *800/544-5712 or 407/396-1212. Fax 407/396-7926.* **Rack rates:** *$23.95–$44.95 double. AE, DC, DISC, MC, V.*

Renaissance Orlando Hotel–Airport
$$–$$$. Airport Area.
Here's the ideal place to stay if you have a limited amount of time and need to be close to the airport on the day you arrive and the day you leave. The hotel is designed for business travelers, with spacious rooms and a big bathroom with TV speaker, hair dryer, and phone. But there's no reason families can't enjoy all the amenities, too, including a whirlpool, a fitness center, a big pool, a sauna, and six golf courses within 10 miles. A shuttle to the theme parks is $26 per person, round trip.

5445 Forbes Pl., at the corner of State 436 and State 528, just east of the Turnpike. ☎ *800/HOTELS-1 or 407/240-1000. Fax 407/240-1005. www.renaissancehotels. com.* **Parking:** *Free self-parking; long-term parking free for guests.* **Rack rates:** *$89–$189 double. MC, V.*

Summerfield Suites
$$–$$$. International Drive.
These two-bedroom suites can sleep up to eight people (if they're really into togetherness). Balconies overlook a courtyard filled with rustling palms. Sun seekers will feel immediately at home in a suite that is more than just a bedroom. Take time away from the theme parks to luxuriate in verdant grounds with the ambiance of a fine resort. Units have homey features such as iron, ironing board, full kitchen, TV in both the living room and the bedrooms, and multiple phones. Continental breakfast is free; extra courses can be purchased. The hotel has a pool, kiddy pool, fitness center, coin-op laundry, video arcade, and 24-hour sundries shop. The shuttle to WDW is $7.

8480 International Dr., between the Bee Line Expressway and Sand Lake Rd. ☎ *800/830-4964 or 407/352-2400. Fax 407/238-0778.* **Rack rates:** *$169–$269 double. AE, CB, DC, DISC, MC, V.*

81

Time-Savers

So you think you want to stay in a Disney hotel, but you're still confused about which one to choose? Call Disney's Central Reservations Office at ☎ 407/ W-DISNEY. These folks can take your reservations at any of the Disney hotels, resorts, villas, official hotels, or Fort Wilderness homes and campsites. They'll be happy to recommend specific accommodations to suit your needs, and they can set you up with a package that includes meals, tickets, and other features.

Walt Disney World Dolphin
Kids
$$$$. Walt Disney World.

The 56-foot-high dolphins that sit atop this 1,509-room hotel can be seen for miles around, so your jaw will already have dropped by the time you enter the lobby of this wildly designed hotel, created by trendy architect Michael Graves. It's pricey and the rooms aren't exactly what I'd call oversized, but the "entertainment" architecture is definitely out of the ordinary. The grounds are lavishly landscaped, and amenities include 24-hour room service, a health club, floodlit tennis courts, boat rental, a 3-mile jogging trail, tennis, a sandy beach, and many restaurants. Camp Dolphin provides supervised kiddy play. The resort shares facilities with the Walt Disney World Swan, next door. You can walk to Epcot or use free WDW transportation.

1500 Epcot Resorts Blvd., off Buena Vista Dr. ☎ *800/227-1500 or 407/ 934-4000. Fax 407/934-4884.* ***Parking:*** *Free self-parking; valet parking $6 nightly.* ***Rack rates:*** *$210–$410 double. AE, CB, DC, DISC, JCB, MC, V.*

Walt Disney World Swan
Kids
$$$$$. Walt Disney World.

Like its dolphin-topped neighbor, this one is capped with 46-foot-high swans that can be seen from afar. Its fascinating design, whether you love it or hate it, is also the work of Michael Graves. Standard rooms with two doubles will be cramped for families; rooms with a king-size bed and sleeper sofa are a better choice. From here, you can walk to Epcot or take WDW transportation to the other parks. Choose from an array of restaurants here and in the Westin-operated Dolphin (above), or order from 24-hour room service. Swim the Olympic-size pool, work out in the fitness center, and let the business center take care of job worries.

1200 Epcot Resorts Blvd., off Buena Vista Dr. ☎ *800/248-7926 or 407/ 228-3000. Fax 407/934-4499.* ***Parking:*** *Free self-parking; valet parking $8 nightly.* ***Rack rates:*** *$280–$410 double; $340–$370 concierge-level double; up to $1,750 suite. Children under age 18 stay free in parents' room. AE, CB, DC, DISC, JCB, MC, V.*

Help! I'm So Confused!

For some of you, the decision may be easy. You want to stay in the nicest hotel closest to the Magic Kindgom, and price is no object. For everybody else, there are tradeoffs to be made among price, location, and convenience.

That's where organization comes into the picture. Some people charge lots of money for getting other people organized, but we'll throw it in free, just because we like you.

Here, then, is a chart. you probably read through the reviews in the preceding section and said, at least a few times, "Hey, that one sounds good." If you put a little red check next to those establishments, you're ahead of the game (if not, we hope you have a good memory), but it would still be a royal pain in the butt to fip around through a few dozen pages comparinga and contrasting them.

So what you want to do is jot down the names and vital statistics of those places in the chart below, get everything lined up and orderly, and then scan the line to see how they stack up against each other. As you rank them in your mind, rank them in the column on the right too; that way you can have your preferences all ready when making reservations, and if there's no room at the inn for choice number 1, you can just move on to number 2.

Hotel Preferences Worksheet		
Hotel	Location	Price per night

Advantages	Disadvantages	Your Ranking (1–10)

Part 3

Learning Your Way Around Walt Disney World & Orlando

You don't have to be a complete idiot to feel a bit overwhelmed by everything going on in Orlando. Negotiating the various sections of Walt Disney World alone can seem daunting, to say nothing of venturing into downtown Orlando and daring the highway traffic.

Rest easy, though. It's not as complicated as it looks at first. Most of the attractions in this book are confined to the area bounded by downtown Orlando to the north, the airport to the east, Walt Disney World to the west, and Kissimmee–St. Cloud to the south. Keep going east from the airport and you end up at the Atlantic Ocean. Keep going west from WDW and you reach Tampa Bay and the Gulf of Mexico beyond.

If you're like a lot of visitors, you might not even make it to downtown Orlando, meaning you'll do less driving and even less navigating. And if you take public transportation everywhere (a very real possibility if you're staying in one of the hotels within WDW), the only maps you'll have to master are the ones of the park.

Chapter 7

Getting Your Bearings

In This Chapter

➤ Getting from point A (the airport) to point B (your bed)

➤ Figuring out the lay of the land

➤ Getting more info once you're here

The flight is over and you're finally here. Now the fun begins, but only after you have maneuvered your way through the airport maze and have survived driving in on I-4, also known as the World's Largest Parking Lot. We even have advice for you if you're one of the few who come by Amtrak.

Your Flight Just Landed—Now What?

The signage at Orlando International Airport is said to be "clear and concise." Well, concise is one thing, but clear is quite another story. There *may* be an airline information desk on your concourse, and it *may* be staffed, and it *may* not have a line that stretches from here to Key West, but chances are you won't see anybody except other confused tourists, all rushing to and fro. You'll have to depend on the signage and your personal radar. If you want to check out what services are available at the airport before you fly, the airport's helpful Web site is http://fcn.state.fl.us/goaa.

When you land and get off the plane, you'll find yourself in what the airport calls an Airside Building. In other words, your journey has one more leg to go: You have to get into the Main Terminal. To get there, you ride the airport's AGT System (in short, a little, automatic train). Look for the big sign that says Shuttle to Terminal & Bag Claim. Don't despair, though; the trains run frequently, and it's only a short hop over to the terminal. If you see one pulling out, another one is just a couple of minutes away. (Since they're automatic, once the doors close, that's that.)

Dollars & Sense

Big savings can be found in the many free magazines and tabloid newspapers found along the interstates and in every hotel lobby, restaurant, shop, rest stop, and gas station. Take one of each. They're filled with coupons good for discounts and freebies. Don't, however, take their advice about the "best" restaurants. Most of them "recommend" only restaurants that advertise with them.

The terminal has two sides, A and B, and you'll hear an announcement on the little train to the Main Terminal about where you should go to collect your bags.

So now you're safely inside the Main Terminal (you're now on level 3, by the way). Baggage claim is downstairs on level 2. There are signs that say BAG CLAIM with arrows pointing the direction you should go. Follow them, or just follow all the people since they're going to the same place you want to be.

You'll find pay phones just inside the doors between the baggage claim and the passenger pickup areas.

If you are coming from another country, you'll go through an Immigration Checkpoint, then baggage claim, then Customs even before you take the little train to the Main Terminal. And, lucky you, you then get to put your bags onto a moving belt so that you can pick them up *again* once you've arrived in the Main Terminal. If you need a Currency Exchange, you'll find booths on the arrival level in the terminal (that's level 3). Their hours coincide with the arrival of international flights, so don't worry if you're arriving outside banker's hours.

Getting Mobile

All the taxis and shuttle vans to hotels and such stop on the same level as baggage claim (that's level 2). If you already have a shuttle reservation, there is probably a space number on it, so just follow the signs to that space to get your ride. Level 2 is also the level where you can be picked up by a friend or relative. City buses and car rentals are on level 1 (that's one level down from baggage claim, and you go here even if the car-rental agency is offsite and picking you up in a courtesy van).

The **city bus (Lynx)** stops at spaces 21 through 23 on level 1 on the A side of the terminal. Buses leave every 30 to 60 minutes daily 6:30am to 8:30pm, with less frequent service on Sundays and holidays. For 75¢ (exact change), you can ride to the main bus depot downtown on Pine Street, but these buses aren't set up to accommodate any more luggage than you can carry in your lap.

Taxis, which stop on level 2, are metered. The fare (for up to eight passengers) from the airport to Walt Disney World is a whopping $40. A trip to International Drive is about $26, to downtown is $17, and to Lake Buena Vista is $32. A taxi may be a good option if you don't need or want a rental car and if there are three or more people in your party ($40 to Walt Disney World is still cheaper than the price of three people in a shuttle).

A **shuttle** ride from the airport to Walt Disney World or Lake Buena Vista costs $25 round-trip for adults, $17 for kids ages 4 to 12 (kids 3 and under are free). Taking a shuttle to International Drive costs a couple of dollars less for the round-trip. It usually costs a little more than half the round-trip price for a one-way ride if you've decided you just can't ever leave Orlando (or if you are getting a ride back to the airport). Shuttle companies that serve Orlando and the attractions area are **Mears** (☎ **407/427-1694;** www.mears-net.com/index1.htm) and **Transtar** (☎ **407/856-7777;** www.thetravelguide.com/transtar/). You can reserve your shuttle ride in advance either by phone or on the company's Web site. (Transtar offers a coupon for $4 off a round-trip fare on their Web site.)

Dollars & Sense

If you have a family, it may be cheaper to rent a car than to take shuttles or taxis around Orlando. Car rentals in Florida are cheaper than almost any place on earth, so even considering what it costs to park and for gas, you may still come out ahead. Besides, a car will give you the freedom to eat at cheaper, out-of-the-World places if you're staying at Mickey's.

Rental-car companies with branches *at* the airport include **Avis** (☎ 800/831-2847), **Budget** (☎ 800/537-0700), **Dollar** (☎ 800/800-4000), and **National** (☎ 800/227-7368). Rental companies *near* the airport provide shuttle service to their facilities. These include **Alamo** (☎ 800/327-9633), **Payless** (☎ 800/729-5377), **Anchor** (☎ 407/438-8996), **Capital** (☎ 407/438-9700), **Demo** (☎ 407/859-3900), **Enterprise** (☎ 800/551-3390), **E-Z** (☎ 507/850-0607), **Florida** (☎ 800/327-3791), **Hertz** (☎ 800/654-3131), **Interamerican** (☎ 407/859-0414), **Thrifty** (☎ 800/367-2277), and **Value** (☎ 800/468-2583). See chapter 4 for consumer tips on how to save when you reserve your car in advance.

If you'll be getting a rental car, collect your bags on level 2 and follow the signs to level 1 or to the Rental Cars area. Here you'll find either a counter with personnel to check you in or, if the rental company is off-site, a bank of free telephones you can use to call for a pickup. The largest companies run continuous shuttles in the bus lane outside level 1. Your wait probably won't be longer than 20 minutes.

The rental-car folks will give you a map. Take time to look it over and get specific directions from the rental agent. Make sure you understand exactly where you need to go as you leave the airport, because things happen fast after that.

Some Directions to Give You Direction

Here are some quick **directions for getting from the airport to Walt Disney World:** Leaving the airport, most people take FL 528 (the Bee Line Highway toll road) west for approximately 12 miles to its intersection with I-4. Go west on I-4 to Exit 26, marked Epcot/Disney Village, and follow the signs. An alternate route is to go southwest on the Central Florida Greenway (FL 417), a toll road. FL 417 will intersect with FL 536; keep left. FL 536 will cross over I-4 and become Epcot Drive. From here, follow the signs to your destination.

North, South, East, West: Getting Yourself Oriented

If you arrive at the airport, you will be almost due east of Walt Disney World, northeast of the Kissimmee–St. Cloud area, and southeast of downtown Orlando. Almost all vacationers to Orlando exit the airport via the **Bee Line Expressway** (also known as FL 528), which is the most direct route to International Drive, Florida's Turnpike, and I-4, the interstate road that links WDW to downtown Orlando.

Any idiot can see on the map that I-4 runs north and south, but the sign painters think of it as an east-west road. From the Bee Line, you'll want to go "east" (or north) to go downtown or to Universal Studios, and "west" (or south) to get to WDW and U.S. 192/Kissimmee. Of course you'll be confused. Everyone is!

The best map is the **Walt Disney World Property Map,** which you can request before you leave home by calling ☎ 407/824-4321.

Tourist Traps

You'll see signs that read Tourist Information everywhere, but most of them are attached to T–shirt shops, operations pitching time-shares and other real-estate deals, and similar tourist traps. Stick with the official information centers listed in this book.

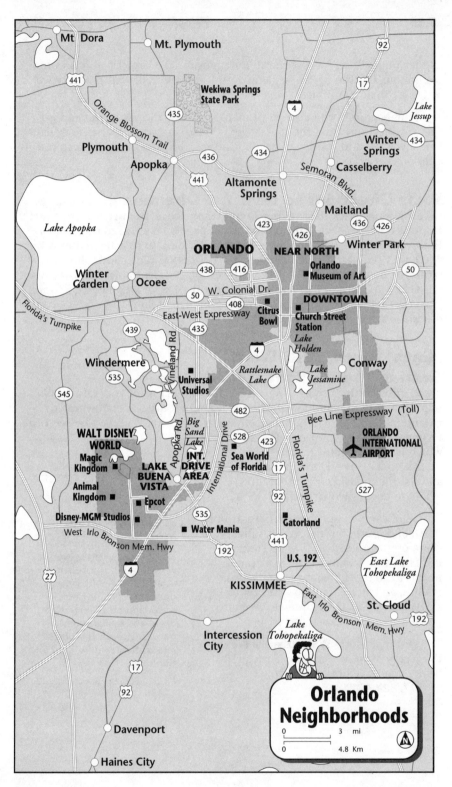

Orlando
Neighborhoods

Walt Disney World

This is the World you've probably come to visit, and it sprawls over 26,000 acres. Walt Disney World is actually not located in Orlando; it's a few miles southwest of the city, and it's really a city unto itself. It contains *several* theme parks (oh, no, one is definitely not enough), plus splashy resorts and hotels of all price ranges, restaurants, and water parks. You want it? Well, they've got it. Disney even has its own transportation system that links everything up into one nicely organized and convenient bundle.

But convenience has its price. The cheapest hotels here cost about twice what you'd pay in nearby Kissimmee for the same accommodations. And if you don't rent a car, you're trapped in a World where everything from meals to spa services is equally high-priced.

Lake Buena Vista Area (Official WDW Hotels)

Lake Buena Vista is Disney's next-door neighbor, where you'll find "official" (though non–Disney-owned) hotels; it's close to the Disney Village, Downtown Disney, and Pleasure Island. Not a bad place, really, if you want to be close to but not quite drowning in all the hubbub, and you'll have free transportation to and from the WDW theme parks (though you're not on the WDW transportation system). There are plenty of places to stay and eat here.

Kissimmee/U.S. 192

This once-sleepy city is actually closer to Walt Disney World than Orlando is, which comes as a surprise to most people. You're just a hop, skip, and jump from the theme parks if you stay here. Your main impression of Kissimmee is likely to be that it's a kind of tacky strip of modest motels and restaurants, including every fast-food place known to man. The main plus? Convenience and bargains.

International Drive Area

This is a 7- to 10-mile stretch of road north of the Disney parks, between FL 535 and the Florida Turnpike. It's where you'll find Sea World and Universal Studios, plus plenty more attractions, not to mention dozens of hotels, motels, restaurants, and shopping centers. You'll probably hear people refer to this as *I-Drive.*

Downtown

Believe it or not, Orlando was a city before the mouse moved in. It was once dying, like many downtowns, but this is an increasingly vibrant neighborhood, with countless bars, restaurants, coffeehouses, and a night-time entertainment complex for adults called Church Street Station. It's near the Orlando Science Center, which just opened in 1997. And there's the new Lymmo, a free shuttle-bus system to get you around.

Near North

These are the suburbs north of downtown Orlando. You'll find many restaurants here that might be worth the drive if you are getting tired of theme parks, but it's a little too far out of the way to stay out here. Just north of "near North" is **Winter Park,** a lovely, unspoiled town with lots of beautiful old-money homes.

Street Smarts: Where to Get Information Once You're Here

It's worth stopping at the Orlando/Orange County Convention & Visitors Bureau's **Official Visitor Center** at 8723 International Dr., at the southeast corner of I-Drive and Austrian Row. Tickets to all attractions and many dinner shows are available at a discount here. You'll save only a few dollars on WDW tickets, but up to 10% to 20% on others. Tickets are sold daily 8am to 7pm except Christmas.

If you're driving down to the Orlando area from points north, stop on I-75 about an hour-and-a-half north of Orlando at the **Disney/AAA Travel Center** at Exit 68, S.R. 200 in Ocala (☎ **904/854-0770**). It's easy-on, easy-off the interstate, and it offers souvenirs, information, tickets, and hotel reservations at attractive discounts. It's open daily 9am to 6pm; in July and August until 7pm.

Local free publications come and go and change their names often, so it's hard to know which one to recommend. *See Magazine* has been around the longest, and it's pretty good.

Chapter 8

Getting Around

> **In This Chapter**
>
> ➤ Using your own two wheels
>
> ➤ The magic bus
>
> ➤ Hoofin' it

One of Orlando's tragedies is that city fathers grabbed greedily for the sudden growth that came with Walt Disney World without planning for the infrastructure that would be required in a major city. To the visitor, this means limited public transportation, horrendous traffic tie-ups, high tolls, ever-increasing taxes on hotels and meals, and very few areas where you can get around on foot. Hundreds of acres of orange groves were bulldozed to make room for subdivisions that were thrown together with little greenspace and no sidewalks.

Fortunately, wonderful tree-shaded pockets of downtown Orlando remain from before the growth explosion. And some of the new areas, such as International Drive, were built with an eye on aesthetics, pedestrians, and sensible transportation systems. Walt Disney World is a model of accessibility, with a superb transportation network and massive neighborhoods, such as Celebration and The BoardWalk, made just for walking. Universal Studios, like WDW, will also be a complete world in itself. As we enter the new millennium, it will have its own hotels with 13,000 rooms.

Time-Savers

State Road 528, locally called the Beeline or Bee Line Expressway, is a toll road. So are the Central Florida Green Way (FL 417) and the East-West Expressway (FL 408). Unmanned toll booths require exact change, so travel with a good supply of quarters. Don't try to avoid the tolls on the Bee Line by taking city streets through Pine Hills between I-4 and Hiawassee. Locals have dubbed the area "Crime Hills." Pay the 75¢.

Not since the Gold Rush has a North American city grown as quickly and haphazardly as Orlando. Anything we write today is subject to change. But once you get a general picture of the city, remember to avoid rush hours, and learn a few shortcuts, you'll find that getting around Orlando is (almost) a breeze.

Note: Details on the Walt Disney World transportation system, which you can use if you choose a hotel in WDW, are in chapter 11.

By Car

Just over half of central Florida's visitors drive there, and most of those who fly in rent a car—so it's safe to assume that Orlando's roads and streets are filled with a lot of people who don't know exactly where they are, just like you. So here are a few tips that will have you negotiating the highways and byways like a native.

➤ Rush hour on I-4 is generally from 7 to 9am and 4 to 7pm. Other busy times include big games or events at the O'rena or Citrus Bowl, or big conventions at the Convention Center. Stay off I-4 if at all possible during these hours; driving any distance during these periods will take at least twice as long as you think.

Time-Savers

As you approach Walt Disney World by car, watch for signs that tell you where to tune on your AM dial to get last-minute tourist information. When you're in other areas, stay tuned to a station such as AM 580, which has frequent traffic reports and advice on avoiding accident scenes and other delays. You can save hours by knowing when to duck off the highway onto an alternate route.

➤ Remember, I-4 runs north and south, but the sign painters think of it as an east-west road. From the Bee Line, you'll want to go "east" (or north) to go downtown or to Universal Studios, and "west" (or south) to get to WDW and U.S. 192/Kissimmee.

➤ Under Florida law, you can turn right on red after coming to a full stop and making sure that the coast is clear (unless signs indicate otherwise). Local drivers will get steamed if you clog up the right-hand lane.

➤ Traffic must stop when school buses are loading or unloading in either direction, except on a divided highway that has either a barrier or a dividing space of 5 feet or more.

➤ International Drive is called I-Drive. Irlo Bronson Memorial Highway is U.S. 192, which nobody calls anything but 192. Florida Route 528 is the Bee Line Expressway. State Road 50 is more commonly called Colonial Drive.

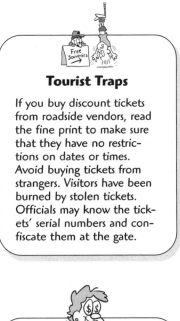

Tourist Traps

If you buy discount tickets from roadside vendors, read the fine print to make sure that they have no restrictions on dates or times. Avoid buying tickets from strangers. Visitors have been burned by stolen tickets. Officials may know the tickets' serial numbers and confiscate them at the gate.

➤ A Florida handicap permit is required for parking in handicap parking places. Handicap permits from other states are honored. A disabled parking plate alone won't do.

➤ Along a 12-mile stretch of U.S. 192 in Kissimmee, 25-foot-high markers start at Walt Disney World and extend to near China, brightly marking the many points of interest. The westernmost marker is Marker 4; the remaining pairs are numbered in sequence and in pairs, one on each side of the highway. If you phone for directions to a restaurant, hotel, or attraction, it's likely that you'll be told that it is "just past Marker so-and-so."

Dollars & Sense

Full-service gas stations charge 3¢ to 6¢ more per gallon than self-service stations. Some stations have two-tier pricing, charging a few cents more per gallon if you use a credit card. Ask before using a credit card.

➤ In an emergency, you can reach the Florida Highway Patrol on your cell phone by dialing *FHP.

A Few Tips on the Local Lingo

Locals have their own vocabulary, and visitors can get lost unless they know that:

➤ OBT or "The Trail" are Orange Blossom Trail, which is also U.S. 441 and U.S. 17–92. Don't confuse it with Orange Avenue, which is also a north-south street, just east of OBT.

➤ OIA and MCO both refer to the airport.

Also, don't confuse Winter Park, Winter Garden, and Winter Haven. They're all towns in Central Florida.

By Bus

Orlando's **Lynx** city bus system is a work of art, with each bus brilliantly designed in a different motif. Bus stops are identified by a lynx paw print. The fare is 75¢ and exact change is required. For more information, call ☎ **407/841-8240.**

Buses *do* run between the airport and downtown, but they aren't the best way for tourists to sightsee, shop, or get to and from hotels, restaurants, and points of interest.

Another bus system, **I-Ride,** operates every 10 to 15 minutes from 7am until midnight every day on International Drive between Sea World and American Way, which is the site of a Howard Johnson's, a Comfort Inn, and a Denny's just west of Kirkman Road (Route 435). One-way fare is 85¢ for adults and 25¢ for seniors, with exact change required. Children under age 12 ride free when accompanied by an adult. Trolleys are air-conditioned. When you get aboard, ask about daily and weekly passes.

Dollars & Sense

Run, don't walk, to the Orlando/Orange County Convention & Visitors Bureau's **Official Visitor Center** at 8723 International Dr., at the southeast corner of I-Drive and Austrian Row. Tickets to all attractions and many dinner shows are available at a discount. You'll save only a few dollars on WDW tickets, but 10% to 20% on others. Tickets are sold daily except Christmas from 8am to 7pm.

Culture Quest, a tour bus of Orlando's top cultural attractions, makes a terrific shuttle system. You can ride the entire circuit, which is good orientation before starting out on your own to visit points of interest, or you can get on and off as you please. The bus operates from five hubs:

➤ Westgate Towers, 7600 W. Hwy. 192, Kissimmee

➤ Florida Plaza, 5730 E. Hwy. 192, Kissimmee

➤ Lake Buena Vista Factory Stores, state roads 535 and 536

➤ The Mercado, 8445 International Dr.

➤ Mystery Fun House, 5767 Major Blvd. (North International Drive area)

Stops include Church Street Station, the Orlando Science Center, Civic Theaters, the Orange County Museum of Art, the Orange County Historical Museum, Leu Gardens, the Cornell Fine Arts Museum, the Winter Park Scenic Boat Tour, the Langford Resort Hotel, Albin Polasek Galleries, The Shoppes of Park Avenue, the Morse Museum of American Art, the Enzian Theater, the Maitland Art Center, the Center for Birds of Prey, the Zora Neale Hurston National Museum of Fine Arts, and the Orlando City Hall Terrace Galleries.

Shuttle tickets—which are available at welcome centers, your hotel's concierge desk, and the hubs—cost $12 for adults and $9 for children ages 4 to 17 for the loop tour; $18 for adults and $12 for children for full service from the hubs to cultural attractions; and $10 for adults and $8 for children for round-trip transportation from the hubs to Church Street Station. For more information, call ☎ **407/855-6434,** or visit their Web site at www.coachlines.com. Shuttles run continuously through the day; the route takes about 1½ hours.

Lymmo is a free bus system that runs in its own lanes in downtown Orlando, stopping at 13 spots including the Orlando Arena, Church Street Station, and City Hall. It stops at an additional six points if passengers want to get off or on. Buses run Monday to Thursday from 6am to 10pm, until midnight on Friday; from 10am to midnight on Saturdays; and from 10am to 10pm on Sundays.

The **Mears Transportation Group** (☎ **407/423-5566**) is the leading operator of tours from Orlando to Cypress Gardens, Kennedy Space Center, Busch Gardens Tampa, and other Central Florida points of interest. Check with your hotel desk for tours offered by Mears and other operators.

Bet You Didn't Know

Downtown Orlando has romantic **horse-drawn carriage rides** from Church Street Station through the downtown area. They run daily 7:30pm to midnight for $25 per couple, or $30 for three or four people.

Put One Foot in Front of the Other

Orlando isn't a walking city like San Francisco or New York, but the downtown grid around Church Street Station has many clubs and restaurants. Winter Park, just north of downtown, is also known for its downtown area of smart shops, restaurants, cafes, and galleries. For other pub crawling, it's best to focus on Downtown Disney, Church Street Station, or The Mercado, where you can stroll from show to shop to bistro.

Need more walking? We doubt it. It'll be the last thing you want to do after spending a day at one of the theme parks.

Part 4

Orlando's Best Restaurants

So you're safely ensconced in your hotel room and exhausted from a day of trav-
eling. And you're probably hungry. Well, you're in luck. Few cities offer so many
dining options, for the simple reason that few cities have so many visitors. Gone
are the days of nothing but fast food and steak houses to choose from. Sure,
there are more IHOPs and Golden Arches than you can shake a stick at, but
Orlando has come a long way, baby.

Now there's a whole range of fresh, new restaurants with innovative chefs, clever
themes (oh, are there ever a lot of themes), and professional service. Because
Orlando attracts visitors from around the globe, you can find lots of kinds of
cuisines here. A lot of ethnic restaurants won't be spicy or authentic enough to
wow jaded New Yorkers or San Franciscans—they're still pretty much geared for
Middle American palates—but there are some exceptions and more surprisingly
good ethnic choices than ever before.

The local restaurants also offer live entertainment or special experiences you just
can't get anywhere else. You can be dining in the most elegant restaurant in
Orlando, light-years away from the theme parks, when suddenly the night sky
lights up as a rocket bursts over Cinderella's Castle.

Chapter 9

The Lowdown on the Orlando Dining Scene

In This Chapter

➤ Tips on Walt Disney World Priority Seating

➤ What's hot now

➤ Choosing where to eat and how much to spend

➤ Dressing the part

➤ Dining with Disney characters

➤ Fast food galore

Orlando's explosive growth has brought with it an explosion in good eating that has lifted the city out of its former bland rut and into a whole new world of exciting opportunities. Top hotels brought in noted chefs to put such restaurants as Dux (in the Peabody Hotel) and Arthur's 27 (in the Buena Vista Palace) on the culinary map. Outside the attractions area, neighborhoods such as Winter Park offer a sophisticated setting for dining and strolling.

Within Disney alone are 64 sit-down restaurants, not including the many food courts, the self-serve snack bars, or any of the restaurants at official Disney hotels in Lake Buena Vista. In recent years, celebrity chefs (like Wolfgang Puck) and just plain celebrities (like Gloria Estefan) have opened restaurants here, adding to the wealth of choices. You can dine in a Victorian time warp at the regal Victoria and Albert's, in a Moroccan palace, in a Japanese tea house, or in a loony bin filled with cackling cartoon characters.

And if you're here from late October to late November, you can partake in the annual **Epcot International Food & Wine Festival,** which takes over the World Showcase with food, wine, and entertainments from more than 30 nations.

Bet You Didn't Know

You can take I-4 to Sanford and embark on a moonlight dinner–dancing cruise aboard the **Rivership Romance** (☎ **800/423-7401** or 407/321–5091; www.rivershiproomance.com). Cruises cost $50 per person, and reservations are required.

The city's near-quixotic quest to keep visitors entertained every minute of every day has spawned dinner theaters galore; currently, about a dozen of them vie for the tourism dollar. You can eat with the Mob one night, in the opera the next night, and with gladiators or knights in armor the third night. It's our experience that it's never the best dinner and never the best theater, but dinner theater is a whale of a bargain. And it's usually PG-rated, with fun for the whole family.

Table for Four Coming Right Up: A Word About WDW Priority Seating

The term "reservations" is not used by most WDW restaurants. Priority Seating is Walt Disney World's method of ensuring that you get the first available table *after you arrive*. A table is not kept empty for you; you will probably still have to wait a few minutes after you get to the restaurant.

The popularity of the Priority Seating system has made it much more difficult to get a table just by walking in. **We strongly recommend calling ahead.** All WDW restaurants can be reserved at ☎ **407/WDW-DINE (939-3463)**.

You can also make priority seating reservations once you are inside the Disney parks. We suggest you do this quickly upon your arrival in the park. At Epcot, go to the restaurants themselves, the Germany Pavilion, Guest Relations, or the Worldkey Information Service Satellites on the main concourse to World Showcase. In the Magic Kingdom, reserve at the restaurants themselves. In Disney-MGM Studios, reserve at the restaurants themselves or at the Hollywood Junction Station on Hollywood Boulevard.

Dollars & Sense

Check free tabloids and magazines, which are stacked everywhere in Orlando hotels, for coupons good for a second meal free, a discount, or a free dessert with a meal. Watch for ads for kids-eat-free specials.

What's Hot Now

The exciting thing about Orlando, even to those who live here, is that new restaurants are popping up faster than you can say "pesto and sundried tomatoes."

Everyone loves the dining-entertainment complexes that are sweeping the city. Park in one spot and you're at the doorsteps of dozens of restaurants, clubs, and shows, so you can stroll and browse around until you find the one that piques your interest. Among the most recent big splashes are Downtown Disney and Pointe Orlando, but even established complexes like Old Town, Pleasure Island, Church Street Station, and the Mercado are still hot.

Downtown Orlando, once almost a ghost town after dark, has become a hotbed of smart clubs and restaurants.

For the kids, there are character breakfasts galore, in and out of the theme parks, plus the Hoop-Dee-Doo Musical Revue, an animated dinner show guaranteed to get a giggle out of the most jaded traveler.

Time-Savers

The least expensive dining facilities in the theme parks offer self-service, sometimes with long lines. You may be tempted to try to eat and run so that you can spend more time riding the rides, but we think your feet will ultimately be happier if you budget time and money for a sit-down place that takes reservations. You'll have more energy throughout the day and avoid fading in the late afternoon.

And, of course, if you're a meat-and-potatoes type and you just want a classic chophouse, drive-thru fast food, a familiar chain restaurant, or deli take-out, Orlando can serve it up in spades. That kind of familiar American fare has been joined by more trendy developments, but it never went away.

Location, Location, Location

➤ **The World Showcase at Epcot** is the ultimate place to wander for a choice of ethnic restaurants, with stunning settings. Each pavilion has two or more venues—usually one for leisurely, sit-down dining and another for quicker, less expensive food.

➤ **Pleasure Island, Downtown Disney, Church Street Station,** and the **Mercado** are complexes that offer a wide array of restaurants plus plenty of bars, shops, and diversions to enjoy before and after dinner. They make for a full evening out.

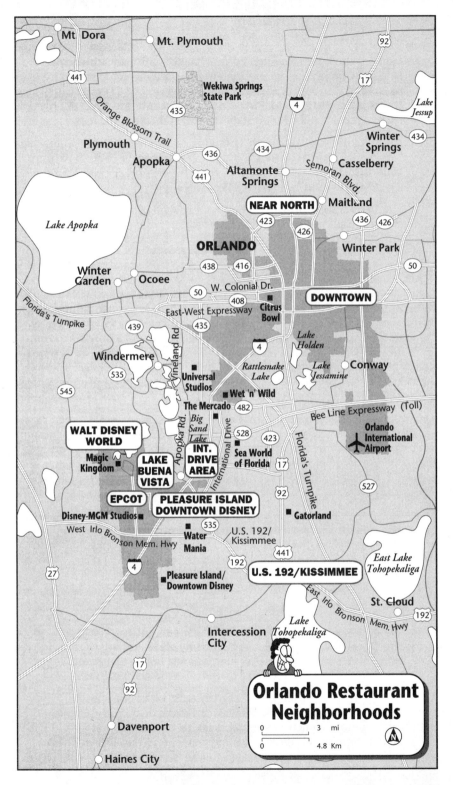

105

➤ Many of the hotels and most of the larger malls have **food courts,** where the family can go in different directions to get their choice of food, then sit down at the same table to eat it. Try **Commander Ragtime's Midway of Fun, Food, and Games** at Church Street Exchange for a riot of food stalls, shops, and coin-op games.

➤ For romantic strolls, window shopping, sidewalk cafes, restaurants, and bars, walk **Fifth Avenue** in Winter Park, **Disney's BoardWalk,** or **Woodland Boulevard** (U.S. 17–92) in downtown DeLand, a little college town an hour north of WDW off I-4.

➤ The **Universal Studios** area also offers good dining and strolling choices. You can get from Cape Cod to San Francisco in a New York minute, with a choice of dining, drinking, and shopping.

The Price Is Right

Naturally, the price of a meal will depend on what you order—if you pig out or order the most expensive dishes on the menu, you'll spend more than if you order moderately. The listings in chapter 10 give you two price elements for each restaurant: a dollar symbol that gives you an idea of what a complete meal will cost, and the price range of the entrees on the menu. The two pieces of information combined should help you choose the place that's right for you and your budget. One dollar sign means inexpensive, and five dollar signs (the maximum) means extravagant.

One important thing to note is that all the listings are for good (often excellent) restaurants where you get a satisfying meal. We didn't list any crummy places just because they were cheap; neither did we list any outrageously expensive places where you pay an arm and a leg for a leaf of well-arranged lettuce. What we did list were restaurants that serve good-quality food at a fair price.

Here's how we've categorized restaurants according to price. If you order an appetizer, a main course, a dessert, and one drink, then add tax and tip, you'll probably spend, per person:

$$$$$	=	$60 and up
$$$$	=	$40 to $60
$$$	=	$25 to $40
$$	=	$15 to $25
$	=	$15 and under

Saving on Drinks

Drinks of any type, even sodas and bottled waters, can add substantially to the cost of a meal. A couple of kids sucking down sodas by the liter can double the price of an inexpensive burger meal. Don't be too shy to ask about the restaurant's policy on refills. At some fast-food restaurants, self-serve drink refills are on the house. Most places refill coffee and iced tea free but charge extra for refills for everything else.

Orlando's deliciously clean tap water is a good idea for both your health and your wallet. In the hot Florida sun, you'll want to drink as much water as you can to keep your cool. Water is also cheerfully served in most restaurants (although you may have to ask for it in a few places). Only in the snootiest places would a waiter assume that you want high-priced bottled water.

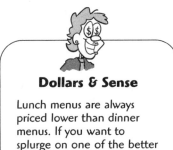

Dollars & Sense

Lunch menus are always priced lower than dinner menus. If you want to splurge on one of the better restaurants, go for lunch or for the early-bird special.

At expensive restaurants, drinks are expensive, too. You might consider having a cocktail at a cheaper place before or after dinner (or in your hotel room) to save money. The prices in your minibar, however, won't be much cheaper than what an expensive restaurant charges you.

A Word About Taxes & Tipping

Taxes on restaurant meals and drinks are 6% to 7% throughout greater Orlando. In addition, you'll need to tip at least 15% in a full-service restaurant and perhaps 12% in a buffet where a server brings your drinks and cleans the table. If you have a drink at the bar first, or special service from the sommelier, don't forget tips for them. The practice of tipping the head waiter has all but disappeared, but money could talk in a crowded restaurant where you want a special table.

No Monkey Suits Required: What to Wear to Orlando Restaurants

Even the fanciest restaurants in the theme parks have a very casual dress code at dinner, because most weary diners have been in the parks all day. Neat and casual is the rule.

Dollars & Sense

Don't overlook Orlando's large, modern supermarkets. Goodings, Albertson's, and Publix have extensive deli sections with large choices of hot and cold foods for takeout. Picnic by the pool, on your balcony, or in a grassy park for little more than a meal you'd prepare at home.

There are a few exceptions, though. Jackets are required in a few of the better spots, including Victoria and Albert's. You won't be overdressed if you wear a tie and jacket in places frequented by people here on business. The better restaurants in the better hotels call for your Sunday best.

If you'll be dining alfresco in the Florida sunshine, cover up those bald heads and pasty arms and legs, at least until you get a base tan. Otherwise, you may start to look like a lobster before you get to eat one. Carry some sunscreen during hot and sticky months, or find a table with an umbrella. Think twice about dining outside in winter months, or at least bring along a sweater. (In fact, we'd suggest taking a sweater or jacket to dinner in any season, because in summer, there's always overzealous air-conditioning to contend with.)

Eek, a Mouse! Dining with Disney Characters

It's a beguiling idea. Combine a meal with a host and hostess who will leave your children wide-eyed: Pocahontas and her friends, Mickey and Minnie, Cinderella, or Aladdin. *Priority Seating is essential and should be made as far in advance as possible.* Note that restaurants inside the theme parks require park admission. Children ages 2 and under eat free. All take American Express, MaterCard, and Visa.

Kids Artist Point

You and your kids can feast on an all-you-can eat breakfast buffet with Pocahontas and friends in a rustic North Woods lodge.

In Disney's Wilderness Lodge, 901 Timberline Dr. ☎ **407/939-3463. Prices:** *$16.95–$24 adults, $5.95 children 3–11. AE, MC, V.* **Open:** *Daily 5:30–11am.*

Beating the Lines

All the theme-park restaurants, cafeterias, and food courts are mobbed between 11:30am and 2pm and between 6 and 9pm. Try to eat at other hours to avoid long lines here. You can ride the most popular rides with shorter lines while everyone else is chowing down!

Kids Cape May Café

Have a generous buffet breakfast or dinner with Chip 'n' Dale, Admiral Goofy, or Pluto. You never know who will show up, but the photo ops are sure to be good.

In Disney's Beach Club Resort, 1800 Epcot Resorts Blvd. ☎ **407/939-3463. Prices:** *$13.50 adults, $8.25 children 3–11. AE, MC, V.* **Open:** *Daily 7–11am, 5:30–9:30pm.*

Kids Chef Mickey's

Chef Mickey will whip up a buffet breakfast or a prime rib dinner buffet, and still find time to schmooze with his pint-sized guests.

In Disney's Contemporary Resort, 4600 N. World Dr. ☎ *407/939-3463. Prices: $14.95 adults, $7.95 children 3–11 for breakfast; $19.95 adults, $8.95 children 3–11 for dinner. AE, MC, V. Open: Daily 7:30–11:30am and 5–9:30pm.*

Kids Garden Grill

This is one of the more entertaining character meals because the Disney gang hosts your ride through desert, prairie, and the Great Plains. The restaurant revolves while you sit in a semicircular booth. The food is hearty American all the way. Park admission is required, of course.

In the Land Pavilion, Epcot. ☎ *407/939-3463. Prices: $14.95 adults, $7.95 children 3–11 for breakfast; $16.95 adults, $9.95 children for lunch; $19.50 adults, $9.95 children for dinner. AE, MC, V. Open: Daily 8:30am–8pm.*

Kids King Stefan's Banquet Hall

What a nice way to start your magical day in the Magic Kingdom! Eat all you want from the buffet while various Disney characters, including Cinderella, shower you with thrown kisses. Park admission is required, of course.

In Cinderella's Castle, Magic Kingdom. ☎ *407/939-3463. Prices: $14.95 adults, $7.95 children 3–11. AE, MC, V. Open: Daily for breakfast (Mon, Thurs, Sat 7:30am–10am; all other days 8am–10am); daily 4pm until park closes for dinner.*

Dollars & Sense

Happy-hour specials are held at almost every bar in town. Some offer two-for-one drinks; others offer free buffets so generous that you won't need dinner. It pays to call ahead to a few bars to ask what's available and when.

Kids Liberty Tree Tavern

In a stately colonial setting, a gaggle of Disney regulars stops by to make sure your kids get plenty to eat from a menu that includes salad, roast chicken, marinated flank steak, sausages, mashed potatoes, rice pilaf, vegetables, and apple crisp with ice cream. Park admission is required, of course.

In Liberty Square, Magic Kingdom. ☎ *407/939-3463. Prices: $19.50 adults, $9.95 children 3–11. AE, MC, V. Open: Daily 4pm–park closing.*

Kids Minnie's Menehune & Mickey's Tropical Luau

The breakfast is Minnie's masterpiece, served family style, while Disney characters help out. Children have a chance to play Polynesian instruments in a daily parade. The Tropical Luau is a shorter version of the Luau Dinner Show, and it's ideal for younger tots who need to eat and go to bed early. The menu is set, serving roast chicken, vegetables, cinnamon bread, and an ice-cream sundae. You'll receive a shell lei as you leave.

In Disney's Polynesian Resort, 1600 Seven Seas Dr. ☎ *407/939-3463. Prices: $13.50 adults, $8.25 children 3–11 for breakfast; $30 adults, $14 children for luau dinner (without characters). AE, MC, V. Open: Daily 7:30–10:30am; luau at 4:30pm.*

Kids 1900 Park Fare

Mary Poppins, Winnie-the-Pooh, Goofy, and Pluto are just a few of the Disney gang who join you here for breakfast or dinner. A mammoth pipe organ makes this one of Disney's most impressive rooms. Breakfast is a lavish buffet. Mickey and Minnie come for a dinner of prime rib, fresh fish, or stuffed pork.

In Disney's Grand Floridian Beach Resort, 4401 Floridian Way. ☎ *407/939-3463. Prices: $15.95 adults, $9.95 children 3–11 for breakfast; $19.95 adults, $9.50 children for dinner. AE, MC, V. Open: Daily 7:30–11:30am and 5:30–9pm.*

Kids Soundstage Restaurant

A cavernous sound stage filled with props is the setting for generous buffets served while Aladdin, Pocahontas, and other characters stop by for autographs.

In Disney-MGM Studios, next to the Magic of Disney Animation exhibit. ☎ *407/939-3463. Prices: $13.95 adults, $7.95 children 3–11 for breakfast; $16.95 adults, $9.95 children for lunch. AE, MC, V. Open: Daily 8:30–11:30am for breakfast, 11:30am–3:30pm for lunch.*

Bet You Didn't Know

A meal plan is available to guests at Walt Disney World resorts. It isn't widely publicized, but you'll save 10% if you're planning to buy all your meals from Walt. Ask about it when you reserve your accommodations.

Kids Watercress Café

Disney characters cavort while you dine from the buffet or order from the menu.

In the Buena Vista Palace, 1900 Buena Vista Dr. ☎ *407/827-2727. No reservations accepted; arrive early. Prices: $12.95 adults; $6.95 children ages 3–11. AE, MC, V. Open: Sun 8–10:30am.*

McFood: Drive-Thrus, Pizzerias & the Chain Gang

Like every city in America, Orlando has its share of familiar restaurant chains, burger joints, and pizzerias (including some that deliver). All of the dining areas we've listed, except Walt Disney World, have a large choice of chain restaurants and fast food for those times when chowing down on a burger is all you want. You won't have to drive more than a few minutes on International Drive or U.S. 192 to find a place that satisfies the whole family. Driving north to south from Kirkman Road on International Drive, you'll find Howard Johnson's, Wendy's, Ponderosa, Pizza Hut, Chili's, Olive Garden, Burger King, Goodings (a chain supermarket with great take-out), Friendly's, and a Bob Evans.

Chapter 10

Restaurants A to Z

In This Chapter

➤ Easy-to-scan indexes of restaurants by location, price, and cuisine

➤ Full reviews of the best restaurants in town

Hungry yet? Stomach growling? Ready to eat this book? Are your kids starting to act like Oliver Twist?

Look no further. We've gone through all of Orlando's restaurants, picked the ones we think are the best (why waste your time reading about places we don't love?), and reviewed them in alphabetical order. We've even thrown in some handy indexes so you can scan them by location, price, and type of cuisine, too. All you have to do is decide where and what you want to eat and how much you want to spend. Pick your restaurants from the indexes up front, then check the review at the end of this chapter.

Note: All sit-down restaurants in Walt Disney World take American Express, MasterCard, and Visa, and all of them have children's menus. All WDW restaurants are no-smoking; you can light up only on patios and terraces. No alcohol is served anywhere in the Magic Kingdom, though it is available at Epcot and Disney-MGM studios restaurants.

Quick Picks: Orlando's Restaurants at a Glance

Restaurant Index by Location

Walt Disney World

Restaurants within all WDW theme parks require park admission, of course. Eat here on days when you want to be in the parks anyway, unless you have a World Hopper Pass that allows you to come in just for a meal (though you'll still have to pay $5 for parking). Pleasure Island has an admission charge, but diners can access its restaurants without buying a ticket to the entire complex. Also remember that no alcohol is served anywhere in the Magic Kingdom.

Akershus (Epcot) $$

Au Petit Café (Epcot) $$

Bistro de Paris (Epcot) $$$$

Columbia (Celebration) $$$

Coral Seas (Epcot) $$$

Fulton's Crab House (Pleasure Island) $$$$

Hollywood Brown Derby (Disney-MGM Studios) $$$

King Stefan's Banquet Hall (Magic Kingdom) $$$

L'Originale Alfredo di Roma Ristorante (Epcot) $$–$$$

Marrakesh (Epcot) $$$

Nine Dragons (Epcot) $$$

Planet Hollywood (Pleasure Island) $$

Plaza Restaurant (Magic Kingdom) $$

Prime Time Café (Disney-MGM Studios) $$–$$$

Sci-Fi Dine-In Theater Restaurant (Disney-MGM Studios) $$–$$$

Victoria and Albert's (Disney's Grand Floridian Beach Resort) $$$$$

Lake Buena Vista

Arthur's 27 $$$$$

U.S. 192/Kissimmee

New Punjab $

International Drive Area

Atlantis $$$$$

B-Line Diner $$–$$$

Bahama Breeze $$

Black Swan $$$$$

Cafe Tu Tu Tango $$

Capriccio $$$

Dux $$$$$

Landry's Seafood House $$–$$$

Michelangelo $$$$

113

Ming Court $$$
New Punjab $
Race Rock $–$$
Wild Jack's $$$

Downtown

Café Europa $$$
La Provence $$$–$$$$
Little Saigon $$
Manuel's on the 28th $$$$$
Numero Uno $$
Thanh Thuy $

Near North

Boston's Fish House $
Bubbaloo's Bodacious BBQ $–$$
Bubble Room $$$
Maison et Jardin $$$$
Rolando's $–$$

Restaurant Index by Price

Our price ranges, assuming that you'll have an appetizer, a main course, a dessert, one drink, tax, and tip, are as follows:

$$$$$	=	$60 and up
$$$$	=	$40 to $60
$$$	=	$25 to $40
$$	=	$15 to $25
$	=	$15 and under

$$$$$

Atlantis (International Drive Area)

Arthur's 27 (Lake Buena Vista)

Black Swan (International Drive Area)

Dux (International Drive Area)

Manuel's on the 28th (Downtown)

Victoria and Albert's (Disney's Grand Floridian Beach Resort)

$$$$

Bistro de Paris (Epcot)

Fulton's Crab House (Pleasure Island)

La Provence (Downtown)

Maison et Jardin (Near North)

Michelangelo (International Drive Area)

$$$

B-Line Diner (International Drive Area)

Bubble Room (Near North)

Café Europa (Downtown)

Capriccio (International Drive Area)

Columbia (Lake Buena Vista)

Coral Seas (Epcot)

Hollywood Brown Derby (Disney-MGM Studios)

King Stefan's Banquet Hall (Magic Kingdom)

L'Originale Alfredo di Roma Ristorante (Epcot)

La Provence (Downtown)

Landry's Seafood House (International Drive Area)

Marrakesh (Epcot)

Ming Court (International Drive Area)

Wild Jacks (International Drive Area)

$$

Akershus (Epcot)

Bahama Breeze (International Drive Area)

Cafe Tu Tu Tango (International Drive Area)

Little Saigon (Downtown)

L'Originale Alfredo di Roma Ristorante (Epcot)

Numero Uno (Downtown)

Planet Hollywood (Pleasure Island)

Plaza Restaurant (Magic Kingdom)

Prime Time Café (Disney-MGM Studios)

Rainforest Cafe (Downtown Disney Marketplace & Animal Kingdom)

Sci-Fi Dine-In Theater Restaurant (Disney-MGM Studios)

$

Au Petit Café (Epcot)

Boston's Fish House (Near North)

Bubbaloo's Bodacious BBQ (Near North)

New Punjab (International Drive Area; also U.S. 192/ Kissimmee)

Race Rock (International Drive Area)

Rolando's (Near North)

Thanh Thuy (Downtown)

Restaurant Index by Cuisine
American

B-Line Diner (International Drive Area) $$–$$$

Bubbaloo's Bodacious BBQ (Near North) $–$$

Bubble Room (Near North) $$$

Hollywood Brown Derby (Disney-MGM Studios) $$$

King Stefan's Banquet Hall (Magic Kingdom) $$$

Planet Hollywood (Pleasure Island) $$

Plaza Restaurant (Magic Kingdom) $$

Prime Time Café (Disney-MGM Studios) $$–$$$

Race Rock (International Drive Area) $–$$

Rainforest Cafe (Downtown Disney Marketplace & Animal Kingdom) $$

Sci-Fi Dine-In Theater Restaurant (Disney-MGM Studios) $$–$$$

Wild Jacks (International Drive Area) $$$

Asian

Little Saigon (Vietnamese; Downtown) $$

Ming Court (Chinese; International Drive Area) $$$

Nine Dragons (Chinese; Epcot) $$$

French

Au Petit Café (Epcot) $$

Bistro de Paris (Epcot) $$$$

La Provence (Downtown) $$$–$$$$

Maison et Jardin (Near North) $$$$

Italian

Capriccio (International Drive Area) $$$

L'Originale Alfredo di Roman Ristoriante (Epcot) $$$

Michelangelo (International Drive Area) $$$$

Other Ethnic

Akershus (Norwegian; Epcot) $$

Bahama Breeze (Caribbean; International Drive Area) $$

Café Europa (German and Hungarian; Downtown) $$$

Columbia (Cuban; Lake Buena Vista) $$$

New Punjab (Indian; International Drive Area and U.S. 192/Kissimmee) $

Marrakesh (Moroccan; Epcot) $$$

Numero Uno (Cuban, Downtown) $$

Thanh Thuy (Indian; Downtown) $

Haute Cuisine

Arthur's 27 (Lake Buena Vista) $$$$$

Atlantis (International Drive Area) $$$$$

Black Swan (Lake Buena Vista) $$$$$

Cafe Tu Tu Tango (International Drive Area) $$

Dux (International Drive Area) $$$$$

Manuel's on the 28th (Downtown) $$$$$

Victoria and Albert's (Grand Floridian Beach Resort) $$$$$

Seafood

Atlantis (International Drive Area) $$$$$

Boston's Fish House (Near North) $

Coral Seas (Epcot) $$$

Fulton's Crab House (Pleasure Island) $$$$

Landry's Seafood House (International Drive Area) $$–$$$

Our Favorite Restaurants A to Z

Akershus
$$. Walt Disney World (Epcot; park admission required). NORWEGIAN.
A huge table spills over with traditional hot and cold dishes of a Scandinavian smorgasbord: venison in cream sauce, gravlax in mustard sauce, smoked pork with honey mustard, red cabbage, boiled potatoes, and, for dessert, a classic "veiled maiden." Wash it down with a frosty Norwegian beer. The setting is all glowing woods, crisp linens, and gleaming crystal. Ask about the child-care center, where kids play while you dine.

Norway Pavilion, World Showcase Epcot.
☎ *407/939-3463. Arranging Priority Seating in advance is recommended.* **Prices:** *Lunch buffet $11.95 adults, $4.50 ages 4–9, free for kids under age 3. Dinner buffet $17.95 adults, $7.50 ages 4–9. A non-smorgasbord child's meal is $4. AE, MC, V.* **Open:** *Daily 11:30am–4pm; 4:15pm–park closing.*

Beating the Lines
If you plan to eat at a restaurant in Walt Disney World, we can't stress this enough: *Make a Priority Seating reservation before you go!!!*

Atlantis
$$$$$. International Drive Area. SEAFOOD/HAUTE CUISINE.
In one of the city's most elegant settings, you can dine on sirloin steak, succulent scallops, or roast rack of lamb, all in a picture-book presentation. Beveled glass, the glint of crystal, and the glow of rich woodwork create a look of rich elegance. Candlelight creates just the right sparkle on tables that gleam with china and silver. Appetizers, soups, salads, and desserts are inspired. Watch out for the after-dinner liqueur cart, though—a sip of some of the brandies can cost more than the rest of the dinner.

In the Renaissance Orlando Resort, 6677 Sea Harbor Dr., across from Sea World.
☎ *407/351-5555. Reservations strongly recommended.* **Main courses:** *$20–$28. AE, DC, DISC, MC, V.* **Open:** *Mon–Sat 6–10pm.*

Arthur's 27
$$$$$. Lake Buena Vista. HAUTE CUISINE.
The views from this splendid, 27th-floor restaurant are spectacular at sunset and when Disney fireworks light the sky. Romantic and mellow, it has the mood of a smart supper club in a 1930s movie, minus the clouds of cigarette smoke. You'll choose from selections such as pan-seared breast of squab with chestnut risotto, or steamed scallops and poached oysters with black capellini pasta. There's an impressive wine list.

In the Buena Vista Palace Resort & Spa, 1900 Lake Buena Vista Dr., just north of Hotel Plaza Blvd. ☎ *407/827-2727. Reservations required.* **Parking:** *Free self-parking or validated valet parking.* **Prices:** *Main courses $20–$30; fixed-price menus $49–$60. AE, DC, DISC, MC, V.* **Open:** *Daily 6:30–10:30pm.*

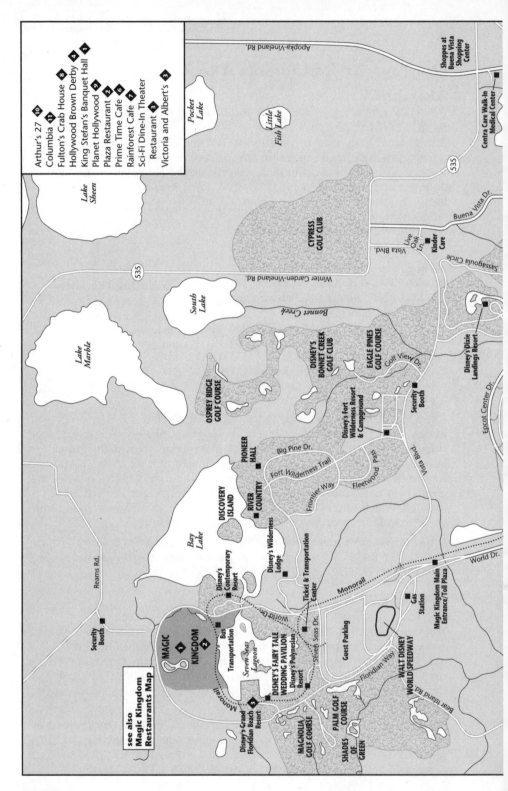

Arthur's 27 ⑩
Columbia ⑪
Fulton's Crab House ⑧
Hollywood Brown Derby ④
King Stefan's Banquet Hall ①
Planet Hollywood ⑨
Plaza Restaurant ②
Prime Time Cafe ⑥
Rainforest Cafe ⑦
Sci-Fi Dine-In Theater
Restaurant ③
Victoria and Albert's ③

see also
Magic Kingdom
Restaurants Map

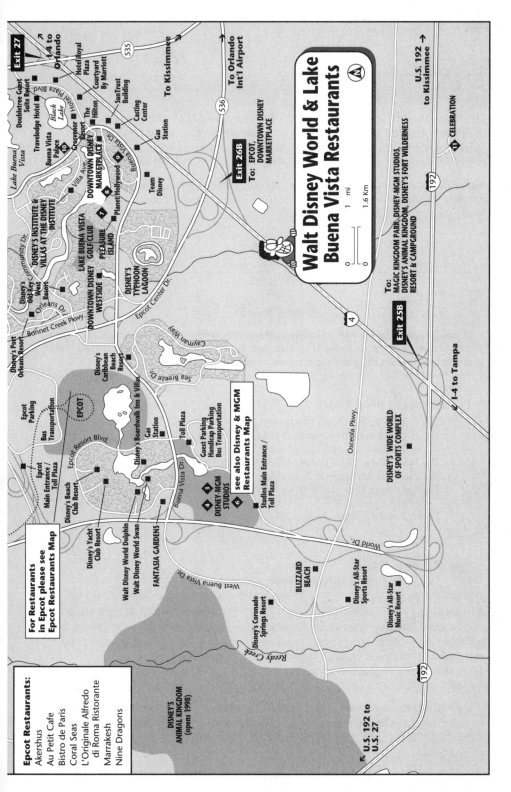

Walt Disney World & Lake Buena Vista Restaurants

Epcot Restaurants:
Akershus
Au Petit Cafe
Bistro de Paris
Coral Seas
L'Originale Alfredo
di Roma Ristorante
Marrakesh
Nine Dragons

For Restaurants
in Epcot please see
Epcot Restaurants Map

Exit 27
I-4 to
Orlando
535

To Orlando
Int'l Airport

To Kissimmee

536

Exit 26B
To: EPCOT,
DOWNTOWN DISNEY
MARKETPLACE

Exit 25B

To:
MAGIC KINGDOM PARK, DISNEY-MGM STUDIOS,
DISNEY'S ANIMAL KINGDOM, DISNEY'S FORT WILDERNESS
RESORT & CAMPGROUND

U.S. 192 →
to Kissimmee

CELEBRATION

192

I-4 to Tampa

0   1 mi
0   1.6 Km

Doubletree Guest Suite Resort
Travelodge Hotel
Buena Vista Palace
Grosvenor Resort
Hotel Royal Plaza
Courtyard By Marriott
The Hilton
SunTrust Building
Casting Center
Gas Station
Hotel Plaza Blvd
Lake Buena Vista
Black Lake
Buena Vista Dr.
Villa Ave.
Team Disney

DOWNTOWN DISNEY MARKETPLACE
Planet Hollywood
PLEASURE ISLAND

DISNEY'S INSTITUTE &
VILLAS AT THE DISNEY
INSTITUTE
Disney's Community Dr.
Disney's Old Key West Resort
Orleans Dr.
Disney's Port Orleans Resort
Bonnet Creek Pkwy

LAKE BUENA VISTA
GOLF CLUB
DOWNTOWN DISNEY WESTSIDE
DISNEY'S TYPHOON LAGOON

Epcot Center Dr.

Cayman Way
Sea Breeze Dr.
Disney's Caribbean Beach Resort

EPCOT
Epcot Parking
Bus Transportation
Epcot Main Entrance / Toll Plaza
Epcot Resort Blvd

Disney's Boardwalk Inn & Villas
Gas Station
Buena Vista Dr.
Toll Plaza
Guest Parking
Handicap Parking
Bus Transportation

see also Disney & MGM
Restaurants Map

DISNEY-MGM STUDIOS
Studios Main Entrance / Toll Plaza

Disney's Beach Club Resort
Disney's Yacht Club Resort
Walt Disney World Dolphin
Walt Disney World Swan
FANTASIA GARDENS

West Buena Vista Dr.
World Dr.

Osceola Pkwy.

DISNEY'S WIDE WORLD
OF SPORTS COMPLEX

BLIZZARD BEACH
Disney's Coronado Springs Resort
Disney's All-Star Sports Resort
Disney's All-Star Music Resort

Reedy Creek

DISNEY'S
ANIMAL KINGDOM
(opens 1998)

U.S. 192 to
U.S. 27
192

119

Au Petit Café
$–$$. Walt Disney World (Epcot; park admission required).
FRENCH.

This sidewalk cafe seems straight out of Nice or Paris. Be seated in time for IllumiNations, and have a light supper of *salade niçoise,* croissant sandwiches, quiche Lorraine, chicken baked in puff pastry, or prawns basted with basil butter. Linger over a glass or two of wine to watch the World go by.

France Pavilion, World Showcase, Epcot. ☎ *407/939-3463. Reservations not accepted.* **Main courses:** *$7.75–$15.50. AE, MC, V.* **Open:** *Daily 11am–an hour before park closing.*

Extra! Extra!

If you're looking for kid-friendly restaurants without mice... there are plenty of other good restaurants to take kids to, even if they don't have Disney characters to keep the youngsters entertained. The food may not be gourmet, but it's a little more interesting than the usual fare served in character dining rooms.

The kids will love the following:

> The Bubble Room (Near North; $$$)
> The B-Line Diner (International Drive Area; $$–$$$)
> Planet Hollywood (Pleasure Island; $$)
> The Prime Time Café (Disney-MGM Studios; $$–$$$)
> Race Rock (International Drive Area; $–$$)
> The Rainforest Cafe (Downtown Disney Marketplace &
>   Animal Kingdom; $$)
> Sci-Fi Dine-In Theater Restaurant (Disney-MGM Studios; $$–$$$)

B-Line Diner
$$–$$$. International Drive Area. AMERICAN

Gleaming chrome and tile create a roadside diner setting for informal, inexpensive eating popular with local bigwigs and visiting celebs. Kids have their own menu. Grownups can order diner classics plus sophisticated specialties, health foods, vegetarian specials, comfort foods, and pastries to eat in or take out. Order drinks from the full bar. An added bonus: it's open round the clock, so this is the place to go when you've just gotta have that 2am cheeseburger.

In the Peabody Orlando, 9801 International Dr. ☎ *407/345-4460. Reservations not accepted.* **Parking:** *Free self-parking; validated valet parking.* **Main courses:** *$8.95–$22 at dinner. AE, CB, DC, DISC, JCB, MC, V.* **Open:** *Daily 24 hours (dinner 5–11pm).*

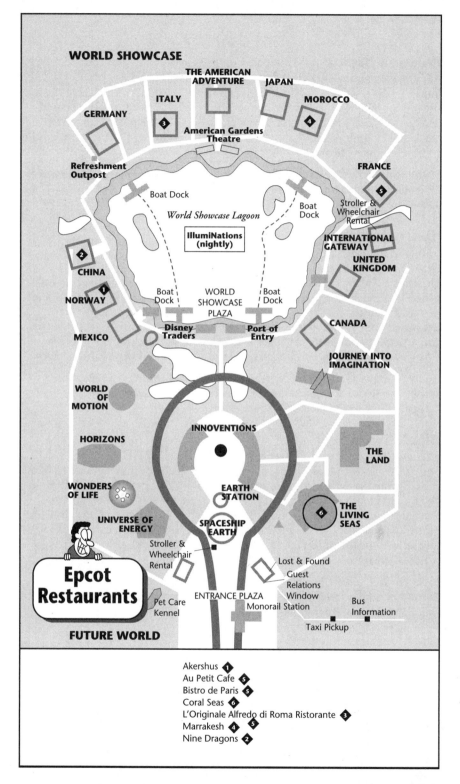

WORLD SHOWCASE

THE AMERICAN ADVENTURE

JAPAN

ITALY ❸

MOROCCO ❹

GERMANY

American Gardens Theatre

Refreshment Outpost

FRANCE ❺

Boat Dock

World Showcase Lagoon

Boat Dock

Stroller & Wheelchair Rental

IllumiNations (nightly)

INTERNATIONAL GATEWAY

CHINA ❷

UNITED KINGDOM

Boat Dock

WORLD SHOWCASE PLAZA

Boat Dock

NORWAY ❶

CANADA

MEXICO

Disney Traders

Port of Entry

JOURNEY INTO IMAGINATION

WORLD OF MOTION

INNOVENTIONS

THE LAND

HORIZONS

EARTH STATION

WONDERS OF LIFE

THE LIVING SEAS ❻

UNIVERSE OF ENERGY

SPACESHIP EARTH

Stroller & Wheelchair Rental

Lost & Found

Epcot Restaurants

Guest Relations Window

Bus Information

Pet Care Kennel

ENTRANCE PLAZA

Monorail Station

Taxi Pickup

FUTURE WORLD

Akershus ❶
Au Petit Cafe ❺
Bistro de Paris ❺
Coral Seas ❻
L'Originale Alfredo di Roma Ristorante ❸
Marrakesh ❹ ❺
Nine Dragons ❷

121

Bahama Breeze
$$. International Drive Area. CARIBBEAN/CREOLE.
Imagine you're in The Bahamas as you dine on island-style specialties in a straw market setting. From the people who created The Olive Garden and Red Lobster, this prototype for a new chain serves paella, coconut curry chicken, key lime pie, and a mean piña colada pudding. Choose from among 50 beers or dare one of the fruity rum drinks.

8849 International Dr. ☎ *407/248-2499. Reservations not accepted.* **Parking:** *No problem, mon.* **Main courses:** *$6.95–$14.95. AE, MC, V.* **Open:** *Sun–Thurs 4pm–1am, Fri–Sat 4pm–1:30am.*

Bistro de Paris
$$$$. Walt Disney World (Epcot; park admission required). CLASSIC FRENCH.
The classic French cuisine here is above reproach, and you'll enjoy it while seated in a plush banquette surrounded by candlelight, snowy linen, and art nouveau touches. You're really a complete idiot if you don't start with renowned chef Paul Bocuse's famous duck foie gras salad with fresh greens and artichoke hearts. Main dishes include roasted red snapper in potato crust, cradled in a bed of spinach and ladled with a red-wine lobster sauce.

France Pavilion, World Showcase, Epcot. ☎ *407/939-3463. Arranging Priority Seating in advance is required.* **Main courses:** *$20.50–$26.95. AE, MC, V.* **Open:** *Daily 4pm–an hour before park closing.*

Black Swan
$$$$$. International Drive Area. HAUTE CUISINE.
This is the perfect place for a romantic dinner accompanied by a fine vintage chosen from an extensive wine list. Try the grilled portobello mushroom in a bed of wilted arugula and a drift of Asiago cheese, then the rack of lamb, roasted to pink perfection, or Southwestern-style chicken served with black beans, roasted corn relish, and cilantro chili fettuccine. You can top off this memorable meal with an apple tart drenched with caramel sauce and whipped cream or one of the dessert wines or liqueurs.

In the Hyatt Regency Grand Cypress, 1 N. Jacaranda, off FL 535. ☎ *407/ 239-1999. Reservations recommended.* **Main courses:** *$25–$34. AE, CB, DC, DISC, JCB, MC, V.* **Open:** *Daily 6–10pm.*

Extra! Extra!

If you're looking for a romantic dinner, head for:

Atlantis (International Drive Area; $$$$$)
Arthur's 27 (Lake Buena Vista; $$$$$)
Bistro de Paris (Epcot; $$$$)
The Black Swan (International Drive Area; $$$$$)
The Bubble Room (Near North; $$$)
Café Europa (Downtown; $$$)
La Provence (Downtown; $$$–$$$$)
Maison et Jardin (Near North; $$$$)
Manuel's on the 28th (Downtown; $$$$$)
Victoria and Albert's (Disney's Grand Floridian Beach Resort; $$$$$)

Boston's Fish House
$. Near North. SEAFOOD.

The fried and broiled seafood dishes here play to a packed house because portions are so generous and prices are so modest. This is a terrific bargain in a no-frills setting. You place your order at the counter and wait at your table until the meal is brought. If you're a light eater, the hearty seafood chowder can make a meal. Or choose from today's catch of ocean or freshwater seafood. For landlubbers, there are chicken dishes and burgers. Dishes arrive piled high with food and fixings, such as french fries, hush puppies, and cole slaw.

In the Aloma Square Plaza, 6860 Aloma Ave. (Route 426), Winter Park.
☎ **407/678-2107.** *Reservations not accepted.* **Main courses:** *$6.75–$11.95. No credit cards.* **Open:** *Fri–Sat 11am–9:30pm; Sun and Tues–Thurs 11am–8:30pm.*

Bubbaloo's Bodacious BBQ
$–$$. Near North. BARBECUE.

If smoke billowing from the chimney indicates a real pit barbecue, this one qualifies. Children love the name and informality of this place, but watch the sauces. Even the Mild is hot for young 'uns, and the Killer is only for those with asbestos taste buds. The pork platter with fixin's is a deal and a half, or try chicken, beef, or clams plus beans and slaw. And it wouldn't be a barbecue without plenty of beer on hand.

5818 Conroy Rd. Take I-4 east to Lee Rd., Exit 45, then left. ☎ **407/295-1212.** *Reservations not accepted.* **Main courses:** *$4.95–$7.95. AE, MC, V.* **Open:** *Sun–Thurs 10am–9:30pm; Fri–Sat 10am–10:30pm.*

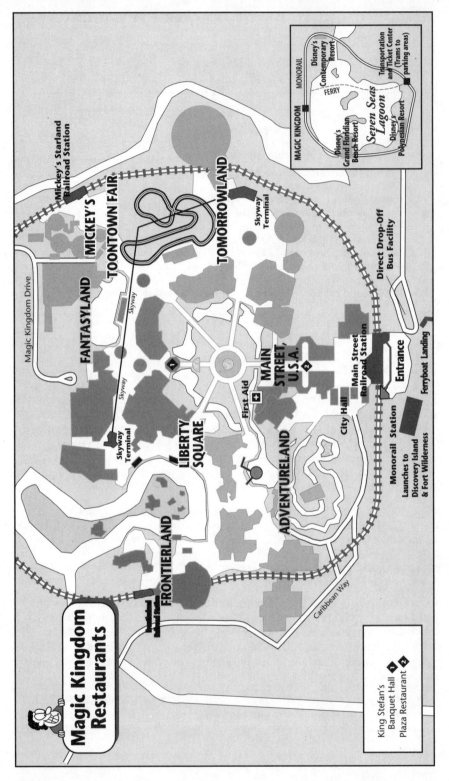

Magic Kingdom Restaurants

King Stefan's Banquet Hall ◆ 1
Plaza Restaurant 2

MICKEY'S TOONTOWN FAIR

Mickey's Starland Railroad Station

TOMORROWLAND

Skyway Terminal

Direct Drop-Off Bus Facility

FANTASYLAND

Magic Kingdom Drive

Skyway

Skyway Terminal

LIBERTY SQUARE

First Aid

MAIN STREET, U.S.A.

Main Street Railroad Station

Entrance

City Hall

Monorail Station

Launches to Discovery Island & Fort Wilderness

Ferryboat Landing

ADVENTURELAND

FRONTIERLAND

Caribbean Way

MONORAIL

Disney's Contemporary Resort

Transportation and Ticket Center (Trams to parking areas)

FERRY

MAGIC KINGDOM

Seven Seas Lagoon

Disney's Grand Floridian Beach Resort

Disney's Polynesian Resort

Kids The Bubble Room
$$$. Near North. AMERICAN.

No matter where you sit, you're surrounded by antiques and junque to talk about while you wait for supersize servings of prime rib, stuffed chicken, turkey and dressing, or steak. Servers ham it up, making this a celebration meal for the whole family. For two, book the Tunnel of Love booth. Locals go ga-ga over the desserts and wacko decor.

1351 S. Orlando Ave., Maitland, 10 min. north of downtown. Take I-4 east to Lee Rd. (Exit 45) then right at the bottom of the ramp and left at Orlando Ave. (U.S. 17–92). ☎ **407/628-3331.** *Reservations recommended.* **Main courses:** *$11.95–$18.95. AE, DISC, MC, V.* **Open:** *Daily 11:30am–4pm; Sun–Thurs 4–11pm; Fri–Sat 4–11pm.*

Café Europa
$$$. Downtown. EASTERN EUROPEAN.

The cabbage rolls, fisherman's pie, and chicken paprika in this *gemütlich* pub are like what Mama used to make (if Mama was a hearty Bavarian). The cookies and coffee for dessert hark back to Vienna. The beer and wine choices are international.

Church Street Market, 55 W. Church St. ☎ **407/872-3388.** *Reservations not needed.* **Parking:** *Use one of the downtown parking lots.* **Main courses:** *$5.95–$17.50. AE, DC, DISC, MC, V.* **Open:** *Mon–Thurs dinner only; lunch and dinner Fri–Sat 4–10pm; Sun noon–10pm.*

Cafe Tu Tu Tango
$$. International Drive Area. TAPAS.

A smart tapas bar where every order comes in a miniature size, this is an ideal spot for grazing. Or make a meal by sharing several tapas around the table. Try Cajun-style egg rolls, tuna sashimi with noodles and spinach in soy vinaigrette, and dozens of other chi-chi appetizers. For dessert, have guava cheesecake with strawberry sauce. *Note that ordering several tapas and drinks can turn this into a $$$ restaurant.*

8625 International Dr., just west of the Mercado. ☎ **407/248-2222.** *Reservations recommended.* **Parking:** *Self-parking is free; valet parking is available.* **Main courses:** *Tapas $3.75–$7.95; even those with the smallest appetites will want to order at least 2 per person. AE, DISC, MC, V.* **Open:** *Sun–Thurs 11:30am–11pm; Fri–Sat 11:30am–midnight.*

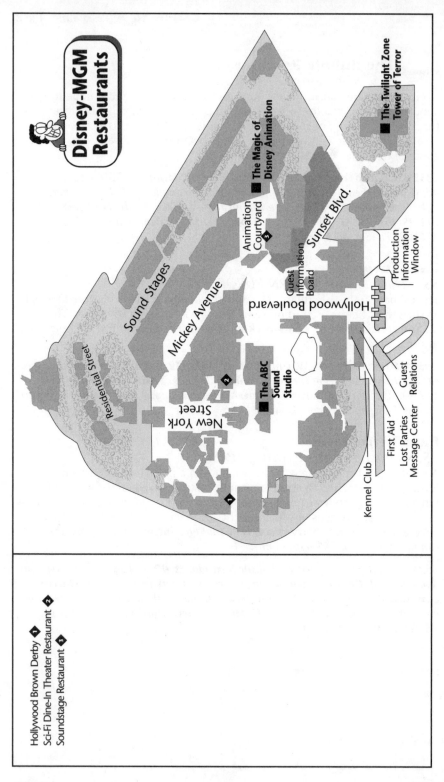

Disney-MGM Restaurants

The Magic of Disney Animation

The Twilight Zone Tower of Terror

Animation Courtyard

Sunset Blvd.

Guest Information Board

Hollywood Boulevard

Production Information Window

Sound Stages

Mickey Avenue

The ABC Sound Studio

Guest Relations

Residential Street

New York Street

First Aid
Lost Parties
Message Center

Kennel Club

Hollywood Brown Derby ●1
Sci-Fi Dine-In Theater Restaurant ●2
Soundstage Restaurant ●3

Capriccio

$$$. International Drive Area. TUSCAN/NORTHERN ITALIAN.
The decor is chic and modern, with Italian flair, including a showcase kitchen with wood-fired pizza ovens. Start with fried calamari, then one of the heavenly pizzas or pastas, or pan-seared tuna with braised fennel and radicchio served with lentil flan. Dip the crusty bread into a puddle of extra-virgin olive oil. For dessert have the *zuppa inglese*. The wine list is extensive.

Extra! Extra!

For child care while you dine, head for:

Akershus (Epcot; $$)
Atlantis (International Drive Area; $$$$$)

In the Peabody Orlando, 9801 International Dr. ☎ ***407/352-4000.*** *Reservations recommended.* **Parking:** *Free self-parking; validated valet parking.* **Main courses:** *$12–$22. AE, CB, DC, DISC, JCB, MC, V.* **Open:** *Tues–Sun 6–11pm.*

Columbia

$$$. Walt Disney World (Celebration). CUBAN.
When the world's most famous mouse and one of Florida's most revered restaurants team up, it's news. The original Columbia was founded in Tampa in 1904 by the great-grandfather of the present operators. It's still a family affair. You'll dine on freshly starched linens in a bright room decorated with touches of old Tampa and old Havana: tiles, shiny woodwork, wrought iron, and bentwood chairs. The 1905 Salad, flan, paella, arroz con pollo, snapper Alicante, and Spanish bean soup are cause for celebration. Cigar smokers are welcome.

649 Front St., in Celebration. ☎ ***407/566-1505.*** *Reservations recommended.* **Main courses:** *$10.95–$21.95. AE, DC, DISC, MC, V.* **Open:** *Daily 11:30am–4pm and 4–10pm.*

Kids Coral Seas

$$$. Walt Disney World (Epcot; park admission required). SEAFOOD.
Classical music and incredible views of the Living Seas aquarium transport diners to a romantic spot under the sea, filled with flickering lights and flitting fish. The seafood is the star here. Meals are unhurried, and the kids don't mind because they are captivated by the kaleidoscope of fish, sharks, and rays.

Living Seas Pavilion, Future World. ☎ ***407/939-3463.*** *Arranging Priority Seating in advance is recommended.* **Main courses:** *$12.15–$23.75. AE, MC, V.* **Open:** *Daily 11am–park closing.*

Dux
$$$$$. International Drive Area. HAUTE CUISINE.
The name refers to the family of live ducks that splashes all day in the marble fountains in the Peabody's grandly formal lobby. This is a favorite of celebrities, who dine here while shooting at Universal Studios. An eclectic international menu changes with the seasons. Sample dishes: dumplings stuffed with portobello mushrooms, scallions, and goat cheese with a garnish of Asiago cheese; lamb chops in Hunan barbecue lacquer; grilled grouper in Cajun spices; hazelnut meringue napoleon topped with ice cream. Choose a wine from a long, inspired list.

In the Peabody Hotel, 9801 International Dr. ☎ **407/345-4550.** *Reservations recommended.* **Parking:** *Free self-parking; validated valet parking.* **Main courses:** *$19–$45. AE, CB, DC, DISC, JCB, MC, V.* **Open:** *Daily 6–10:30pm.*

Fulton's Crab House
$$$$$. Walt Disney World (Pleasure Island). SEAFOOD.
Lose yourself in a world of brass, shining mahogany, and river charts. Today's catch can be presented charcoal-grilled, broiled, fried with a dusting of cornmeal, blackened, or steamed. The cioppino is a feast of lobster, clams, mussels, red potatoes, and corn. Or have the filet mignon with whipped potatoes. The wine list is comprehensive; there's a full bar. For dessert, don't miss the milk-chocolate crème brûlée.

Dollars & Sense

You don't have to buy admission to Pleasure Island to dine at Fulton's Crab House, the Fireworks Factory, Planet Hollywood, or the Portobello Yacht Club.

Aboard the Riverboat at Pleasure Island. ☎ **407/939-3463.** *Reservations not accepted.* **Parking:** *Free self-parking; valet parking $5.* **Main courses:** *$14.95–$50. AE, MC, V.* **Open:** *Daily 4pm–midnight; snacks available 11:30am–2am.*

Hollywood Brown Derby
$$$. Walt Disney World (Disney-MGM Studios; park admission required). AMERICAN.
The place where Hollywood's stars gathered during the 1930s and '40s is realistically replicated in a parklike setting. Caricatures of the stars who were regulars at the California original line the walls here. Dine on fresh grouper served atop a creamy pasta, followed by the famous grapefruit cake with cream-cheese frosting, or the white chocolate cheesecake.

Hollywood Blvd., Disney-MGM Studios. ☎ **407/939-3463.** *Arranging Priority Seating in advance is recommended.* **Main courses:** *$16.50–$23.75; early-bird dinner $15.75. AE, MC, V.* **Open:** *Daily 11am–park closing.*

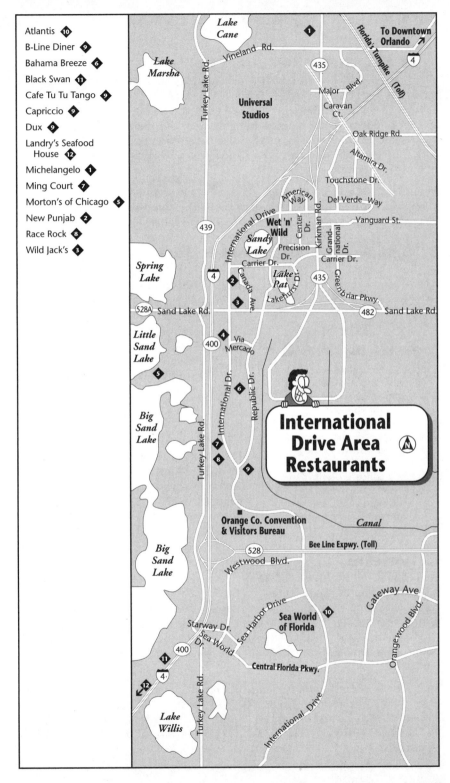

Atlantis **10**
B-Line Diner **9**
Bahama Breeze **6**
Black Swan **11**
Cafe Tu Tu Tango **9**
Capriccio **9**
Dux **9**
Landry's Seafood House **12**
Michelangelo **1**
Ming Court **7**
Morton's of Chicago **5**
New Punjab **2**
Race Rock **8**
Wild Jack's **3**

International Drive Area Restaurants

King Stefan's Banquet Hall

$$$–$$$$. Walt Disney World (Magic Kingdom; park admission required). AMERICAN/ENGLISH.

Cinderella will probably be on hand to greet you before you dine in Gothic splendor under knights' banners hanging from the vaulted ceiling. Here you'll feast on chicken, fish, or king-size cuts of prime rib or sirloin served with fresh vegetables and a hearty soup. For openers, try the elegant breaded Brie with tangy lingonberry.

In Cinderella's Castle, in the Magic Kingdom. ☎ *407/939-3463. Arranging Priority Seating in advance is recommended.* **Main courses:** *$17.50–$25.75 at dinner; cheaper at lunch. AE, MC, V.* **Open:** *Daily 11am–park closing.*

L'Originale Alfredo di Roma Ristorante

$$–$$$. Walt Disney World (Epcot; park admission required). ITALIAN/MEDITERRANEAN.

Discover fettuccine Alfredo made just as the recipe's originator made it. Sample southern Italian cuisine in a "seaside" Italian palazzo evoked by huge murals. Try veal scaloppine with roasted potatoes, a vegetarian plate of grilled vegetables, or a divine linguine pesto, then tiramisu for dessert. The three-course early-bird dinner is a bargain.

Bet You Didn't Know

If you have special dietary needs (if you're a diabetic, a vegetarian, or a struggling dieter, or if you keep kosher), you won't have to worry about finding something you can eat in the Disney parks. Disney has made a concerted effort to add healthier foods to its menus, even at the cafeterias and fast-food counters.

Italy Pavilion, World Showcase, Epcot. ☎ *407/939-3463. Arranging Priority Seating in advance is recommended.* **Main courses:** *$9.25–$24.75. A $15.75 fixed-price dinner is served 4:30–6pm.* **Open:** *Daily 11am–an hour before park closing.*

La Provence

$$$–$$$$. Downtown. CLASSIC FRENCH.

A stately setting transports guests to the French Riviera, where fine wines are paired with sophisticated cuisine. Order à la carte: an authentic foie gras or terrine, then lobster bisque and a fish, game, meat, or vegetarian main dish. Or choose the fixed-price *menu gastronomique* or the simpler *menu du marche*. Both offer a parade of courses at fair prices. Live jazz plays in the library-style lounge.

50 E. Pine St., 1 block north of Church St., just east of Court. (Note that Orange Ave. is 1-way southbound here.) ☎ *407/843-4410. Reservations strongly recommended.* **Parking:** *A parking garage is just east on Pine St., between Magnolia and Rosalind.* **Main courses:** *$19–$29.95. Fixed-price menus $25.95 and $51.* **Open:** *Mon–Thurs 5:30–9:30pm, Fri–Sat 5:30–10:30pm.*

Landry's Seafood House

$$–$$$. International Drive Area. SEAFOOD.

This is the local outpost of a chain that originated in Texas. Its accent is on seafood with Cajun and Caribbean touches. Salmon with lemon butter is simple and flavorful. Or have the fresh catch of the day, which could be grouper, mahimahi, or snapper. For starters, try the seafood-stuffed mushrooms. Key lime pie is the favorite dessert here.

8800 Vineland Ave. (FL 535), east of I-4. ☎ **407/827-6466.** *Reservations accepted for parties of 8 or more.* **Main courses:** *$11.95–$15.95. AE, DC, DISC, MC, V.* **Open:** *Mon–Fri 4–11pm, Sat–Sun 11:30am–11pm.*

Little Saigon

$$. Downtown. VIETNAMESE.

In the heart of a tiny but vibrant Vietnamese neighborhood, this treasure is run by and for its regulars. Order food by number, and if you need a description of the dish, ask for the manager, whose English is better than that of many of the servers. Don't miss the summer rolls with peanut sauce. A few beers and wines are available.

131

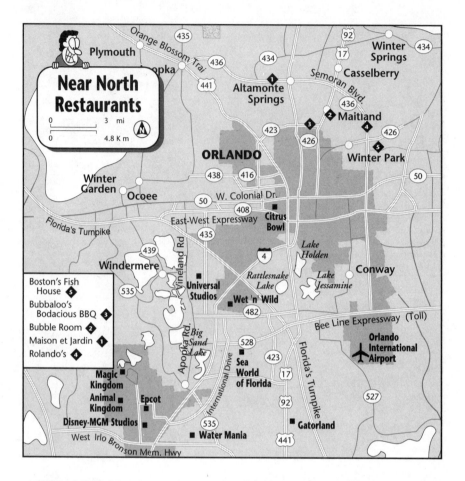

Near North Restaurants

0 ────── 3 mi
0 ────── 4.8 K m

Boston's Fish House ❺
Bubbaloo's Bodacious BBQ ❸
Bubble Room ❷
Maison et Jardin ❶
Rolando's ❹

1106 E. Colonial Dr. From I-4, take the Colonial Exit (Hwy. 50) and go east; look for the fish mural between Mills and Thornton. ☎ **407/423-8539.** *Reservations required.* **Main courses:** *$4.25–$7. AE, DISC, MC, V.* **Open:** *Daily 10am–9pm.*

Maison et Jardin
$$$$. Near North. CLASSIC FRENCH.

Formal and romantic, Maison et Jardin (*House and Garden* just sounds so much prettier in French, doesn't it?) is a time-honored local favorite and a consistent award winner. The menu has just the right mix of dishes, including the signature beef Wellington or medallions of elk served with raspberry sauce. The wine list is impressive.

430 Wymore Rd., Altamonte Springs, 10 min. north of Orlando. Take I-4 east to Maitland Blvd. East exit, then right at Lake Destiny Rd. At the next light, turn left onto Wymore Rd. ☎ **407/862-4410.** *Reservations recommended.* **Main courses:** *$18.50–$28.50. AE, DC, DISC, MC, V.* **Open:** *Mon–Sat 6–10pm; Sun brunch 11am–2pm and dinner 6–9pm.*

Manuel's on the 28th
$$$$$. Downtown. HAUTE CUISINE.

Take the elevator to the 28th floor for a stunning after-dark view of the sparkling, sprawling metropolis that Orlando has become. At most "view" restaurants, the food can't match the scenery; at Manuel's, the cuisine may even outstrip the surroundings, especially when it is delivered by a friendly and professional staff. They'll help you pair the perfect wine with rack of lamb, a veal-chop-and-scampi combination plate, or a steak wreathed in fresh vegetables.

390 N. Orange Ave., in the Barnett Bank building. ☎ *407/246-6580. Reservations required.* **Main courses:** *$24–$32. AE, DC, DISC, MC, V.* **Open:** *Tues–Sat 6–10pm.*

Marrakesh
$$$. Walt Disney World (Epcot; park admission required). MOROCCAN.

Hand-laid mosaics in intricate patterns set the scene for lavish North African dining, complete with belly dancers. Try the Moroccan *diffa* (traditional feast) to sample saffron-seasoned harina soup made with lamb and lentils, beef *brewats* in a broth of spices and a cloak of pastry, roast lamb with rice pilaf, chicken with green olives, couscous with vegetables, Moroccan pastries, and mint tea.

Morocco Pavilion, World Showcase, Epcot. ☎ *407/939-3463. Arranging Priority Seating in advance is recommended.* **Main courses:** *$13.75–$19.95. A fixed-price diffa is served for $29.95 for 2 people at lunch, for $49.95 for 2 people at dinner. AE, MC, V.* **Open:** *Daily 11am–an hour before park closing.*

Ming Court
$$$. International Drive Area. CHINESE.

Dine in an ethereal setting graced with lotus ponds filled with glowing goldfish while you're entertained by zither music. You'll rub elbows with more locals than tourists here. Try the crisp chicken in a tangy tangerine sauce, spicy Szechuan beef or shrimp, or butter-tender filet mignon with crisp-tender vegetables.

9188 International Dr., between Sand Lake Rd. and the Bee Line Expressway. ☎ *407/ 351-9988. Reservations recommended.* **Main courses:** *$7.95–$16.95. AE, CB, DC, DISC, MC, V.* **Open:** *Daily 11am–2:30pm and 4:30pm–midnight.*

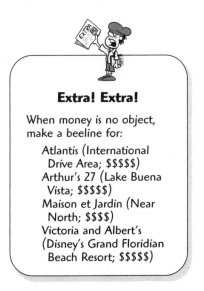

Extra! Extra!

When money is no object, make a beeline for:

Atlantis (International Drive Area; $$$$$)

Arthur's 27 (Lake Buena Vista; $$$$$)

Maison et Jardin (Near North; $$$$)

Victoria and Albert's (Disney's Grand Floridian Beach Resort; $$$$$)

Michelangelo
$$$$. International Drive Area. ITALIAN/MEDITERRANEAN.
The veal Michelangelo here is meltingly tender, and the marinated prime rib is a feast. Order homemade pastas as a side dish or main course. A substantial menu offers a nice choice of appetizers, soup, main dishes, and desserts. There's a full bar and a decent wine list.

4898 Kirkman Rd., in the Kirkman Shoppes, ¼ mile north of Universal Studios.
☎ *407/297-6666. Reservations recommended.* **Main courses:** *$13.95–$28.95. AE, DC, DISC, MC, V.* **Open:** *Daily 6–11pm.*

Morton's of Chicago
$$$$. International Drive Area. STEAKHOUSE.
Chicago knows beef, which is served here in straightforward meat-and-potatoes style. The cuts are costly, but they are butter-tender and aged to perfection. Side dishes are à la carte, which can add up to an expensive evening if you go overboard. The no-smoking section could be larger and more smoke free. There's a full bar.

7600 Dr. Phillips Blvd., in the Marketplace at Dr. Phillips. ☎ *407/248-3485. Reservations recommended.* **Main courses:** *$16.95–$29.95. AE, DC, MC, V.* **Open:** *Mon–Sat 5:30–11pm; Sun 5–10pm.*

New Punjab
$. International Drive Area/another branch on U.S. 192, Kissimmee. INDIAN.
Whether you have a yen for vegetarian cooking, a fiery curry, or a tangy tandoori, these cozy restaurants serve them up without pretense in a comfortable, informal setting decorated with Indian motifs. Have lamb tandoori, chicken with spinach, vegetables masala, or a spicy vindaloo, followed by a fruity ice dessert to put out the fire. Beer and wine are available.

7451 International Dr. ☎ *407/352-7887. Or 3404 Vine St., Kissimmee.*
☎ *407/931-2449. Reservations not accepted.* **Main courses:** *$7.95–$14.95. AE, MC, V.* **Open:** *Tues–Sat 11:30am–11pm; Sun–Mon 5–11pm.*

Extra! Extra!

For a knockout view after dark, your best bets are:

Arthur's 27 (Lake Buena Vista; $$$$$)

Manuel's on the 28th (Downtown; $$$$$)

Nine Dragons
$$$. Walt Disney World (Epcot; park admission required unless you're a guest at the Swan or Dolphin hotels). CHINESE.
This is one of the loveliest World Showcase restaurants, with intricately carved rosewood paneling and an amazing dragon-motif ceiling. Order shredded duck with sweet peppers and Chinese pancakes, spicy Szechuan shrimp, stir-fried chicken with rafts of vegetables, or

sliced sirloin stir-fried with broccoli and oyster sauce. The fresh fruit juices are delicious, with or without an alcohol kicker. For dessert, try the sweet red-bean ice cream with fried banana.

China Pavilion, Epcot. ☎ *407/939-3463. Arranging Priority Seating in advance is recommended. **Main courses:** $10.50–$23.75; a fixed-price dinner is $11.50. AE, MC, V. **Open:** Daily 11am–an hour before park closing.*

Numero Uno
$$. Downtown. CUBAN.

This family-operated hole in the wall isn't fancy, but you won't notice the decor once the paella hits your table. Or have *ropa vieja* (literally "old clothes" because the beef is so tender), roast pork, or a remarkable arroz con pollo. Dishes come with plantains and refried beans. Dessert is the traditional three-milk cake. Beer and wine only.

2499 S. Orange Ave. ☎ *407/841-3840. Reservations recommended. Parking is tight, but free. **Main courses:** $7.95–$18.95. AE, DC, DISC, MC, V. **Open:** Mon–Fri 11am–3pm; Mon–Sat 5:30–9pm.*

✦Kids✦ Planet Hollywood
$$. Pleasure Island. AMERICAN.

Your kids already know about it, and they're probably clamoring to go. This place is part restaurant and part showcase for Hollywood memorabilia. Diners are surrounded by clips from soon-to-be-released movies and more than 300 show-biz artifacts ranging from Peter O'Toole's *Lawrence of Arabia* costume to the front end of the bus from *Speed!* And although you might expect mediocre food amidst all the hype, it's pretty good. You can nosh on appetizers like hickory-smoked buffalo wings, pot stickers, or nachos, or try out the selection of burgers, sandwiches, pastas, and pizzas.

1506 E. Buena Vista Dr., Pleasure Island. ☎ *407/827-7827. Reservations not accepted. **Main courses:** $7.50–$18.95 (most under $13). AE, DC, MC, V. **Open:** Daily 11am–2am.*

Bet You Didn't Know

Once in a while, a deep, double booming noise shakes things up a little. No, it's not a roller coaster crashing—it's the sound of the space shuttle landing at Cape Canaveral. It produces a twin sonic boom when it reenters the atmosphere that can be heard throughout three counties.

Plaza Restaurant
$$. Walt Disney World (Magic Kingdom; park admission required). AMERICAN.

Take a breather from the hot sun and teeming crowds with a lunch break at everyone's hometown restaurant, located appropriately enough at the end of Main Street in the Magic Kingdom. The menu offers burgers plain or fancy,

135

sandwiches hot or cold (try the Reuben or the double-decker hot roast beef), salads big and small, and milkshakes in three flavors.

Magic Kingdom, Walt Disney World. ☎ *407/939-3463. Arranging Priority Seating in advance is recommended.* **Main courses:** *$7.75–$10.75. AE, MC, V.* **Open:** *Daily 11am–park closing.*

Prime Time Café
$$–$$$. Walt Disney World (Disney-MGM Studios; park admission required). AMERICAN.

Return to the age when TVs were black and white and Mom made you finish your vegetables before you could have dessert. Comfort foods like meatloaf and mashed potatoes, pot roast like Grandma's, and Dad's chili are served in a 1950s kitchen, where tables are covered with the familiar boomerang-pattern Formica. Mom (your server) will scold you if you put your elbows on the table or don't clean your plate, but order the banana split anyway. While you eat, *I Love Lucy* reruns play on the flickering TVs.

Disney-MGM Studios, near the Indiana Jones Stunt Spectacular. ☎ *407/939-3463. Arranging Priority Seating in advance is recommended.* **Main courses:** *$11.95–$20.25 at dinner; cheaper at lunch. AE, MC, V.* **Open:** *Daily 11am–park closing.*

Kids Race Rock
$–$$. International Drive Area. AMERICAN.

Gearheads of all ages love this pit stop, where burly burgers, pizza, egg rolls, soups, salads, and sandwiches are served up while heart-stopping race scenes play on a giant screen. Live and in person are the biggest monster trucks in the world, dragsters, and hydroplanes. Kids have their own Quarter Midget Menu with games and coloring.

8986 International Dr., just south of Sand Lake Rd. ☎ *407/248-9876. Reservations accepted only for groups.* **Main courses:** *Prime rib is $17.95; sand-wiches are $6.95–$7.95. AE, DC, DISC, MC, V.* **Open:** *Daily 11am–11pm or later if it's crowded.*

Kids Rainforest Cafe
$$. Downtown Disney Marketplace & Animal Kingdom. AMERICAN.

Kids love this place! The food's pretty respectable, but it's really the decor that makes this restaurant. As its name suggests, entering the Rainforest Cafe is like walking into a tropical jungle—there are lifelike silk plants all over, Animatronic monkeys chattering, and occasional rain and thunder rum-blings. The extensive menu features California-influenced house specialties like Chicken Monsoon with shrimp and linguine, and Rasta Pasta (bow-tie noodles with a variety of vegetables and a creamy garlic-pesto sauce). Another branch is scheduled to open soon in the Animal Kingdom.

In the Downtown Disney Marketplace, 1800 E. Buena Vista Dr., Lake Buena Vista.
☎ **407/827-8500.** *Reservations not accepted. The other restaurant will be located in Disney's Animal Kingdom near the main entrance.* **Main courses:** *$5.50–$17.95. AE, DISC, MC, V.* **Open:** *Sun–Thurs 10:30am–11pm; Fri–Sat 10:30am–midnight.*

Rolando's
$–$$. Near North. CUBAN.

Mountainous platters of traditional Cuban food make for memorable dining in an unpretentious setting of hanging plants and Formica tables. Order traditional pork, red snapper, tamale pie, or chicken with a hearty rice pudding for dessert.

870 E. Semoran (FL 436), between Red Bug Rd. and U.S. 17–92. Take I-4 east to the East-West Expressway, then east, then left on Semoran Blvd. (FL 436). ☎ **407/767-9677.** *Reservations not accepted.* **Main courses:** *$7.75–$17.50. AE, DISC, MC, V.* **Open:** *Tues–Sat 11am–10pm; Sun 1–8pm.*

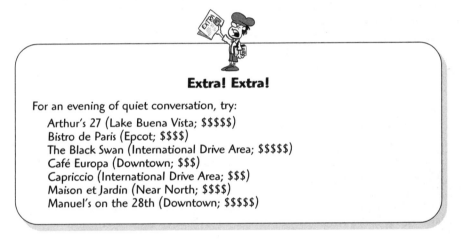

Extra! Extra!

For an evening of quiet conversation, try:
- Arthur's 27 (Lake Buena Vista; $$$$$)
- Bistro de Paris (Epcot; $$$$)
- The Black Swan (International Drive Area; $$$$$)
- Café Europa (Downtown; $$$)
- Capriccio (International Drive Area; $$$)
- Maison et Jardin (Near North; $$$$)
- Manuel's on the 28th (Downtown; $$$$$)

Kids Sci-Fi Dine-in Theater Restaurant
$$–$$$. Walt Disney World (Disney-MGM Studios; park admission required). AMERICAN.

Picture a drive-in movie in the 1940s, when carhops brought your burger and malt. Kids love the seating in a real car. Horror flicks that are too hokey to be scary play on the screen while you dine on barbecued ribs with vegetables and fries, Cajun-style grilled chicken, free popcorn, and, for dessert, The Cheesecake That Ate New York. Have a milkshake or order from the full bar.

Disney-MGM Studios, near the Monster Sound Show. ☎ **407/939-3463.** *Arranging Priority Seating in advance is recommended.* **Main courses:** *$9.50–$22.75 at dinner; cheaper at lunch. AE, MC, V.* **Open:** *Daily 11am–park closing.*

137

Thanh Thuy
$. Downtown. VIETNAMESE.
Here's the place to find a filling, family meal in an unpretentious room in Orlando's growing Vietnamese community. Start the meal with one of the fried spring rolls, then a hot soup or one of the chicken, pork, or beef combinations. The flashy tableside presentation menu is great fun to watch and to eat as course after course comes to the table. Beer and wine are available.

1227 N. Mills Ave., about 12 blocks north of Colonial Dr. ☎ *407/898-8011. Reservations not accepted. Limited self-parking is free.* **Main courses:** *$3.75–$7.95. AE, DC, DISC, MC, V.* **Open:** *Daily 10am–10pm.*

Victoria and Albert's
$$$$$. Walt Disney World. HAUTE CUISINE.
This is the most memorable (and memorably expensive) restaurant in Orlando. If money is no object and you're serious about food (or romance), head here. You're greeted by a harpist or violinist at the entryway of this plush, intimate dining room, which has exquisitely appointed tables. The cuisine is impeccable and is presented with a flourish by the attentive and professional staff. You can also reserve weeks ahead for a private dinner, served in a special kitchen alcove, by chef Scott Hunnell and his staff. You could come here for a regular dinner at $80 per dinner plus $30 for a wine pairing, but here is a chance to gild the lily. The dining experience lasts 3 to 4 hours, but you will remember it for a lifetime. The menu changes each time but is sure to be a dazzler.

In the Grand Floridian Beach Resort, 4401 Floridian Way, Walt Disney World. ☎ *407/939-3463 or 407/824-1089. Reservations required well in advance.* **Parking:** *Self-parking is free; valet parking is validated.* **Prices:** *The chef decides each night's menu, which costs $115 per person without wine and $160 per person with 5 wines served course by course. AE, MC, V.* **Open:** *Two dinner seatings nightly at 5:45 and 9pm. The chef's kitchen is by special reservation only.*

Wild Jacks
$$$. International Drive Area. AMERICAN.
Raw-boned meat-and-potato diners dote on this chuck wagon, with its mounted buffalo heads, wagon-wheel chandeliers, and open kitchen aflurry with steaks on the open-pit grill. Order a Texas-size chunk of cow with jalapeño mashed potatoes and corn on the cob, skewered shrimp, tacos, chicken, or pasta. Wash it all down with an iced longneck from the bar. For dessert, have peach cobbler a la mode. There are other Wild Jacks in Altamonte Springs and Kissimmee.

7364 International Dr., between Sand Lake Rd. and Carrier Dr. ☎ *407/ 352-4407. Reservations not accepted.* **Parking:** *Plenty, pardner, and it's free.* **Main courses:** *$6.95–$17.95. AE, CB, DC, DISC, JCB, MC, V.* **Open:** *Sun–Thurs 4:30–10pm, Fri–Sat 4–11pm.*

Part 5

Exploring Walt Disney World & Orlando

You've decided where to stay. You know where to eat. So what are you going to do now?

You're going to Disney World!

Of course, so is the Super Bowl–winning quarterback, not to mention half the people who watched the game on television. That means literally thousands of people trying to see the same characters your kids want to meet, thousands of kids trying to ride the same rides, and hundreds of people at each restaurant, food court, and hot dog stand trying to eat the same foods. You'll enjoy your visit to the parks a whole lot more if you have an idea of which rides and attractions are worth the long lines and which are skippable.

In this section, we'll talk about the myriad kingdoms in the vast Disney empire and tell you how to negotiate all of them. And there's a whole lot more to Orlando than just Disney, so we'll also talk about the fun you can have at Universal Studios, Sea World, Cypress Gardens, and all the other parks competing for your tourist dollars. We'll tell you which ones are worth a special trip and which ones will have your kids saying, "Mom, I'm bored." We'll help you design a personalized itinerary that will appeal to everybody in your family and maximize your park time.

Chapter 11

The Wonderful World of Disney

In This Chapter

➤ What and where are the Disney parks?

➤ Getting around

➤ Tickets and passes

➤ Tips on maximizing your fun and minimizing your stress

We've been to Walt Disney World dozens of times since it opened in 1971, and we still feel like complete idiots when planning a new trip. It's so big, so spectacular. And every day it seems to sprout another new hotel, a new ride, a new razzle-dazzle show, or a fancy new restaurant. On May 6, 1998, it will add an entire new park, Disney's Animal Kingdom (bigger than all the other Disney parks *combined*).

About 14 million people a year visit the Magic Kingdom, almost 12 million visit Epcot, and attendance at Disney-MGM Studios is about 10 million. According to *Amusement Business* magazine, Universal Studios Florida, Sea World of Florida, and Busch Gardens Tampa are all among the nation's top 10 theme parks.

So whether this is your first trip or your 40th (some Floridians buy yearly passes and come once a week!), it's worth taking a few minutes to get your bearings and plan a little strategy.

First, realize that you're not the only rookie in town. Most of those folks around you are first-timers, too, and a lot of them don't even have this book to show them around. So you're already way ahead of the game.

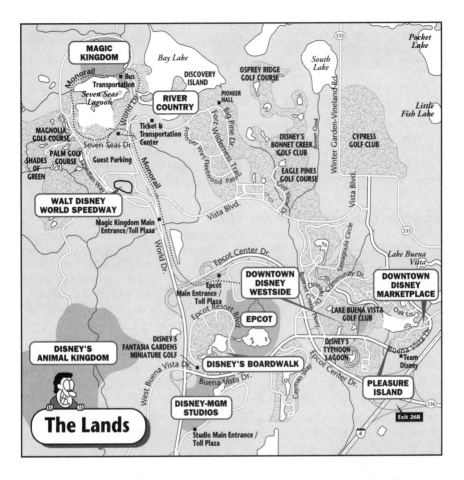

Also realize that things at Disney are constantly being evaluated and improved. Old gardens are constantly replaced with new blooms. Lines are reconfigured to ease congestion and pedestrian traffic jams. A popcorn wagon relocates under a shade tree to keep the people waiting in line cooler. A marching band materializes on the street. Entertainers spring to action in a plaza. Mickey or Goofy rambles by and poses for your camera. With luck, you're chosen to participate in a show.

We understand the pressure you feel. You want this trip to live up to all that you and your family dream of. You're probably also anxious about the expense. It's costing up to $60 per person per day just to get *into* the parks, where everything—food, drinks, souvenirs, film—is premium priced. But let's break it down into manageable bites and take it step by step.

In addition to the general information here, we've included suggested itineraries for enjoying each of the major attractions in the chapters that follow; you'll also find details on all the services and facilities available in each park in those chapters.

Bet You Didn't Know

More than 1,400 couples are married each year at WDW. Many of the ceremonies take place in an elegant Victorian summerhouse on its own island near Disney's Grand Floridian Beach Resort (☎ **407/828-3400**). Walt Disney World is also the single most popular honeymoon destination in the United States.

What in the World *Is* All This?

The universe known as Walt Disney World actually consists of four separate theme parks plus an assortment of other villages and shopping areas. But even WDW veterans make the mistake of saying "Disney World" when they mean the Magic Kingdom—the flagship park where Mickey and Donald mingle with guests looking to ride the rides, visit Cinderella's Castle, and watch the daily parade down Main Street U.S.A. The other three parks in the World are Epcot, Disney-MGM Studios, and, beginning in May 1998, Disney's Animal Kingdom. A short summary of each park follows here. Chapter 12 covers the Magic Kingdom and gives you strategies for maximum enjoyment. Chapter 13 is devoted exclusively to Epcot, and chapter 14 tells you how to tackle Disney-MGM Studios. Chapter 15 gives you a preview of what to expect when Disney's Animal Kingdom opens later in 1998.

➤ **The Magic Kingdom,** symbolized by Cinderella's Castle, is the first and still the most popular of WDW's theme parks. Everyone should give it at least 1 day. In our view, it has the most to offer children, so we recommend that families allot 2 or more days. It's divided into several distinct sections: Main Street U.S.A., Adventureland, Frontierland, Liberty Square, Fantasyland, Mickey's Toontown Fair, and Tomorrowland.

Bet You Didn't Know

So how come you never see Mickey relaxing with his head off or Winnie-the-Pooh taking a cigarette break? It's because the employees inside those character costumes are kept to a very strict code of conduct, which includes no talking and no stepping out of character. The "cast" travels around the park through an intricate system of underground tunnels that are strictly off-limits to the public.

➤ **Epcot,** basically an exposition of human achievement and new technology, is symbolized by the awesome Spaceship Earth. As you enter Future World, you'll find exhibits dealing with innovations. Then you pass into the World Showcase, in which pavilions of a dozen nations surround a placid lagoon. Allow at least 2 days to see all the shows and rides, sample the varied ethnic restaurants, and loiter through all the specialty shops.

➤ **Disney-MGM Studios** is the Tinseltown of the 1930s and 1940s, filled with studio tours, animated and live shows based on timeless movies and television shows, and rides such as the chilling "Twilight Zone Tower of Terror." It's worth 1 day, more if you're a film freak.

➤ **Disney's Animal Kingdom** is the new kid on the block. It's symbolized by a 14-story Tree of Life, which is to this park what Cinderella's Castle is to the Magic Kingdom. This new theme park, set to debut in 1998, is a combination wildlife park, zoo, and theme park filled with thrill rides, combined as only Disney could do it.

But wait—there's more! In addition to the four major theme parks, there are several other types of attractions in the Disney empire. These are covered in greater detail in chapter 17.

➤ **The Walt Disney Wide World of Sports™** complex has a 7,500-seat baseball stadium and facilities for more than 30 sports, including soccer, softball, basketball, and track and field. It's the spring-training home of the Atlanta Braves and the training site of the Harlem Globetrotters.

➤ **Walt Disney World Speedway** has a stock car racing tri-oval track that fields daily races throughout September, with additional events in October and November. Year-round, visitors can sign up for the **Richard Petty Driving Experience,** in which you can learn to drive at speeds of up to 145 miles an hour. Call ☎ **407/939-0130** for details.

➤ **Water parks.** WDW has three splashy water parks, each worth as many hours as you can spare for floating lazy rivers, surfing, screaming down water slides, and staying cool. They'll seem pretty appealing when it's 90 degrees and 90% humidity. They are **Blizzard Beach,** surrounding "snow"-covered Mount Gushmore; **River Country,** based on Tom Sawyer's ol' swimmin' hole; and **Typhoon Lagoon,** where you're shipwrecked on Mt. Mayday.

Bet You Didn't Know

Chewing gum is allowed in the theme parks but is not sold there; cigarettes are sold in all the parks, but smoking is allowed only outdoors.

Rounding out the Disney universe are several shopping villages, malls, marketplaces, and nightlife areas. These are covered more fully in chapters 18, 20, and 21.

Disney's BoardWalk is a free attraction where you can stroll the waterfront, dine, dance, or linger in an eye-popping sports bar where even the rest rooms have televisions.

Downtown Disney, new in 1997, comprises **Pleasure Island,** which opened in 1989 as a theme park for adults, as well as **Downtown Disney Marketplace,** with dining and shopping, and **Downtown Disney West Side,** with more shopping, dining, and a 24-screen movie theater complex.

Discovery Island is a nature retreat that is reached by boat from the Contemporary Resort or Fort Wilderness. It has its own programs, admission, and pleasures.

Disney Institute is another kind of vacation, where you'll sleep and dine in a luxury resort while attending seminars, classes, and sessions on anything from animation to rock climbing, gourmet cooking to cinema. The Institute has its own health club, spa, performance center, amphitheater, television and radio studios, demonstration kitchens, and tennis courts, and it's in the heart of the **Lake Buena Vista Golf Course.**

In addition to the marvelous shops found in the theme parks, **Disney Village Marketplace** is a parklike mall filled with shops and restaurants. Admission is free.

Behind-the-Scenes Tours

If you'd like to get an insider's look at how Disney makes its magic, behind-the-scenes tours are available. **Hidden Treasures of World Showcase** features the architecture and culture of Epcot's pavilions. **Gardens of the World** is a tour of Epcot's gardens, narrated by a horticulturist. **Keys to the Kingdom** is a backstage look at the high-tech wonders that make the magic. **Wonders of Walt Disney World,** for children ages 10 to 15, offers several programs. All are at an added cost, and all require advance arrangements, which you can make by calling ☎ 407/939-8687.

How Do I Get to All This?

If you're driving to Walt Disney World, take I-4 to exits 25, 26, or 27. From there, you'll see colorful signs directing you to individual parks.

Parking is easy. Just do what the people in the yellow-striped shirts tell you to do. If you park at the humongous Magic Kingdom parking lot, you'll probably want to ride the tram to the front gate, but at Epcot and Disney-MGM it's probably faster to walk unless you've got really small children. Parking costs $5.

If you didn't choose to rent a car, or if you'd prefer not to take it, you still have options. If you're staying in a Disney resort, you can take the Disney transportation system to get into the parks (see below). And even if you didn't choose a Disney hotel, most accommodations in the area offer park shuttles for a fee. We've noted all these in the hotel reviews.

Time-Savers

Write down your car's location. We can't stress this enough. You'll never remember where you parked the car at the end of a day spent trying to remember all the rides you wanted to see. All the rental cars look alike, and the increasing number of sport utility vehicles and minivans may block your view of your car from afar. This is especially important at Epcot and MGM, where lots are not as well marked as in the Magic Kingdom. (And by the way, if you're disabled, a handicap permit is required to park in special spaces at WDW; a Disabled Veteran license won't do.)

Getting Around the World

If you can read a subway schedule or bus timetable, you'll ace the WDW transportation system immediately. Most transportation runs continuously; you *can* get anywhere you want to go, but it could involve as many as two transfers and long waits.

Getting from your hotel to any park usually involves only one ride. Things get more complicated if you want to get from one resort to another, so consider the complications if you want to dine in a hotel far from your own. If you have a car, it's often easier to drive.

Tourist Traps

Some restaurants in the WDW parks have started adding an "instant tip" of 10%. Check your bill before adding your tip—you don't want to pay twice!

The famed **monorail** is just part of the huge transportation web, which also consists of buses and ferryboats. Served by the monorail are the Contemporary Resort, Polynesian Resort, Grand Floridian, Transportation and Ticket Center (TTC), and Magic Kingdom. The Magic Kingdom is also served by ferryboat. A monorail runs to Epcot from the Ticket and Transportation Center.

Some pointers on using the WDW transportation system:

➤ If you're staying at a Disney hotel, keep your hotel ID handy. During the most crowded times, WDW guests are given preference. If you can't prove that you are staying in a WDW hotel, you'll have to wait in line with the non-Disney guests.

➤ Eating and drinking aren't permitted on board.

➤ Strollers must be folded and out of the aisles during transport. A better idea is to leave your stroller in the car and use one of the rentals provided at the park entrance.

➤ All WDW transportation is wheelchair accessible, usually via the rear entry. Everybody else should therefore board through the front doors. Don't sit in seats that are reserved for the disabled. If they're needed, you'll be asked to move.

➤ During peak periods, you may have to stand.

What in the World Does All This Cost?

If you've got an itinerary, chances are the folks at Disney have already thought of a ticket package to match it. The following table lists the most popular plans. Kids ages 10 and over pay adult prices; those under age 3 are admitted free. Prices do not include sales tax and are subject to change.

Disney World Admission Prices

Ticket Package and Description	Admission Price	
	Adult	Ages 3–9
Any one park (1 day)	$42	$34
Four-day Value Pass (1 day each at the Magic Kingdom, Disney-MGM Studios, and Epcot, plus another day at the park of your choice)	$149	$119
Five-day Park Hopper Pass (unlimited in-and-out admission to the theme parks, including any combination on any day)	$189	$151
Six-day All-in-One Hopper Pass (unlimited admission to the theme parks, in any combination, for 5 days, plus admission to the water parks and Pleasure Island for 7 days from date of first use)	$249	$199
Seven-day All-in-One Hopper Pass (same as above, with one extra day)	$274	$219
Theme Park Annual Pass (unlimited admission to the theme parks for 1 year)	$309	$259
Premium Annual Pass (unlimited admission for a year to the theme parks, water parks, and Pleasure Island)	$415	$355
Discovery Island Excursion	$11.95	$6.50
River Country (1 day)	$15.95	$12.50
Water Parks (Typhoon Lagoon or Blizzard Beach) for 1 day	$25.95	$20.50
Pleasure Island (1 evening)	$18.95	N.A.
Disney's Wide World of Sports (1 day)	$8	$6.75

Getting the Most out of the World

Face it. You can't possibly do everything. You're going to have to miss out on some of the splendor, no matter how much time you spend in each park. Your kids aren't going to want to leave at the end of the day, and they won't want to let you sleep late the next morning. But there are a few things you can do to get the most out of each day. We'll supply some specific instructions for each park in subsequent chapters, but you'll enjoy your trip a lot more if you follow some sound advice.

Clever engineers arranged for the parks' most popular rides to be distributed evenly throughout the park so that the massive crowds don't choke any one area. The downside (for you) is that you may have to crisscross the entire park several times to get to all the blockbuster rides. Don't think this isn't on purpose. What better way to get you to stop at a restaurant to buy a cold drink, stop in a store to buy a T-shirt, or ride one of the less-crowded rides before undertaking Space Mountain a second time? So a little advance planning is in order.

Beating the Lines

The best way we know to beat the lines is to go to the theme parks during low-traffic times of the year. On high-volume days, make sure you allot plenty of time for each park and budget your time sensibly. Plan to spend all morning in one section of the park and all afternoon in another. That way, you won't waste time and energy running back and forth between Fantasyland and Tomorrowland. Spend 2 days if necessary. Always look for signs that give you information about waiting times. They usually read something like "The wait time from this point is approximately XXX minutes." Ask (or read) about height or health considerations before you get in line. You don't want to wait for nothing.

Buy Your Tickets in Advance

Tickets to all the parks are available in most hotels (sometimes at discounted rates) and at more places than we can name. It's a small savings in time, but your kids will be jumping out of their pants if you get that close to the main gate and then have to wait in line to buy tickets.

Get a Show Schedule As Soon As You Enter the Park

This is essential. Spend a few minutes looking over the schedule as you enter the park, noting where you need to be, and when. Many attractions are non-stop, but others occur only at certain times or only once a day.

Go Where the Crowds Aren't
Duh!

It sounds obvious, but you'd be surprised how many people follow a crowd just because it's a crowd. Head to the left when the rush is moving to the right. Make a beeline for the ride you most care about first thing in the morning, but after that, save the major attractions for late in the day. Eat when other people are riding rides (that is, before noon or after 2pm), and ride the rides when others are eating lunch (noon to 2pm).

Avoid Rush Hour
I-4 is woefully over capacity, especially during rush hour (7 to 9am and 4:30 to 6pm). In addition to the thousands of people looking to spend the day in the parks are the thousands of people who work in the parks. For the most part, you want to get to the park early. But the days when people staying in WDW resorts are allowed to enter the park before it opens are more crowded than other mornings. If you're not entitled to this privilege, sleep late on that day.

Pace Yourself & Take Care of Yourself
You've got all day in the hot sun, and you'll be doing plenty of walking. Wear sneakers or good walking shoes and comfortable clothing, and don't forget the sunscreen. (Locals spot tourists by their painful bright-red glow.) Take breaks periodically for water or simply to sit under a shade tree for a few minutes. Stagger long lines with air-conditioned shows. If you are staying at a WDW hotel, go back to your hotel room for a late-afternoon nap or a dip in the pool before returning to the park for more attractions and the closing shows.

Make Dining Reservations Ahead of Time
If a sit-down dinner at a certain venue is important to you, be sure to get Priority Seating reservations either before your visit or when you enter the park. We also recommend making time for a sit-down lunch at an off-hour so that you can recharge your batteries.

Travel Light
Resist the temptation to schlep along half of your belongings. You will be cursing your heavy bag or overloaded purse by mid-afternoon. And don't carry large amounts of cash. The Pirates of the Caribbean aren't the only thieves in WDW. There are ATM machines in all the parks if you run short of cash.

Chapter 12

The Magic Kingdom

In This Chapter

➤ Logistics and services

➤ A detailed look at the rides, shows, and attractions

➤ Parades and fireworks

➤ Suggested itineraries

If you have young kids, you might as well head here on your first full day in Orlando since this is the park they want to visit most (and they'll probably want to come back on the second day). It's the most popular park in the Disney enterprise, attracting more than 14 million visitors each year.

That's more than a million people each month; a quarter of a million people each week; 40,000 people a day! This makes Mickey's house the most formidable park in all of Disney World.

You'll park in a lot the size of Asia and spend an eternity just to get to the entry, so do get here early. As you take the tram to the gate, drivers will remind you where you're parked. Don't forget it. You'll never find your car if you do. In fact, *write down your location and put it in your wallet or purse*. Then you don't have to remember anything. If you ignore everything else we say, follow that piece of advice. You'll thank us!

OK, OK, that's it. No more planning. You're off to meet Mickey! We won't attempt to list every ride in every park (a little spontaneity is a good thing, after all), but this chapter rounds up the highlights. *Our tour of the Magic Kingdom starts at the front gate and moves counter-clockwise from section to section*. Your own path through the park won't be nearly so orderly (see the suggested itineraries below), and you'll probably double back a few times or end up taking the long way from Tomorrowland to Frontierland, but so what? The only thing that matters is that you're having fun.

What You Need to Know About the Park

Hours: Or When Is the Official Opening Time Not Really the Opening Time?

The Magic Kingdom is open every day from 9am to 7pm. That's what they *say*, but there are exceptions—and the gates almost always open earlier than the "official" opening time. If you follow our advice and arrive extra early (up to an hour before the official opening), you might be rewarded big time. (As if your kids were going to let you sleep late that day anyway!) You'll also beat the traffic, and you may even be able to park closer to the gate. The park stays open longer in summer and on holidays. During special events, it may be open as late as midnight.

Services & Facilities

➤ **ATMs** are located at the main entrance, the SunTrust Bank on Main Street, and in Tomorrowland.

➤ **Baby-Changing Facilities** are located next to the Crystal Palace at the end of Main Street, and they include rocking chairs and toddler-size toilets. Disposable diapers, formula, baby food, and pacifiers are for sale. Changing tables are located here as well as in all women's rest rooms and some men's rest rooms. Disposable diapers are also sold at Guest Services.

➤ **The First Aid Center,** staffed by registered nurses, is located alongside the Crystal Palace.

➤ **Lockers** can be found in an arcade underneath the Main Street Railroad Station. The cost is $6, including a $2 refundable deposit.

➤ **Lost Children.** If your kids get lost, somebody will most likely take them to City Hall or the Baby Care Center, where lost children logbooks are kept. Children under 7 should wear name tags.

➤ **Packages** can be sent from any store to Guest Relations in the Plaza area, so you can pick them up all at once at the end of the day and you don't have to schlep all those souvenirs around.

➤ Make **Priority Seating** arrangements when you enter the park if you care about having a sit-down meal at a special venue. See chapter 9 for more details.

➤ **Special Shows.** When you enter the park, study the *Entertainment Show Schedule*, which lists all the special events of the day. You might find special concerts, otherwise unannounced visits from Disney characters, and information about fireworks and parades. Plan these events first, as they're the only ones that you won't get a second chance to see.

➤ **Strollers** can be rented at the Stroller Shop near the entrance for $6 a day, including a $1 deposit.

Meeting Characters

So your little boy has his heart set on meeting Mickey, but you're not sure where you're supposed to find Johnny's favorite rodent in all these crowds?

Just ask any employee, and if they don't know, they'll be able to make a quick phone call and find out for you. You're very likely to spot characters right away at City Hall on Main Street as you enter the park. Another good bet is Mickey's Toontown. You'll also see many of them in the afternoon and evening parades.

Most characters will sign autographs (though they can't really carry pens in those costumes), pose for pictures, or hug your child. Characters in heads are not allowed to talk, though, because they wouldn't get the classic voices right.

Also, don't be surprised if your kids turn a little shy or become overwhelmed (those costume heads are pretty big). You'll want to stay close to toddlers as they meet their cartoon pals.

Extra! Extra!

Wheelchairs can be rented at the Transportation and Ticket Center or the Stroller and Wheelchair Shop just inside the main entrance. The cost is $6 for a regular wheelchair and $32 for an electric.

Main Street, U.S.A.

Main Street is a place to lose yourself in pleasant nostalgia for yesteryear—although we recommend passing through quickly when you first enter the park. (Get thee to the popular rides right away before the lines get too bad!) You'll have to pass through it again at a leisurely pace as you *exit* the park at the end of the day.

You don't have to pay admission to the **Main Street Cinema,** where you can watch Disney cartoons—although no seating is available. There's also a lot of shopping here, for Disney gift items, old-fashioned candy, crystal animals, sports memorabilia, and more.

From here, you can take the **Walt Disney World Railroad** on a free loop around the park, or get off at stops in Frontierland or Mickey's Toontown Fair. Other vehicles departing Main Street include horse-drawn trolleys, horseless carriages, jitneys, buses, and fire engines.

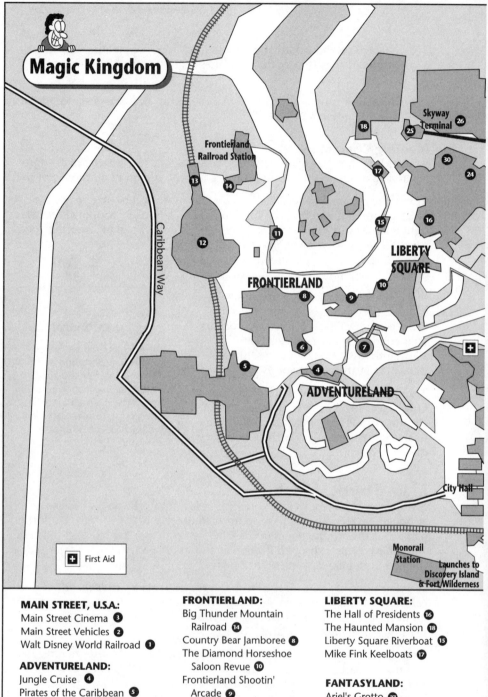

Magic Kingdom

Skyway Terminal

FrontierLand Railroad Station

LIBERTY SQUARE

FRONTIERLAND

ADVENTURELAND

Caribbean Way

City Hall

Monorail Station — Launches to Discovery Island & Fort/Wilderness

First Aid

MAIN STREET, U.S.A.:
Main Street Cinema ❸
Main Street Vehicles ❷
Walt Disney World Railroad ❶

ADVENTURELAND:
Jungle Cruise ❹
Pirates of the Caribbean ❺
Swiss Family Treehouse ❼
Tropical Serenade with the
Enchanted Tiki Birds ❻

FRONTIERLAND:
Big Thunder Mountain
Railroad ❶⓸
Country Bear Jamboree ❽
The Diamond Horseshoe
Saloon Revue ❿
Frontierland Shootin'
Arcade ❾
Splash Mountain ⓬
Tom Sawyer Island ⓫
Walt Disney World Railroad ⓭

LIBERTY SQUARE:
The Hall of Presidents ⓰
The Haunted Mansion ⓲
Liberty Square Riverboat ⓯
Mike Fink Keelboats ⓱

FANTASYLAND:
Ariel's Grotto ㉗
Castle Forecourt Stage ⓳
Cinderella's Castle ⓴
Cinderella's Golden Carousel ㉑

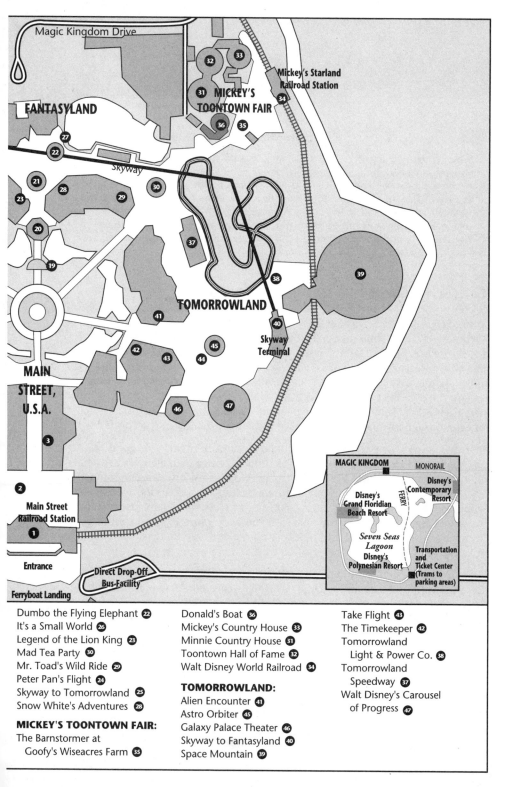

Magic Kingdom Drive

FANTASYLAND

Skyway

Mickey's Starland Railroad Station

MICKEY'S TOONTOWN FAIR

TOMORROWLAND

Skyway Terminal

MAIN STREET, U.S.A.

Main Street Railroad Station

Entrance

Direct Drop-Off Bus-Facility

Ferryboat Landing

MAGIC KINGDOM   MONORAIL

Disney's Grand Floridian Beach Resort

Disney's Contemporary Resort

FERRY

Seven Seas Lagoon

Disney's Polynesian Resort

Transportation and Ticket Center (Trams to parking areas)

Dumbo the Flying Elephant 22
It's a Small World 26
Legend of the Lion King 23
Mad Tea Party 30
Mr. Toad's Wild Ride 29
Peter Pan's Flight 24
Skyway to Tomorrowland 25
Snow White's Adventures 28

MICKEY'S TOONTOWN FAIR:
The Barnstormer at
  Goofy's Wiseacres Farm 35

Donald's Boat 36
Mickey's Country House 33
Minnie Country House 31
Toontown Hall of Fame 32
Walt Disney World Railroad 34

TOMORROWLAND:
Alien Encounter 41
Astro Orbiter 45
Galaxy Palace Theater 46
Skyway to Fantasyland 40
Space Mountain 39

Take Flight 43
The Timekeeper 42
Tomorrowland
  Light & Power Co. 38
Tomorrowland
  Speedway 37
Walt Disney's Carousel
  of Progress 47

Time-Savers

When entering the park, agree on a family meeting spot inside the park in case you get separated, and write it down for everyone. Even older children soon become disoriented and can't find their way back to "that bench" or "under this tree." They must be able to explain to a park official that they need to get to City Hall or the rest rooms at the Main Entrance. Make sure everyone understands they must not go through the turnstile and try to reach the car. The crush of people and cars makes this a dangerous place at closing time.

Tomorrowland

Disney completely overhauled Tomorrowland back in 1994 because its vision of the future (when it was designed in the 1970s) was starting to look too retro. Originally, it imagined a 21st century with neither computers nor answering machines. The updated take on the future enlisted the talents of *Star Wars* director George Lucas, among others, and has now been souped up to be a whole lot more high tech (*read:* more aliens and robots, and state-of-the-art video games). The new Tomorrowland is where older kids will want to start their Magic Kingdom adventure, and where they'll be begging you to buy them the cool space toys and Star Wars memorabilia in the shops.

First things first. One of the most popular rides in the park—for good reason—**Space Mountain,** like Alien Encounter, brings teenagers and adrenaline junkies rushing here as soon as the park opens, so lines can be long. Get here immediately if you can, or head here during any off hours, such as lunch or when crowds thin in the evening. It's a classic roller coaster, with the added fears of being lost in space, in the dark, plunging and spinning. It's for ages 10 through 12 and older. Thrill-seekers take the first cars. You must be 44 inches tall to ride.

Lucas helped design **The ExtraTERRORestrial Alien Encounter,** an extremely popular ride and another white-knuckle experience. It brings a terrifying creature from outer space right into the terrified audience. The ride is recommended for ages 10 and older.

The **Astro Orbiter** whirls passengers high into the galaxy in colorful rockets. It's fine for ages 8 and under.

Take Flight, recommended for ages 6 and older, whirls you through the barn-storming, wing-walking days of early aviation.

The Timekeeper is a rousing robot show that combines IMAX scenes with Circle Vision and AudioAnimatronics. You'll go from the dinosaur era through medieval times and into outer space. It's for ages 10 and older.

The **Tomorrowland Speedway** puts you behind the wheel. Children ages 6 through 15 could ride it all day. It's tame because you can't get above about 7 miles per hour. Children must be 52 inches tall (4'4") to drive alone.

The **Galaxy Space Theater** stars Mickey Mouse and his friends in a talent show. Young kids won't want to miss it.

Skyway to Fantasyland is a cable-car ride for all ages. It beats walking from one section of the Magic Kingdom to another, and it provides an exciting view of the park.

The **Tomorrowland Transit Authority** is ideal for all ages. Unique linear-induction motors propel cars on an elevated people-mover. You'll wind around Tomorrowland and into Space Mountain.

Beating the Lines

The slowest lines in the Magic Kingdom, alas, seem to lead to those rides that little kids want most: Dumbo, Mad Tea Party, the Carousel, and the Astro Orbiter. Since these rides have a fixed number of riders and everybody gets on and off at once, the lines move in fits and starts. Check these lines first, and promise your kids to come back later if the wait seems too long. With so many wonders to choose from, it's best to keep on the move. Signs at several rides indicate how long you'll have to wait from that point and provide a good reference point.

Mickey's Toontown Fair

If you have young kids, go here first. (If you don't want to walk, you can get here on the WDW Railroad from Main Street.) This is a gentler section of the park, largely geared to little ones, so older kids might be bored. Here you can meet **Mickey** and **Minnie Mouse, Donald Duck, Goofy,** and countless other Disney characters. **Barnstormer** is a kiddie roller coaster that will be a blast for ages 4 through 8.

Fantasyland

The rides and attractions here are based on the Disney movies we all grew up with way back when, as well as new rides based on some of the more recent additions to the Disney treasure trove of film classics. Young kids will want to spend lots of time here.

The symbol of the Magic Kingdom, **Cinderella's Castle** is at the end of Main Street, right in the center of the park. You'll want to take family photos here, just for the view. If you come at the right time, Cinderella herself might pay you a visit.

Cinderella's Golden Carousel is a gorgeous merry-go-round that will delight young children. The organ plays—what else would you expect?—Disney classics like "When You Wish Upon a Star."

Ariel's Grotto is a splashy (literally—kids get wet) area with fountains and the Little Mermaid, in person. Waits can be long, but at the end of the line is a chance to meet and photograph Ariel herself.

It's a Small World is so very, very cute that older brothers may threaten to barf, but it's a must-ride for every trip to the Magic Kingdom, if only to hear that awful song again (and again and again). You'll glide around the world meeting Russian dancers, Chinese acrobats, French cancan dancers, a Venetian gondolier, and an Arabian doll on a magic carpet. For ages 2 and up.

Dollars & Sense

Your entertainment dollars go further if you don't try to see an entire park in a day. With a multiday pass, you can relax and not feel panicked that you have to see every attraction in a blur. Leave the park at midday, have a picnic or inexpensive lunch at your hotel, and then have a nap or a swim before returning to the park for the afternoon and evening.

Mr. Toad's Wild Ride hurtles you in colorful cars through dark rooms, where you crash into solid objects, are menaced by scary creatures and loud noises, and even land in hell itself. It's a scary one, all right, and only for older kids, but it's been a longtime favorite. At this writing, we had heard that officials at Disney were considering modifying and retooling Mr. Toad, but nothing's official yet.

Dumbo, the Flying Elephant won't do it for adrenaline-addicted older kids, but it's a favorite for ages 2 through 8 or so. Ride Dumbo, whose big ears keep you airborne for a gentle, circular flight, with a few little dips.

Legend of the Lion King is a lavish stage show starring Simba and his friends as they tell the beloved jungle story. Children under age 4 might get fussy; those over age 12 might find it too childish.

The Mad Tea Party is a ride that can be wild or mild, depending on how much you choose to spin the teacup that is your chariot. The ride is based on *Alice in Wonderland* and is suitable for ages 4 and up.

Peter Pan's Flight will delight children aged 4 through 10 with its pirate galleons and a flight over London in search of Captain Hook, Tiger Lily, and the Lost Boys.

Snow White's Adventure takes you to the dwarfs' cottage and the wishing well, and ends with the prince's kiss to break the evil spell. It's less scary now than when it was introduced in 1971, when it was really dark and menacing, but we don't recommend it for children under age 7 or 8.

Skyway to Tomorrowland is a real cable-car ride that takes you from Small World, over Mickey's Toontown Fair, to Space Mountain. It's good transportation and a great ride for all ages.

The shops here include a great place to pick up Disney Christmas items and ornaments.

Liberty Square

Right in the center of the park is Liberty Square, a re-creation of Revolutionary-era America. Much of the historical touches (like the 13 lanterns symbolizing the original 13 colonies) will be lost on younger visitors, but they'll delight in seeing a fife-and-drum corps marching along the cobblestone streets.

The **Hall of Presidents** will appeal to adults and bright children over age 10, but the program may drag for younger children. It's a magnificent, inspiring production, based on painstaking research. Presidents come alive and talk to the audience.

The **Haunted Mansion** is another favorite; it doesn't get much scarier than spooky music, eerie howling, things that go bump in the night, weird flying objects, and sudden shocks that'll scare the pants off you. Don't take the very little ones, but older kids (say, over 8 or so) will love it.

Beating the Lines

Most rides and shows continue throughout the parade, but because thousands of people are drawn to the parade route, the lines at popular attractions such as Space Mountain, Splash Mountain, Pirates of the Caribbean, and Alien Encounter, become much shorter. If you don't care much about the parade, this is your chance. Check with a uniformed staffer, however, to learn what routes or transportation close during parades. Once crowds form at parade sites, you can't move.

Boat rides aboard the *Liberty Belle* and Mike Fink Keelboats take you through the Rivers of America. You may tangle with a few pirates or rustlers, but mostly this is a pleasant way to rest tired feet and imagine that you're on the Tennessee River in Davy Crockett's day. Kids over 6 will be beguiled; younger children, if they are tired, will enjoy the lulling ride.

There's shopping here, too, for antiques, gifts relating to American history, and all kinds of foods from a genuine country store.

Frontierland

Frontierland is dressed up to look like the Old West, with rustic log cabins, wooden sidewalks, swinging-door saloons, and Disney cast members (employees) dressed like cowboys and frontier women.

The real highlight here is **Splash Mountain,** one of the Magic Kingdom's favorite thrill rides. Teenagers rush here first and take the trip time after time. It's a scary ride that travels 40 miles per hour. Your log canoe makes it through swamps, waterfalls, and a heart-stopping, five-story fall. It's recommended for ages 10 and up. Riders must be at least 44 inches tall.

Big Thunder Mountain Railroad is also too intense for children under age 9 or 10, but older kids (riders must be at least 40 inches tall) will love it. You'll jounce around an old mining track, barely escaping floods, a bridge collapse, a rock slide, and other mayhem.

Tom Sawyer Island takes you across a narrow "river" by log raft to a real island where you'll find Injun Joe's Cave, swinging bridges that threaten to throw you into the gaping chasm below, and an abandoned mine. It's a must for ages 4 through 14. Have lunch or a snack at **Aunt Polly's,** which overlooks the "river."

Country Bear Jamboree is 15-minute animation show featuring bears who sing country-and-western style. There's enough noise and variety to keep most toddlers wide-eyed, but it's best for ages 4 and up.

The **Diamond Horseshoe Saloon Revue & Medicine Show** takes you back to the rootin-tootin' West where fancy ladies, honky-tonk piano, and gamblers entertain. It's air-conditioned, which is a big plus on a sweltering day, and is suitable for ages 5 and over. Seven shows play daily. Come for lunch and choose from a menu of popular sandwiches.

Time-Savers

Attendants allow parents to split up just before entry to scary rides, so one parent can stay with any children who are too small to ride. When the other parent and older kids finish the ride, the family can unite again. The second parent is now in position to ride without going through the line again. Rules vary, so ask the first attendant you see and keep asking as you move through the line.

The **Frontierland Shootin' Arcade** is probably the most elaborate shooting gallery you'll ever play. And because you're not trying to win a prize, it's only 2¢ a shot. Infrared bullets are shot from real rifles into a world where fog creeps in, thunder claps, coyotes yowl, and the graveyard comes alive. It's best for ages 8 and over.

Adventureland

Adventureland is back toward the park entrance, just west of Main Street. "Swashbuckling" is the operative word here. Kids can envision being in the jungle or the forest, walking through dense tropical foliage (complete with vines), or marauding through bamboo and thatch-roofed huts.

Pirates of the Caribbean has reopened by public demand, but it has been completely keel-hauled to be more politically correct. The pirates are now less scary, too. It's jolly good fun for all ages, a 10-minute joyride well worth standing in the long lines, though maybe a little scary for kids under 5.

Jungle Cruise, for ages 4 and over, is a funny-scary, 10 minute–long narrated sail on the Congo, the Amazon, and the Nile, where you'll see jungle "animals," lush foliage, a temple-of-doom-type encampment, and lots of surprises.

Nearby, the **Swiss Family Treehouse** can captivate ages 4 through 12 for hours of swinging, exploring, crawling fun. The beloved Joann Wyss story of the Swiss Family Robinson, who made a comfortable home from things they salvaged from their ship or found on their desert island, comes alive here.

Tropical Serenade, best for ages 2 through 10, is a sweet sing-along staged by four birds perched on an enchanted fountain, and their chorus of 250 tropical-bird friends. Children are mesmerized by the "tiki, tiki, tiki" song, and you'll all leave this theater humming a happy tune.

There's fun shopping in Adventureland, too, for gift items from Africa, Mexico, and beyond, plus nature- and animal-themed souvenirs.

Oohs & Aahs, Parades & Fireworks

Remember the Magic is the afternoon parade. Check your show schedule as you enter the park. It usually marches at 3pm on Main Street, through Liberty Square, and into Frontierland. Get your seat early—but don't sit on the grass or you'll be asked to move.

Spectro-Magic is the dazzling, after-dark parade, held nightly in summer and on special nights during holiday periods. Thousands of lights create an

Time-Savers

If you have only 1 day in the Magic Kingdom, skip lengthy meals. Instead, enjoy a character breakfast or elaborate dinner on some other day, like the day you saved for sunning and swimming at your hotel.

spectacle. It follows the same parade route as Remember the
ause a parade this impressive doesn't happen every day, it's
good viewing spot. Stake your claim even earlier to a curbside

Fireworks are a nightly spectacle in the Magic Kingdom in summer and
during peak holiday periods. The show starts with a flight of Peter Pan from
the pinnacles of Cinderella's Castle, followed by a fortune's worth of
pyrotechnics that light up the sky like it's the 4th of July. Liberty Square,
Frontierland, and Mickey's Toontown Fair are good viewing spots, as are
some of the Disney hotels closest to the park.

Have a Goofy Day: Some Suggested Itineraries

Whew! That's a lot to digest, much less try to fit into 1 or 2 days. And that's
without waiting on lines or stopping to eat, drink, shop, or tie the little ones'
shoes.

Undoubtedly you'll have your own ideas about what you'd like to do most,
but here's some advice in case you don't know which type of fun to have
first. We've planned two itineraries for the Magic Kingdom. The first one will
primarily interest families with younger children. The second one will have
more appeal for adults and teenagers (if they can stand to be seen with their
parents).

Each itinerary is for 1 day. If you spend a second day at the Magic Kingdom,
even a complete idiot won't need an itinerary to remember which rides and
attractions he liked best and wants to repeat.

The Magic Kingdom in a Day with Kids

1. Make a Priority Seating reservation at **King Stefan's Banquet Hall**,
   located inside Cinderella's Castle.

2. If you have very young kids, go straight to the **Walt Disney World
   Railroad** station on Main Street and take the first train out. Get off at
   Mickey's Toontown Fair, where the tots will be wowed by the sight
   of Mickey, Minnie, and the gang. They can ride their own roller coaster, see where Mickey lives, and see all their dreams come true before
   the day even begins.

3. Then walk just west of Toontown to **Fantasyland.** Ride **Dumbo the
   Flying Elephant** and **Peter Pan's Flight.** See the **Legend of the
   Lion King** and **It's a Small World.** For very young children, linger
   longer in Fantasyland to ride **Cinderella's Golden Carousel** and perhaps ride Dumbo again.

4. Take the **Skyway to Tomorrowland,** where preteens will want to do
   all the thrill rides. Or, for younger children, see the 22-minute **Walt
   Disney's Carousel of Progress.**

5. Is it lunchtime already? Have a hot dog, deli plate, or barbecue at **Cosmic Ray's Starlight Café** and enjoy the stage show.

6. Due west of Tomorrowland is **Liberty Square** with its restful **boat ride,** patriotic theme, and **Hall of Presidents,** which is best for ages 10 and older. If you didn't eat in Tomorrowland, have lunch in the **Liberty Square Tavern,** which specializes in down-home American meals such as turkey and stuffing or pot roast with mashed potatoes.

7. When you finish in Liberty Square, proceed through Frontierland, resisting its temptations for now, to board the train at the **Frontierland Railroad Station.** It's a delightful, restful ride around the entire Magic Kingdom. Take it all the way around and end up back in Frontierland. Older children will now want to ride **Big Thunder Mountain Railroad** and **Splash Mountain.** Suitable for all ages are **Tom Sawyer Island,** the **Diamond Horseshoe Saloon Revue & Medicine Show** (food is available), and the **Country Bear Jamboree.**

Bet You Didn't Know

Mickey Mouse has 80 different costumes, including his scuba diving outfit and a full dress tuxedo.

8. Check the time of today's parade. Start hunting for good spots along the route about an hour beforehand. If you're not sure whether you've picked a good spot, ask a cast member (a Disney employee, preferably one in costume). You don't want to be shooed off the grass once the parade starts.

9. Head over to Adventureland and ride **Pirates of the Caribbean,** the **Jungle Cruise,** and the **Tropical Serenade.** Older kids like the **Swiss Family Treehouse.**

10. Keep an eye on your watch to be back at King Stefan's in time for your dinner seating. Then check the entertainment schedule for after-dark fireworks or parades.

The Magic Kingdom in a Day for Teenagers & Adults

1. Make Priority Seating reservations for dinner at the **Liberty Tree Tavern** for a feast served family-style, **Tony's Town Square** for grilled fish or steaks, **Plaza Restaurant** for burgers and salads, or the **Crystal Palace** for carvery meats and a sundae bar.

2. On the right-hand side of Main Street as you walk in, be at the Plaza Pavilion Restaurant when the barrier opens; go through the restaurant to Tomorrowland to ride **Space Mountain** and then **The Extra-TERRORestrial Alien Encounter** pronto. Check out the video arcades and any other of the rides or shows you wanted to see here.

3. Cross back through the center of the park, through Liberty Square, to Frontierland, and get in line to ride **Splash Mountain.** The line won't get any shorter all day.

4. Leaving Splash Mountain, veer left to ride **Big Thunder Mountain Railroad,** and then do the **Haunted Mansion.** Head back toward Cinderella's Castle and Fantasyland, where you can see **Legend of the Lion King** in a huge theater that seats 500. Lines move quickly here.

5. Start thinking about lunch at 11 or 11:30am before the crowds get too thick, unless you have Priority Seating somewhere. While you're eating, work out plans to view the afternoon parade. People start staking out the best spots an hour in advance.

6. The **Hall of Presidents,** in Liberty Square, is a great way to beat the midday heat. You get to sit in a comfortable seat in an air-conditioned theater while watching a show that is both educational and extremely entertaining.

7. Fantasyland is the most toddler-friendly section of the park, so visitors with older children and teens will probably want to split quickly (although **It's a Small World** has a cult following among Disney regulars who remember it from their childhood) and take the **Skyway** to Tomorrowland and back. It's a great ride.

8. If you want to see the **parade,** stake out your spot around now (about an hour before parade time). If you're in doubt about whether the spot is a good one, ask a uniformed cast member. You don't want to be rousted at the last minute from an area that is cleared at parade time. The parade is worth the wait; even jaded teenagers will love it. However, this is also a good chance to try those rides and shows that were too crowded at other times. The parade draws some of the mobs away.

9. If you're really into Mickey and Minnie, check out **Mickey's Toontown Fair,** just east of Fantasyland. Kids of all ages (including grandparents) love it. This is a good place to catch the train that circles the entire Magic Kingdom. It's an entertaining, breezy ride that will give you a breather and good views of the various parts of the park.

10. Get off the train at the Main Street Station and head into Adventureland to ride the **Jungle Cruise** and **Pirates of the Caribbean,** which was revamped and made more PC in 1997. Play in the **Swiss Family Treehouse** and, if you're really into animation, see the **Tropical Serenade with the Enchanted Tiki Birds.** Beware, though; like It's a Small World, this attraction gives some people the screaming meemies. (That song will be stuck in your head all day!) Try your luck in the **Frontierland Shootin' Arcade.**

11. Have dinner and enjoy the evening parade and fireworks. After the rest of the park closes, Main Street stays open for strolling and shopping.

Epcot

What's an Epcot?

Well, it's somewhere between an amusement park and a museum with lots of interactive, hands-on experiences. Think of it as a trip around the world without the jet lag (though some would say it's just as draining). If the Magic Kingdom is every tot's shining dream brought to life, Epcot appeals to the imagination and fantasies of older children and adults.

Walt Disney himself originally envisioned the Experimental Prototype Community Of Tomorrow (EPCOT) as a high-tech city with 20,000 residents. But after Walt's death, what was built instead turned out to be more theme park than community, and the name became simply Epcot.

We strongly suggest at least a 2-day visit because the park is so large and varied. In the World Showcase, you can experience exotic, far-flung lands without a passport. With the luxury of time, you can sit on a park bench in downtown London and watch the world go by. You can sit in a sidewalk cafe in Paris, sipping an aperitif, or ride Norway's roaring Maelstrom for a true sense of Viking legend.

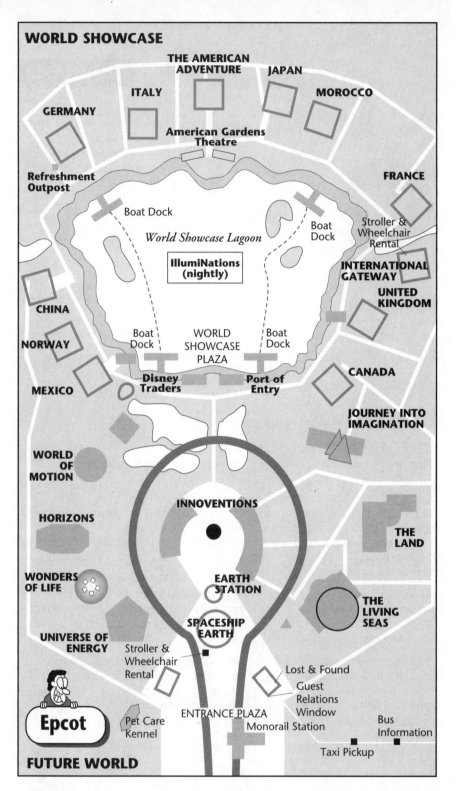

In Future World you can touch, taste, hear, and ride the new millennium as you learn about the latest cutting-edge technology. Yes, there are thrill rides, but you'll actually learn something, and it'll be pretty painless. When the kids get back to school, they'll have a new mental hook on which to hang aquaculture, oceanography, nutrition, computers, transportation, and many other studies. Future World puts them in a real context.

For some of WDW's best dining, shows, rides, and simple strolling in a pretty setting, Epcot is a standout.

What You Need to Know About the Park

➤ **Hours.** Epcot is generally open daily from 9am to 9pm, and as late as midnight on special days in summer and on holidays.

As with the Magic Kingdom, you really need to arrive about an hour before the "official" opening time because the gates almost always open earlier than the announced opening time. You'll also beat the traffic that way, and you may even be able to park closer to the gate.

➤ **ATMs** are located at the front of the park, in the Germany pavilion, and on the bridge between World Showcase and Future World.

➤ **Baby-Changing Facilities** are located in Future World, near the Odyssey Restaurant, and are furnished with rocking chairs and toddler-size toilets. Disposable diapers, formula, baby food, and pacifiers are for sale. There are changing tables here as well as in all women's rest rooms and some men's rest rooms. Disposable diapers are also sold at Guest Services.

➤ **The First Aid Center,** staffed by registered nurses, is located in Future World, near the Odyssey Restaurant.

➤ **Lockers** can be found just west of Spaceship Earth, outside the Entrance Plaza, and near the Bus Information Center near the bus parking lot. Cost is $3 plus a refundable $2 deposit.

Time-Savers

Even though strollers can be a nuisance and are not allowed on some park transportation, they are lifesavers, even for an older child who will be grateful to be able to collapse into one when little feet are tired. Stroller deposit at most parks is only $1 or $2, so some people just abandon them rather than stand in line for a refund.

➤ **Lost Children.** If your kids get lost, somebody will most likely take them to Earth Center or the Baby Care Center, where lost children logbooks are kept. Children under age 7 should wear name tags.

➤ **Package Pickup.** If you buy something early in the day and don't want to schlep it around with you, have the clerk send it to Guest Relations, which is just inside the Entrance Plaza. The service takes about 3 hours, and you can pick up all your purchases on the way out.

➤ **Strollers** can be rented at stands on the east side of the Entrance Plaza and at the World Showcase International Gateway. It costs $6 per day, including a $1 refundable deposit.

➤ **Video cameras** can be rented at the Kodak Camera Center at the Entrance Plaza, at the Lagoon's Edge World Traveler between Future World and the World Showcase, or at Cameras and Film in the Journey Into Imagination pavilion. The cost is $25 per day plus a $300 deposit. You can buy disposable cameras throughout the park.

First Things First

➤ **Write Down Your Parking Space Number Before You Enter the Park!!!**

➤ **Make Your Priority Seating Arrangements for Epcot Restaurants Pronto!** Remember all this advice from the dining chapter? No? Well, Priority Seating is as close to a reservation as you can get in Walt Disney World. It's especially important at Epcot, since this is the park with the best Disney restaurants. You can book ahead by calling ☎ **407/WDW-DINE** (939-3463) up to 60 days in advance. We strongly recommend calling ahead. But if you didn't, make a bee-line for the Worldkey Interactive Terminals at Guest Relations in Innoventions East or in World Showcase. You can also do this by stopping in the restaurants themselves. We think the Living Seas is a terrific relaxing choice for lunch; and for dinner, France, Japan, and Morocco have the best food of all the "countries" in the World Showcase.

➤ **Pick Up an Epcot Map and Entertainment Schedule at the Guest Relations Lobby.** Take a minute in the morning to look over the map so that you can plan what shows and entertainment you want to schedule throughout your day.

Future World

Future World comprises the front, or northern, section of the park (even though it will probably be at the bottom of most maps, including the one in this book). It consists of themed pavilions surrounding the giant silver golf ball that Disney calls Spaceship Earth. Each area is sponsored by a major corporation and focuses on discoveries and scientific achievement in different fields. Following is an alphabetical list and a brief description of each pavilion; for advice on how to see and do it all (and which pavilions not to miss), check the "Suggested Itineraries" section later in this chapter.

Horizons

Horizons puts you in a gondola for a 15-minute glide through a vision of the future, some of it portrayed on 80-foot-high IMAX screens. It's best for ages 8 and older.

Note: Rumor is that Horizons will close January 17, 1998 for either a facelift or replacement. Talk is that it may be replaced with a roller coaster that bursts out of the building.

Innoventions

Innoventions is located in two half moon–shaped buildings just beyond Spaceship Earth. Here's where you'll see state-of-the-art electronics long before they arrive in stores. (HDTV and Virtual Reality are already old hat here.) Kids will flock to test out as-yet-unreleased computer programs and Sega games. It's for ages 8 and over.

Time-Savers

Agree on an exact meeting spot in case anybody in your family gets lost. (Put name tags on children under age 7.) Individual pavilions are so large that you have to specify *where* you'll meet in Germany or The Land.

Journey Into Imagination

This is where you can catch the ***Honey I Shrunk the Audience*** 3-D film. Vibrating seats and other visual and tactile stimuli give the audience the feel that they are ant-sized creatures being pursued by cats and mice.

The **Journey Into Imagination Ride,** suitable for ages 6 and over, ends at **Image Works,** where you can act in a TV drama, paint on a magic palette, draw with laser beams, and find your way through the **Rainbow Corridor** sensor maze. It's an ideal adventure for the family to enjoy together.

The Land

The Land is the largest Future World pavilion. Its educational rides, displays, films, and shows make agriculture, a seemingly ho-hum subject, come to life. It has something for just about everyone, although children under age 8 might get restless.

The **Food Rocks** attraction does for nutrition what the old "Schoolhouse Rock" animated shorts did for grammar, multiplication, and U.S. history with songs like Neil Moussaka's "Don't Take My Squash Away" and the Refrigerator Police's "Every Bite You Take."

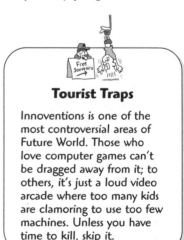

Tourist Traps

Innoventions is one of the most controversial areas of Future World. Those who love computer games can't be dragged away from it; to others, it's just a loud video arcade where too many kids are clamoring to use too few machines. Unless you have time to kill, skip it.

The Living Seas

The Living Seas is one of Florida's premier aquariums, a 5.7 million–gallon tank filled with more than 4,000 sea creatures including sharks, colorful reef fish, rays, and dolphins. You'll see a brief film, and then descend to **Seabase Alpha** to see an ocean research base of the future. Unless children are intensely interested in the sea, those under age 12 will soon lose interest.

If you're a certified diver, you can sign up in advance to get into the tank by calling ☎ **407/937-8687.**

Also offered at Living Seas is **D.E.E.P., Disney's Dolphin Exploration and Education Program.** In a 3-hour program, offered on weekdays, you'll get a behind-the-scenes lesson in dolphin behavior. Call ☎ **407/ WDW-TOUR** for more info.

Spaceship Earth

Spaceship Earth is the big geodesic dome you've seen in all the commercials. Inside is a low-key 15-minute ride, suitable for all ages, where you'll observe the development of human communications from Cro-Magnon Man through the space age. After the journey, enjoy the interactive computer fun.

Avoid Spaceship Earth early in the day, when it is most crowded. Come back in the afternoon, when most of the crowds have gone on to other areas and you'll have an easier time getting to use the computers.

Beating the Lines

If lines are too long at Spaceship Earth, consider taking a break at Global Neighborhood, the electronic playground at the far side, or exit area, of the sphere.

Test Track

Test Track, sponsored by General Motors, is a new Epcot exhibit based on auto testing. You'll feel braking, cornering, climbing, curving hills, and driving on long straight-aways. It's best for ages 8 and over. This ride was scheduled to open in 1997, but has been delayed until mid-1998.

The Universe of Energy

The Universe of Energy is the first building to the left of Spaceship Earth. It takes you on a half-hour thrill ride through the history of energy. It's fine for ages 8 and older.

The Wonders of Life

The Wonders of Life, for ages 8 and older, takes a humorous look at health, fitness, and the human body. In **Body Wars,** you are miniaturized to molecule size so that you can travel through human blood vessels. Germs attack. Corpuscles come to the rescue, and the good guys win. In the film *The Making of Me,* conception and birth are described tastefully.

World Showcase

Surrounding a sparkling lagoon are pavilions representing a spectrum of nations. Each has shops, food, and displays or a show, as well as gardens or streetscapes authentic to that country. One of the most pleasant ways to spend time here is to find a park bench in "England" or "France" and pretend you're overseas.

We always see a lot of small tykes here, but children under age 8 or 10 usually tire quickly of this part of the park.

The pavilions are listed alphabetically here, but you'll probably just go clockwise or counterclockwise around the lagoon. See the suggested itinerary later in this chapter for advice on what to see and do in each "country."

Don't forget to return here for the **IllumiNations** presentation after dark. This fireworks, light, and laser show is synchronized to the fountains in the World Showcase Lagoon. It's a must-see for everyone in the family, even jaded teenagers and tired 6-year-olds. Check your show schedule when you enter the World Showcase, and then find a seat anywhere around the lagoon about a half hour before show time.

The American Adventure

The American Adventure is a half-hour show that speeds through the United States. It's filled with joy, pride, and poignancy. As you enter the park, check the Entertainment Schedule to see if anything is playing in the America Gardens Theater.

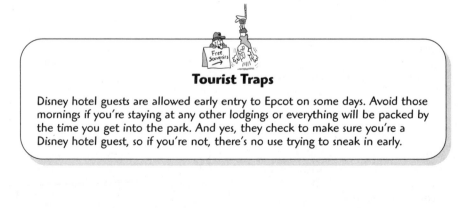

Tourist Traps

Disney hotel guests are allowed early entry to Epcot on some days. Avoid those mornings if you're staying at any other lodgings or everything will be packed by the time you get into the park. And yes, they check to make sure you're a Disney hotel guest, so if you're not, there's no use trying to sneak in early.

Canada

Canada offers an awesome 360° Circle-Vision movie that surrounds you with Royal Canadian Mounties, plunges you into Niagara Falls, takes you into the Canadian Rockies, and shows you an ocean of northern wildflowers.

China

China shows a 360° Circle-Vision film on the *Wonders of China.* Guests stand throughout the film, which is tiring, but you'll want to keep turning around to see the entire screen.

France

France's offering is an elegant, wide-angle film, ***Impressions de France,*** shown in a plush, sit-down theater. Linger on the grounds to see the replica Eiffel Tower, flowering trees, and formal Parisian gardens. Then dine in one of the restaurants, which are among the best in the World, if not the world.

Beating the Lines

Line up for continuous presentations (like the France movie) just after one show begins. You'll have to wait 20 minutes for the next show, but you'll be one of the first in line and you'll get the best seats. Some rides, such as the Maelstrom in Norway, can add additional seating as crowds grow, so the wait won't be as long as you think.

Germany

Germany offers a change of pace, with a rollicking beer garden, oompah bands, a cobblestone courtyard, and a Hummel store where you'll probably see an artist at work creating actual Hummel figures. There are no rides; the show is the year-round Oktoberfest that plays in the *bierstube.*

Italy

Italy is a favorite for its warm scenes straight from the old country: gondolas floating in the lagoon, a bell tower, a piazza with pretty fountain, olive trees, and street performers presenting *commedia dell'arte.*

Japan

Japan presents traditional music, dance, magic, and other skills. Check your show schedule as you enter the park. The dining is superb and the gardens are some of the most restful respites in the Showcase. Take time to study the red Gate of Honor on the lagoon, the pagoda, pebbled footpaths, and other traditional touches, all masterfully done.

Mexico
Mexico does a fine job of presenting snippets of its varied cultures. You'll see a Mayan pyramid, get a glimpse of the volcano Popocatapetl, see traditional dances, and end your voyage on the River of Life at a fiesta.

Morocco
Morocco is one of the most beautiful and exotic "countries" in the World Showcase. You'll enter the old city through an arched gate and view a masterpiece of mosaics. Musicians play around the fountain. Diners are entertained by a belly dancer. Don't miss the garden, with its olive trees and date palms.

Norway
Norway presents the most exciting ride in the World Showcase: a voyage with the Vikings through the terrifying **Maelstrom.** A 13th-century church sits aside the cobblestone village square. There's also a charming 70mm film on the history of Norway.

United Kingdom
The U.K. pavilion is authentic right down to the pub, thatched cottage, flagstone pathways, and blooming rosebushes galore. Check your show schedule so that you don't miss a performance of the street players; they're a hoot, and you may be recruited to join in.

The Whole World in Your Hands: Some Suggested Itineraries
To see Epcot really requires 2 or more days. Lots of people try to do it in a single day, giving rise to the joke that EPCOT really stands for "Every Person Comes Out Tired." Do yourself a favor and budget 2 days for this park, and don't go crazy trying to do everything. You'll be happier spending parts of each day here and saving some energy for swimming, sleeping late, or just hanging out by your hotel pool.

We've written up both a 2-day itinerary and a 1-day schedule for people whose time is extremely limited. Be forewarned, though, that the 1-day itinerary may feel rushed and exhausting. You'll see as much of the park as is physically possible in 1 day, but you might derive more pleasure out of a more leisurely pace.

Time-Savers

Because much of the IllumiNations show takes place in the air, you won't miss much by failing to stake out a prime spot long before the show. Spend your time seeing and doing things right up until showtime.

It's a Small World After All: Epcot in 2 Days

It's tempting to skip around the park for variety's sake, and sometimes it's essential to leapfrog pavilions and then backtrack to avoid long lines. Still, we prefer taking Future World in a clockwise or counterclockwise direction on the first day, and then looping the World Showcases on the other day. Epcot is a very large park compared to the other Disney parks. Long distances between pavilions must be considered if your budget for time or energy is limited.

On Day 1:

1. At the base of the big sphere in Earth Station, go to **Guest Relations** to get a park map and show schedule and to book Priority Seating for lunch and dinner if you haven't already. Ask if any rides or attractions are closed today, and find out the official opening time for tomorrow.

2. Ride the 16-minute **Spaceship Earth,** one of Epcot's premier rides for all ages from preschoolers to grandparents. This is also the obvious first choice for everyone else, so if you don't beat the crowds, move it to the end of your day. Unless you're among the first in line, you won't have another good shot at it until after 5pm. As you exit this ride, you'll see a small playground called **Global Neighborhood,** with high-tech activities for all ages—and there's no wait.

3. Proceed to the next attraction on the circle, **Universe of Energy.** Lines here can be long, but it's a big theater and turnover is swift. You'll probably wait no longer than 40 minutes for 8 minutes of pre-show and a 26-minute show about energy. Very young children may find the dinosaurs scary, and the educational parts can be a snore, but overall, the show is a must. It's filled with special effects, fast-moving visuals, and superb sound.

4. **Wonders of Life** is the home of **Body Wars,** a rip-roaring ride simulator that is a must for ages 8 through adults (though it's not for the most senior of senior citizens, pregnant women, or people prone to seasickness or claustrophobia). Also in this pavilion is **Cranium Command,** an animated and funny show about the brain, which is suitable for all ages. **The Making of Me** is a humorous, tasteful handling of the birds and bees story. The very young won't get some of it, but it will answer a lot of questions for ages 7 and up. The show takes 14 minutes; waiting time will be about half an hour.

5. **Horizons** is a 15-minute ride that operates continuously, so it tends to be overwhelmed just after **Universe of Energy** lets out. Still, lines move steadily along and you shouldn't have to wait more than half an hour even if 700 to 800 people are in line ahead of you. The show has plenty of appeal for all ages, taking you through friendly farms and villages of the next millennium.

6. General Motors' **Test Track** takes you on a simulated test ride for a new car. It's more commercial than most rides, but so innovative and exciting (with roller coaster segments) that you won't mind the hype. The 5-minute romp is ideal for all ages.

7. Cut through Innoventions to the Living Seas and have **lunch.**

8. After lunch, either do the entire **Living Seas** attraction and short ride, or proceed to **Journey Into Imagination** and work your way back to the entrance before closing. If you'll be dining in the World Showcase and/or staying for IllumiNations, stay at Living Seas and work your way back toward the lagoon.

9. **The Land Pavilion** has three restaurants, so it can get crowded during meal hours. But in the later afternoon, it should be cleared out, allowing you to take the boat ride through a greenhouse filled with real crops. It's the best show here. **Food Rocks** is a silly nutrition show with a needed message; waits are never long. **Circle of Life** is a 12-minute film with more of the environmental messaging. Its saving grace is a cast from *The Lion King.*

10. **Journey Into Imagination** is a good place to end your first day, or to wait for dinner and **IllumiNations** because you can watch the "leaping water" fountains forever. We never tire of these random blops of water on their happy romp across the heads of passing crowds. Take the **Journey Into Imagination fantasy ride,** suitable for all ages. **Image Works** is an electronic playground where you can pass time pleasantly while gearing up for this pavilion's blockbuster 3-D film, **Honey, I Shrunk the Audience.** It's a must-see for ages 6 and up, but can be scary for preschoolers.

Beating the Lines

When crowds are heaviest, you might consider just getting away for a while. Try making dinner reservations at the Swan, Dolphin, or BoardWalk resorts, which you can walk to from Epcot. After you leave the park and retrieve the car, drive over to the hotel where you are having dinner. After dinner, *walk* back into the park for IllumiNations. When the show is over, leave through the International Gateway between France and the United Kingdom to get back to your car; you'll have to fight a lot less traffic. Or continue your evening at BoardWalk until the wee hours, when there's hardly any traffic anywhere.

On Day 2:

1. If you arrive when the park opens, repeat any **Future World** rides or shows that you missed. Or sleep a little later and arrive in time to take up your position at the Port of Entry to the **World Showcase.** Horse-drawn trolleys cover the route and boats crisscross the lagoon, but we prefer to walk it.

2. Start in **Canada.** The movie is uplifting and entertaining. Don't miss it before moving into the **United Kingdom** for shopping, street shows, people-watching, and a stop at the very authentic pub.

3. Proceed to **France** and see a lovely lyrical movie that will captivate all but the very young. Check out the restaurants here if you'll be return-ing for lunch or dinner, and then proceed to **Morocco** to find a color-ful casbah with merchants, fabulous Moorish tile and arts, and little passageways that put you in Bergman-Bogart Land. There's no show here, but the restaurant with its belly dancers is one of Epcot's best-kept secrets.

4. Check the schedule for programs at the **American Gardens Theater,** and then stop at **Japan** if you have time. The store here is packed with enticements, but don't miss the overall grandeur of the architecture and grounds.

5. **The American Adventure,** which anchors this part of Epcot, is a stately, patriotic triumph of audio-animated characters. The theater is huge, so waits are rarely long. Proceed to **Italy** for shopping and a snack. You find yourself in St. Mark's Square in **Venice,** complete with a 105-foot bell tower. Photo opportunities are superb, but there's no show except for singing servers in the restaurant.

6. **Germany** is a good place for lunch or supper because it's a nonstop Oktoberfest with oompah band, yodelers, beer, and wursts. Don't miss the model railway and the Bavarian-looking shops.

7. Next you'll come to **China,** with its good food, bargain buys, gardens and ponds, and a 360° movie. Position yourself to be one of the first to exit, and then rush to the **Norway** pavilion and get on line for the **Maelstrom** ahead of the throngs who will have the same idea. This much-too-short boat ride is one of Epcot's most thrilling rides.

8. At **Mexico,** you have completed the circle. Take time to look at the ancient artifacts around the pavilion, and then take the easygoing boat ride through a cliche version of the history of Mexico.

9. Have dinner, and then position yourself for **IllumiNations,** which will take place not long after dark.

It's a Mad, Mad, Mad, Mad World: Epcot in 1 Day

Put your jogging shoes on and pack your Filofax, because to do Epcot in 1 day, you'll have to be organized and move quickly.

1. Book a Priority Seating lunch at **Living Seas** and dinner at one of the ethnic restaurants in the World Showcase in advance. Make sure you arrive 1 hour before the "official" opening time. Grab a park map and show schedule at **Guest Relations**, just left of the big sphere. Ask a cast member if anything is closed today so that you don't waste any time.

Time-Savers

Buy park admission tickets and make Priority Seating arrangements ahead of time, so you don't waste precious time and energy standing in two additional lines.

2. World Showcase opens 2 hours later than the front of the park, so spend your early morning in **Future World.** Skip **Spaceship Earth** for now. It will be much too crowded and time-consuming; come back later in the day, preferably when most people are eating lunch or after 5pm. Go straight to **Test Track,** the newest thrill ride.

3. Proceed to **Journey Into Imagination,** where adults and kids of all ages will delight in the *Honey, I Shrunk the Audience* ride.

4. Located next to Journey Into Imagination is **The Land.** Take the **Living with the Land** boat tour. It's educational and a respite from the noise and crowds outside.

5. If you like thrill rides, cross through the center of Future World to the **Wonders of Life Pavilion** and get in line for **Body Wars,** the journey through the human bloodstream. The ride is jerky and loud, so it might not be everyone's cup of tea.

6. Cross back to **Living Seas,** where you can watch the huge aquarium forever. Relax with **lunch.** The food is excellent and the mood mellow—the perfect retreat after the heat and bright sun. Now is also a good time to backtrack to **Spaceship Earth.**

7. Unless you're eager to see (or repeat) something else in Future World, proceed to the **World Showcase,** which is, in our view, the best part of Epcot. Pavilions surround a big lagoon, which you can cross by boat, walk around, or ride around in a trolley. We prefer to walk it clockwise when pressed for time.

8. Start at the **Norway Pavilion** and ride the **Maelstrom.** It's charming and only a little scary. **China** has a fabulous 360° movie. In **Germany** or **Italy,** enjoy the architecture and shops. If you're thirsty, the **Biergarten** in Germany, with its oompah music, is a good place to take a break.

175

9. Something is always going on at the **American Adventure.** See the 30-minute show or catch the outdoor concert at the America Gardens Theater. The **Japan** and **Morocco** pavilions are both notable for their design and architecture; Japan also boasts a **show of traditional music and dance** that is one of Epcot's best. Check your show schedule regularly so that you don't miss it.

10. In the **France** pavilion, be sure to see the movie ***Impressions de France.*** This is a good place for dinner or a snack at the *boulangerie* (bakery). If you haven't yet made dinner reservations, make them now.

11. Proceed to the **United Kingdom** and try to catch a performance of the street theater. The shopping is good for Scottish, English, Welsh, and Irish goods, and the pub pulls an authentic, but overpriced, pint. The London-like park in the back of the pavilion is a quiet place to rest, except during **IllumiNations** when it fills up quickly with waiting spectators. The film at the **Canada** pavilion is a beaut. If you've got any energy left, make sure to catch it.

12. You've now made the rounds of World Showcase and are headed back to Future World to fill in any time that remains between now and your dinner seating. With luck you'll have a lagoon-front table where you can also watch **IllumiNations,** but the jockeying for views can get vicious no matter where you are. People start settling in as much as 2 hours before the show.

13. After the show, your choice is either to join the suffocating press of people trying to get to the parking lot or shuttles, or join the suffocating press of people who are staying on in the shops until they close. Everyone is pretty good-natured, so be prepared for long waits and keep your sense of humor.

Chapter 14

Disney–MGM Studios

Anyone who loves movies or remembers the golden age of Hollywood will enjoy wandering the realistic streets, shops, and sets of this combination theme park and working studio. Lots of filming is done here, so you never know whether you're seeing shtick or an actual taping. That's part of the fun of wandering these 110 acres.

You might be approached by Louella Parsons for an interview, or a script girl who scolds you for being late on the set. A "fight" might break out at Hollywood and Vine between a cabbie, who illegally parked his ancient Checker Cab, and a Keystone cop.

Movie Wars: Disney–MGM or Universal Studios?

Pity the visitor who has to choose between these two stellar theme parks. Both are absolute musts for movie buffs. For older adults who remember the golden age of Hollywood, Disney–MGM Studios gets the nod for nostalgia appeal. For visitors with little children, we'd give an edge to Universal Studios for its Nickelodeon, E.T., Fievel, and Hanna-Barbera attractions. Both parks have unavoidably long lines at the most spine-jarring thrill rides. Universal has the most exciting rides, including Kongfrontation, Jaws, Earthquake, and the upcoming Twister, but they break down often and end up closed for the day. Universal is physically larger, meaning more walking, but not as congested, meaning less people-dodging.

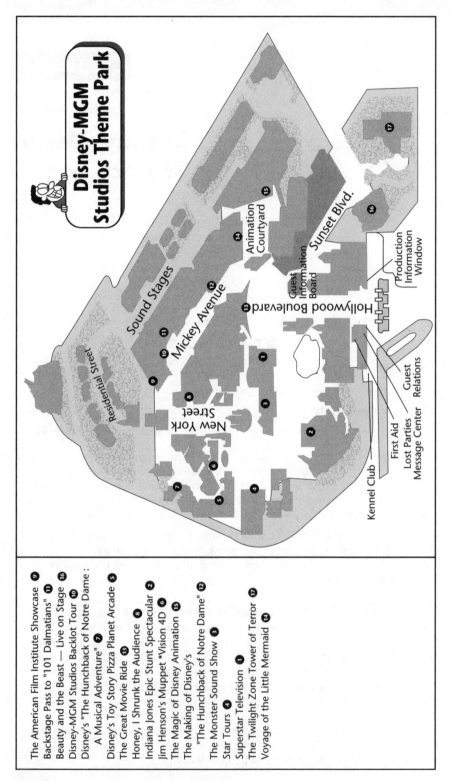

Disney-MGM Studios Theme Park

Sound Stages

Residential Street

New York Street

Mickey Avenue

Hollywood Boulevard

Sunset Blvd.

Animation Courtyard

Guest Information Board

Production Information Window

Guest Relations

First Aid
Lost Parties Message Center

Kennel Club

The American Film Institute Showcase **9**
Backstage Pass to "101 Dalmatians" **11**
Beauty and the Beast — Live on Stage **16**
Disney-MGM Studios Backlot Tour **10**
Disney's "The Hunchback of Notre Dame :
A Musical Adventure" **7**
Disney's Toy Story Pizza Planet Arcade **5**
The Great Movie Ride **13**
Honey, I Shrunk the Audience **8**
Indiana Jones Epic Stunt Spectacular **2**
Jim Henson's Muppet *Vision 4D **6**
The Magic of Disney Animation **15**
The Making of Disney's
"The Hunchback of Notre Dame" **12**
The Monster Sound Show **3**
Star Tours **4**
Superstar Television **1**
The Twilight Zone Tower of Terror **17**
Voyage of the Little Mermaid **14**

178

At both parks, collectors will find mountains of merchandise. Disney-MGM has the best selection of pricey movie memorabilia, including items actually owned or autographed by stars. Universal's shops have the best appeal to collectors of souvenirs themed to today's hits. As for dining, Universal has the ubiquitous Hard Rock Cafe; only at Disney-MGM can you find a Brown Derby. Admission prices are the same, but one park could have an advantage over the other depending on what multiday passes you buy.

What You Need to Know About the Park

➤ **Hours.** Disney-MGM is generally open daily from 9am to 7pm, and as late as midnight on special days in summer and on holidays. Get there about an hour beforehand if you can, because as in the other Disney park, the gates almost always open earlier than the "official" opening time. You'll also beat the traffic, and you may even be able to park closer to the gate.

➤ **ATMs** are located at the park's main entrance.

➤ **Baby-Changing Facilities** are located at the Baby Care Center, which also sells diapers, formula, baby food, and pacifiers. There are changing tables here as well as in all women's rest rooms and some men's rest rooms. Disposable diapers are also sold at Guest Services.

➤ **The First Aid Center,** staffed by registered nurses, is located in the Entrance Plaza next to Guest Services.

➤ **Lockers** can be found to the right of the Entrance Plaza, next to Oscar's Classic Car Souvenirs. Cost is $3 to $5, depending on the size.

➤ **Lost Children.** If your kids get lost, somebody will most likely take them to Guest Services, where lost children logbooks are kept. Children under 7 should wear name tags.

Time-Savers

Make a note of where you park at Disney–MGM Studios. The parking here is more convenient to the entry than at the other parks, but the lot isn't as well marked. Trams are available, but unless you are carrying two handfuls of kids, walking is a faster option. As soon as you enter, get a show schedule and work out a plan of action.

➤ **Package Pickup.** If you buy something early in the day and don't want to carry it around with you all day, have the clerk send it to Guest Services, which is just inside the Entrance Plaza. The service takes about 3 hours. Don't forget to pick up your package on the way out.

➤ **Strollers** can be rented at Oscar's Super Service, just inside the main entrance. The cost is $6 per day.

➤ **Video cameras** can be rented at Hollywood Boulevard for $30 per day plus a $450 deposit. You can buy disposable cameras throughout the park.

G-Rated Attractions & Rides

Children under 10 will be frightened by some of the attractions at this park and bored by others, but they will be thrilled by the movies and productions geared specifically for them. Children over 10 will think the kiddy rides too baby-ish for them, but will marvel at the more adult attractions. Divvy up your day here with a keen eye on what's appropriate for your kids.

Backstage Pass to 101 Dalmatians shows some of the secrets of the making of the live-action version of this movie. A furry flurry of real Dalmatians is part of the show. Kids and adults of all ages will love it.

Jim Henson's Muppet-Vision 4-D is a delight for all ages. It's an in-your-face spectacle filled with surprises and slapstick from Miss Piggy, Kermit, and the gang.

Monster Sound Show is an inside look at how all those loud and weird sound effects make it into the movies. Yell loud enough, and you may be chosen to try to replicate some sound effects for use in a real movie. Then you get to compare your version to the way it would sound when done by a professional.

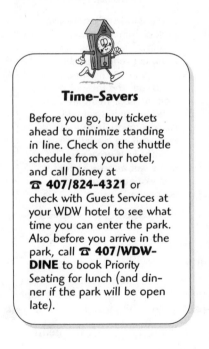

Time-Savers

Before you go, buy tickets ahead to minimize standing in line. Check on the shuttle schedule from your hotel, and call Disney at ☎ **407/824-4321** or check with Guest Services at your WDW hotel to see what time you can enter the park. Also before you arrive in the park, call ☎ **407/WDW-DINE** to book Priority Seating for lunch (and dinner if the park will be open late).

Theater of the Stars stages vibrant, live productions that last about 25 minutes. An adaptation of *Beauty and the Beast* played here for a long run before giving way to the current production, Disney's *The Hunchback of Notre Dame: A Musical Adventure*. The show could change again in the future, so check before waiting in line, which could last a half hour or more.

Voyage of the Little Mermaid re-creates the underwater world of the movie, with live performances, movie clips, puppetry, and special effects. You'll get to hear Sebastian sing "Under the Sea" and see Ariel's live performance of "Part of Your World." The Voyage has some scary scenes, but just like the movie (which every kid has most likely seen), it has a happy ending.

PG-Rated Attractions & Rides

These productions aren't designed to appeal to the littlest tots.

American Film Institute Showcase is a walk through Hollywood history and memorabilia. It gives visitors an appreciation of all the people who pitch in to turn an idea into a feature motion picture.

Backstage Studio Tour is an entertaining 25-minute tram tour that takes you behind the scenes to Disney's costume collection (the world's largest), sets from popular (and not-so-popular) TV shows, and the domain of the special-effects wizards. The highlight is the portion of the ride through Catastrophe Canyon, where you live through an earthquake that alternately threatens to burn, crush, or flood you to death. Real movie fans may want to do it twice.

The **Great Movie Ride** is like a trip through movie history. You enter through a replica of the famous Mann's Chinese Theatre in Hollywood (complete with hand- and footprints of the stars). If you can think of a famous scene in movie history, it's probably here, from Rhett carrying Scarlett up the stairs in *Gone With the Wind* to Bogey and Bergman's long goodbye in *Casablanca* to Gene Kelly's signature dance from *Singin' in the Rain*.

Indiana Jones Epic Stunt Spectacular is an eye-popping look at how stunts are done. Real actors barely escape getting burned, blown up, beheaded, shot, or otherwise eliminated, so it's very exciting—especially for those audience members who are asked to take part. This is one of the most popular rides in the park, but children under age 6 may find it too scary.

Beating the Lines

The best time to find shorter lines at the most popular rides, such as Star Tours and the Twilight Zone Tower of Terror, is during the Indiana Jones Stunt Spectacular or the parade.

Time-Savers

Blocks of shops in the theme parks are connected although they look like separate shops from the outside. When streets are crowded, you can often make better time getting from Point A to Point B inside the shops.

Star Tours is a topsy-turvy, turbulent ride through space in a simulator that soars, jiggles, and jounces. The theater never moves and the movie screen stays stationary, but the seats rock and rumble and careen in coordination with what you see on the screen, faithfully replicating a ride on a *Star Wars*-like spacecraft with R2-D2 and C3PO. It's more realistic and bone-jarring than even the most intense roller coaster, and weary adults may want to skip it. It's been around a while, but it's still one of the best thrill rides in all the Disney parks.

Superstar Television is a chance to bring out the ham in you. "Casting directors" choose audience volunteers to recreate 15 famous television scenes—everything from the classic "I Love Lucy" chocolate factory episode to scenes from "Cheers" and "The Golden Girls." Come early if you want a part in the show.

Twilight Zone Tower of Terror has been torqued to new thrills since its introduction in 1994. It's scarier than ever. You enter an abandoned hotel during a thunderstorm and ride through a lot of spooky stuff and nonsense before your elevator plunges 13 stories. This may be the best thrill ride in the whole park. You must be 44 inches tall to ride.

Time-Savers

When entering the theme parks you'll be dazzled, but don't rush to the first thing you see. By studying the map, making a plan, and noting which attractions are closed, you'll save time and shoe leather.

Oohs & Aahs: Parades, Shows, & Fireworks

➤ **Hercules: Zero to Hero Victory Parade** is a rip-roaring daily parade down Hollywood Boulevard featuring Disney's newest full-length animated hero. Consult your show schedule.

➤ *Honey, I Shrunk the Kids* **Movie Set Adventure** is an enormous playground with something for all children: toddlers to age 10. More than a playground, it's entertainment complete with sound effects and filled with Disney's magic touches.

➤ **Sorcery in the Sky** is this park's fireworks spectacle, playing nightly. Consult your show schedule.

➤ **Fantasmic,** opening Fall 1998, is an after-dark spectacular with a cast of 50-plus lasers, music, and lights.

So Many Rides, So Little Time: A Suggested Itinerary

Unlike Epcot and the Magic Kingdom, Disney-MGM is a park you can manage in a single day. If you're a real movie buff, spend one day here and one day at Universal Studios Florida, and then return to the park you liked best if you have a third day.

1. Get here an hour before you'll be allowed to enter. Note the number of your parking place and walk to the entry. Trams are available, but the walk is short compared to other parks. Put a name tag on all children age 7 and under. Agree on a meeting spot in case you're separated, and write it down. If you haven't made Priority Seating arrangements for sit-down dining, do so at the kiosk at Hollywood and Vine.

2. Rush directly to the **Twilight Zone Tower of Terror.** It's a socko ride except for the youngest children and claustrophobes, and long lines soon form. After riding, go back toward the park entrance and Guest Relations for a map of the park and a show schedule. Ask a cast member if any rides or shows are closed.

3. The park is small, so backtracking isn't the concern here that it is at other parks. Consider passing up attractions that have long lines and come back at a better time. Waits can be long at the **Great Movie Ride,** which lasts a half hour, and **Star Tours,** which takes 15 to 20 minutes after you board. Both are absolute musts. So is the **Indiana Jones Epic Stunt Spectacular,** which allows people to enter up to 5 minutes after the show begins. Unless the theater is filled to capacity, you can dash in after everyone else is inside and avoid a long wait in line. If you have a choice, sit at the far right of the stage and you'll exit sooner.

Time-Savers

If you're not a guest at a WDW hotel, avoid going to theme parks on days when WDW guests are allowed early entry. By the time you get in, long lines will have already formed at every ride. Don't try to fake it. They check for proof that you're a WDW guest.

4. **Voyage of the Little Mermaid** is a must for little ones. After the first show, it plays continuously. Ask a cast member or note the sign indicating the waiting time. If it's a half hour or less, it's probably the best you can do. See **MuppetVision 4-D** or, if you're not a Muppets fan, spend time in the shops or pick a park bench in one of the street sets and enjoy the passing scene. It's deliciously realistic.

5. With luck, you've made it through all the above before lunch at the **Prime Time Café,** which we recommended for a noisy, good-times atmosphere with comfort foods, or the **Brown Derby** for a quieter setting and California cuisine.

6. Tour **The Magic of Disney Animation,** and then the **Backlot Tour.** These attractions take about an hour and have appeal for the whole family.

7. Check the schedule for afternoon shows and parades. This park, even more than the others, themes its entertainments heavily toward Disney films with emphasis on the current hits, so shows change often. **ABC Sound Studio** and **SuperStar Television** are always good entertainment, and you can also see what's going on at the **Theater of the Stars** and the **Backlot Theater.**

8. Leave an hour before the 7pm closing or, if the park is open late tonight, have cocktails and a leisurely dinner before the after-dark entertainments. On your way out, shop along Hollywood Boulevard, have your picture taken, and price the movie memorabilia.

183

Chapter 15

The Mouse That Roars: Disney's Animal Kingdom

In This Chapter

➤ The story behind Disney's latest blockbuster

➤ A preview of the rides and shows

➤ Dining tips at the Animal Kingdom

Disney's fourth park opened in spring of 1998, and although it's the baby of the bunch, it wouldn't be a Disney park unless it was constantly being updated, tinkered with, debugged, and perfected. So don't be surprised if names and even locations of rides, theaters, or sections of this park have been changed, relocated, modified, or com-pletely removed when you visit.

Animal Kingdom currently consists of five "habitats": The Oasis Safari Village, DinoLand U.S.A., Camp Minnie-Mickey, and Africa. (A sixth habitat, Asia, is scheduled to open in 1999.) The park covers more than 500 acres, and at the heart of it all is the 14-story "Tree of Life," an intricately carved representation of animals hand-crafted by Disney artists.

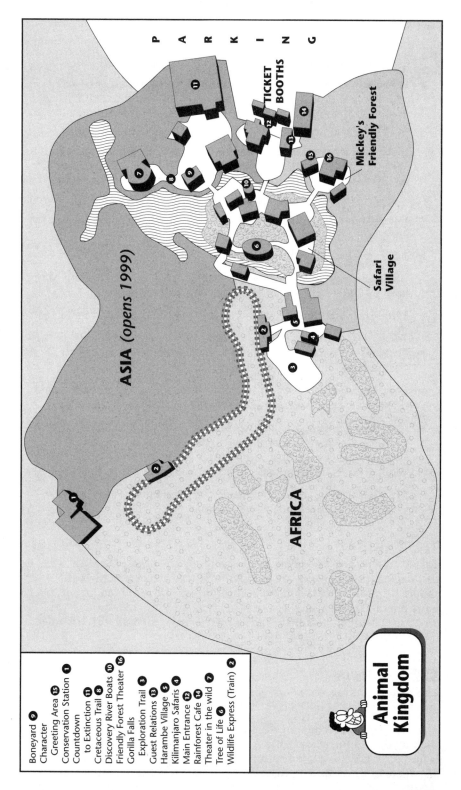

PARKING

TICKET BOOTHS

Mickey's Friendly Forest

Safari Village

ASIA (opens 1999)

AFRICA

Boneyard **9**
Character
  Greeting Area **15**
Conservation Station **1**
Countdown
  to Extinction **11**
Cretaceous Trail **8**
Discovery River Boats **10**
Friendly Forest Theater **16**
Gorilla Falls
  Exploration Trail **13**
Guest Relations **3**
Harambe Village **5**
Kilimanjaro Safaris **4**
Main Entrance **12**
Rainforest Cafe **14**
Theater in the wild **7**
Tree of Life **6**
Wildlife Express (Train) **2**

Animal Kingdom

Logistics & Services

➤ **Directions.** Animal Kingdom is in the southwest corner of WDW, near Blizzard Beach and the All-Star resorts. Take I-4 to Exit 25B, the main WDW entrance, and then follow the signs to the Animal Kingdom.

➤ **Hours and Admission.** Animal Kingdom is open daily from 8am to 5pm. Admission is $42 for adults, $34 for children ages 3–9, free for younger kids. See the chart on p. 146 for a rundown of prices for Disney's multi-park passes.

➤ **Parking** already seems insufficient for the number of visitors, so get here *early.*

➤ **ATMs** are located at the main entrance and at Safari Village.

➤ **Baby-Changing Facilities** are located in Safari Village. Many shops have disposable diapers behind the counter. Just ask.

➤ **The First Aid Center,** staffed by registered nurses, is located in Safari Village.

➤ **Lockers** can be found just inside the main entrance. They cost $3 plus a refundable $2 deposit.

➤ **Lost Children.** If your kids get lost, somebody will most likely take them to Guest Services. Children under 7 should wear name tags.

➤ **Package Pickup.** If you buy something early in the day and don't want to carry it around with you all day, have the clerk send it to Garden Gate Gifts, which is just inside the Entrance Plaza. It takes about 3 hours. Don't forget to pick up your package on the way out!

➤ **Strollers** can be rented just inside the main entrance to the right. Cost is $5 plus a refundable $1 deposit.

The Oasis

This is the first area you come to after entering the park. Like Main Street in the Magic Kingdom, there are no rides or attractions here. Rather, this area simply helps to create the mood (imagine you're not in Orlando, but in a far more remote place). Waterfalls, tropical trees, and flowers surround you. You'll see few reminders that this is all man-made. After all, this is Disney magic at work.

Safari Village

This is Animal Kingdom's central shopping, dining, and service area, all located on an island in the center of the park.

The 140-foot-high **Tree of Life** is the focal point of Animal Kingdom in the way that Cinderella's Castle is for the Magic Kingdom or Spaceship Earth is for Epcot. It's also a good landmark, since you can see it from almost anywhere in the park. The Tree of Life is home to a theater attraction (called "It's Tough to Be a Bug") based on the recent Disney/Pixar film *A Bug's Life*. This attraction is usually crowded.

You can access all of the theme areas from Safari Village; take the **Discovery River Boats** to "Africa," or linger here in the shops and restaurants.

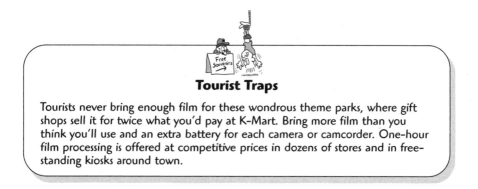

Tourist Traps

Tourists never bring enough film for these wondrous theme parks, where gift shops sell it for twice what you'd pay at K-Mart. Bring more film than you think you'll use and an extra battery for each camera or camcorder. One-hour film processing is offered at competitive prices in dozens of stores and in free-standing kiosks around town.

Camp Minnie-Mickey

This area of the park is located left of Safari Village. Any Disney character that can be said to belong in the forest or jungle will be on hand here for handshakes, autographs, and photo opportunities. That means Simba and other *Lion King* characters, Ballou and other characters from *The Jungle Book*, plus Snow White, Chip 'n' Dale, and numerous others. Mickey, Minnie, Goofy, Pluto, Donald, Daisy, and the usual headliners will also put in appearances at varying times. There's also a very good stage show here you won't want to miss called **"Festival of the Lion King."**

DinoLand USA

Located to the right of Safari Village, DinoLand USA is Disney's attempt to capitalize on the dinosaur craze inspired by *Jurassic Park* and Barney.

It's home to the **Countdown to Extinction** adventure ride, in which you "time travel" past snarling dinosaurs. You must be 46 inches tall to participate in this nonstop thrill ride.

The other major attraction in DinoLand USA is the 1,500-seat **Theater in the Wild,** which hosts a stage show called **"Journey Into Jungle Book."** **The Boneyard** is a playground where kids can "dig up" the "bones" of Tyrannosaurus Rexes, Triceratopses, and other dinosaurs.

Africa

Everybody heads here—this is where the wild things are! The **Kilimanjaro Safaris** takes 32 passengers at a time on a 25-minute photo safari through a world of rhinos, lions, wildebeests, impalas, gazelles, elephants, and other African creatures.

Strategic placement of watering holes and salt licks brings the animals out to where people can see them, while seemingly invisible barriers separate predators from prey (and passengers).

The ride is scripted, with a pro-environmentalist voiceover, as well as a finale in which riders happen upon poachers, chase them down, and deliver them to the proper authorities. The ride ends at the entrance to the **Gorilla Falls Exploration Trail,** which winds through habitats occupied not only by gorillas, but also by hippos.

The other major attraction in Africa is the **Wildlife Express** train ride through the belly of the park to a **Conservation Station** at the far end of Africa. The conservation station includes a nursery for young animals and **The Affection Section,** an animal petting area that's sure to be a hit with kids. The train ride itself is not the thrill ride of Kilimanjaro Safaris, but it allows visitors to see many of the same animals.

Please Feed the People: Food at Disney's Animal Kingdom
Animal Kingdom has surprisingly few restaurants so far. Instead, most of the feeding sites (for people) are of the counter-service and fast-food variety.

Try **Restaurantosaurus** in DinoLand USA for burgers and fries or **Pizzafari** in Safari Village.

The only full-service restaurant is the long-anticipated **Rainforest Cafe.** Like the Hard Rock Cafe at Universal Studios, it's accessible from both inside and outside the park. You can dine here without paying park admission.

Chapter 16

Universal Studios

Just when everyone in Orlando thought that Walt Disney World was the be-all and end-all, Universal Studios moved in and knocked our socks off. When people ask about our favorite park, we just can't decide, but we *can* concede that Universal can compete in a Disney town.

Universal is big and getting bigger. Its rides are utterly startling in their quality and complexity. Its grounds are groomed down to the last blade of grass to make you think you're in New York, New England, or San Francisco.

Most lay people don't follow the studios enough to know who produces what, but in Orlando you soon get the big picture literally and figuratively. Both Universal and Disney-MGM Studios spend a lot of their dollars and your time in shamelessly plugging their own films and characters. At Universal, that means *Earthquake, Hercules* (the live-action show, not the animated feature), *Terminator, Back to the Future*, Barney, Yogi Bear, *Jaws, E.T.*, and many more favorites.

This is not just a theme park, but a working movie studio where visitors often see a film being made. Among films shot here were cable television's *The Swamp Thing, Clarissa Explains it All*, and *SeaQuest*.

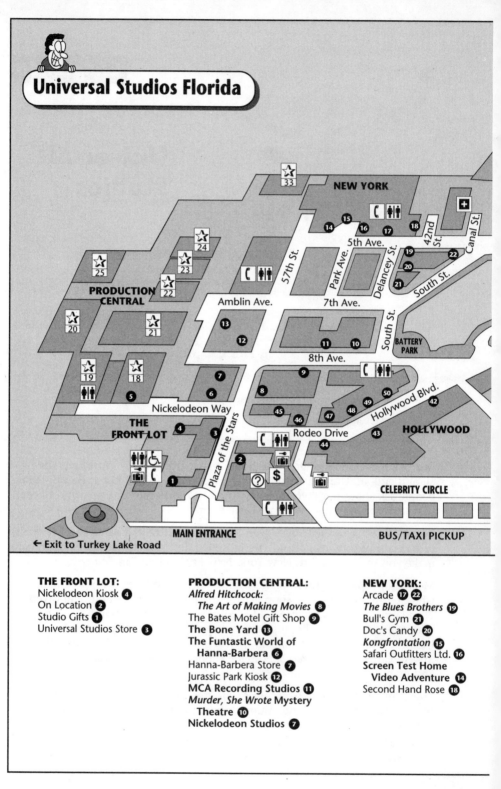

Universal Studios Florida

THE FRONT LOT:
Nickelodeon Kiosk ❹
On Location ❷
Studio Gifts ❶
Universal Studios Store ❸

PRODUCTION CENTRAL:
Alfred Hitchcock:
The Art of Making Movies ❽
The Bates Motel Gift Shop ❾
The Bone Yard ⓭
The Funtastic World of
Hanna-Barbera ❻
Hanna-Barbera Store ❼
Jurassic Park Kiosk ⓬
MCA Recording Studios ⓫
Murder, She Wrote Mystery
Theatre ❿
Nickelodeon Studios ❼

NEW YORK:
Arcade ⓱ ㉒
The Blues Brothers ⓳
Bull's Gym ㉑
Doc's Candy ⓴
Kongfrontation ⓯
Safari Outfitters Ltd. ⓰
Screen Test Home
Video Adventure ⓮
Second Hand Rose ⓲

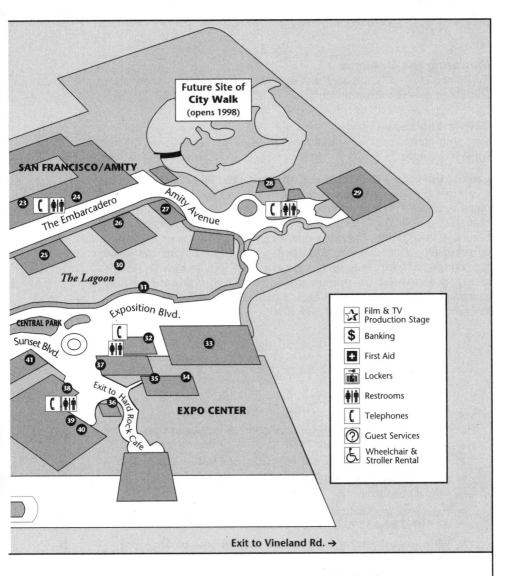

SAN FRANCISCO/AMITY:
Beetlejuice's
    Graveyard Revue **23**
Dynamite Night
    Stuntacular **30**
Earthquake —
    The Big One **24**
Jaws! **28**
Quint's Nautical Treasures **27**
Salty's Sketches **26**
Shaiken's Souvenirs **25**
Wild West Stunt Show **29**

EXPO CENTER:
Animal Actors Stage **37**
Back to the Future Gifts **32**
Back to the Future
    ...The Ride **33**
The Barney Store **35**
A Day in the Park
    with Barney **34**
E.T. Adventure **40**
E.T.'s Toy Closet **39**
Expo Art **31**
Fievel's Playland **36**
Universal Cartoon Store **38**

HOLLYWOOD:
AT&T at the Movies **41**
Brown Derby Hat Shop **47**
Cyber Image **43**
The Dark Room **44**
The Gory, Gruesome
    & Grotesque Horror
    Make-Up Show **42**
Lucy, A Tribute **46**
It's a Wrap **48**
Movietime Portrait &
    Celebrity News **50**
Silver Screen Collectibles **45**
TERMINATOR 2: 3-D
    BATTLE ACROSS TIME **44**

Mastering the Universe

In this section you'll find all the details to make your trip to Universal Studios go a little more smoothly.

Before You Leave Home

Start your planning early so that you can make the most of your days at Universal Studios.

Call the **Universal City Travel Company (☎ 800/224-3838** or 407/363-8000) and ask for theme park and travel package information. In a couple of years when the first Universal hotels open, you will have more options. For now, packages involve nearby hotels in a large choice of locations and price ranges. Packages that include a cruise, car rental, airfare, airport transfers, beach add-on, and tickets to other attractions are available at big savings. Extras include such perks as a Nickelodeon Kids Travel Tote, early park admission, or complimentary transportation from your hotel to Universal. The mailing address for the park is Universal Studios Florida, 1000 Universal Studio Plaza, Orlando, FL 32819.

Time-Savers

Here's what you can do in advance so that you don't have to waste any of your precious park time standing in line or dealing with arrangements:

➤ Check on the shuttle schedule from your hotel to Universal Studios.

➤ Call Universal at ☎ **407/363-8000** the day before to ask tomorrow's official open time.

➤ If you have small kids, make reservations for a character breakfast by calling ☎ **407/224-6339.**

➤ When you arrive at the park, **make a note of your parking space number.**

➤ Get in the right line (entrance, tickets, voucher redemptions) 45 minutes before opening.

➤ Get today's show schedule and a park map. Note what special filmings are going on today at Nickelodeon that would be of interest to the children and ask what attractions are closed today.

➤ Put a name tag on each child under age 7. Agree on a family meeting spot in case you get separated.

You can **book a character breakfast** ahead of time at ☎ **407/224-6339.** You'll eat in the International Food Bazaar with stars such as the Flintstones, Barney, Fievel, and Yogi Bear; you also experience lots of surprises.

For current news of special events at the park, check the Web at **www.oso@aol.com** where the *Orlando Sentinel* offers a special section called Theme Park Central.

If you belong to AAA, discounted tickets to Universal can be purchased through your local AAA office. Don't forget to bring your card to the theme park; it's good for discounts at shops and restaurants, too.

What Does It Cost?

Like the Disney folks, the people at Universal Studios give you a dizzying array of ticket options from which to choose, hoping that discounted prices will encourage you to spend more than 1 day here.

In our opinion, the best deal is the **Orlando FlexTicket,** which comes in 7- and 10-day varieties. During some promotions, everyone gets a second day free or Florida residents get a special discount (proof of residency is required). For studio passes or FlexTickets ahead of time, call ☎ **800/224-3838;** for annual passes, call ☎ **800/889-7275.**

The following table lists the most popular plans. Kids 10 and over pay adult prices; those under age 3 are admitted free. Note also that you pay the highest single-day price if you buy your tickets at the gate. Check to see if your hotel offers discounted admission packages. Prices include sales tax and are subject to change.

Universal Studios Florida Admissions Prices

Ticket Package and Description	Admission Price	
	Adult	Ages 3–9
One-day ticket	$44.52	$36.04
Two-day pass	$65.72	$55.12
Annual Celebrity Pass	$84.80	$68.90
Orlando 7-Day FlexTicket (unlimited admission for up to 7 days to Universal Studios, Sea World of Florida, and Wet 'n Wild)	$105.95	$87.93
Orlando 10-Day FlexTicket (unlimited admission for up to 10 days to Universal Studios, Sea World of Florida, and Wet 'n Wild)	$137.75	$114.43
5-hour VIP Tour (lets you cut the lines all day)	$110	$110 (per person)
8-hour Exclusive VIP Tour (you are escorted to the front of the line all day)	$1,200 for up to 15 people	

What You Need to Know About the Park

➤ **Directions.** Take I-4 to Exit 30B, which is Kirkman Road, off Florida Route 435. Get into the far right lane and follow the signs. It will feel like you're going in the wrong direction, but you're not. The signs will deliver you to the correct place.

➤ **Parking.** Universal is the only theme park in Florida that offers covered parking, which is a boon in this blistering sun. *Be sure to make a note of where you leave the car so that you can find it later.* Parking is $6 for cars, $7 for RVs, and $12 for valet parking.

➤ **Park Hours.** The park is open every day from 9am to 7pm except during Halloween Horror Nights when it closes at 5pm and reopens from 7pm to midnight. It's open later for special events such as Mardi Gras and New Year's Eve. Call ahead to find out the schedule.

➤ **ATMs** are found just inside and just outside the main entrance.

➤ **Baby-Changing Facilities** are found in all men's and women's rest rooms. There is also a nursing area at Guest Relations.

➤ The **First Aid Center** is located between New York and San Francisco, next to Louie's Restaurant.

➤ **Lockers** are located just across from Guest Relations and rent for $1 per day.

➤ **Lost children** will most likely be delivered to Guest Relations near the main entrance or to Security (behind Louie's Restaurant, between New York and San Francisco). Children under age 7 should wear name tags.

➤ **Strollers** are available for rent in Amity and at Guest Relations. Cost is $6 for a single stroller, $12 for a double-wide.

It's a Ride. No, It's a Movie. Actually, It's Both!—Universal's Top Attractions

Most of the attractions here use cutting-edge technology such as giant IMAX screens and other special effects. While you wait in line, you'll be entertained by pre-shows that are even better than the ones down the road at Disney.

Attractions are listed here alphabetically. Check the section "Exploring the Universe: Some Suggested Itineraries" later in this chapter for advice on which attractions are worth the long waits.

Back to the Future: The Ride

Blast off into space and time through volcanic tunnels, glaciers, and canyons. Among other pleasures, you'll be swallowed by a dinosaur. The ride is exceedingly bumpy and raucous, not suitable for the faint of heart (or back). For the best views, sit in the back of the car. Recommended ages are 8 to adult. You must be at least 40 inches tall.

Beetlejuice's Graveyard Revue

Horrible creatures including Dracula and Wolfman show up to scare you skinny. It's too loud and scary for very small children (say, under 6), but teenagers love the rock music and pyrotechnics. Let your kids go on this one by themselves; most adults find it pretty silly.

Time-Savers

Universal's VIP Package provides a 5-hour guided tour with priority entrance to rides and special seating in theaters. Prices start at $359, including 3 hotel nights, a 3-night FlexTicket, and one dinner.

A Day in the Park with Barney

Your kids have already made you get the Barney pajamas, the Barney plush stuffed animal, countless Barney videos, and that stupid song stuck in your head. What other Barney paraphernalia could there be? How about an environmental message from the purple dinosaur, complete with singing and dancing by Barney, Baby Bop, and BJ? Anyone pint sized will be enchanted; anyone over the age of 6 will barf.

Dynamite Nights Stuntacular

Boats roar around the lagoon, which is alight with flames and fireworks. This show is well worth staying in the park to the last, even though it means joining the crowds that then flock to the parking lot.

Earthquake: The Big One

You're riding the BART train in San Francisco when The Big One hits. All around you is bedlam: Water mains burst, buildings buckle, and a propane truck explodes. It is heart-stopping and not suitable for claustrophobes, frail folks, and little kids (under 8 or so, and they have to be over 40 inches tall and accompanied by an adult).

E.T. Adventure

For many families, this now-classic adventure is worth the price of park admission all by itself. The wait is made more pleasant by a glade of cool trees. You'll fly with E.T. by bicycle on a mission to save his planet while being serenaded by the familiar movie music.

The Funtastic World of Hanna-Barbera

Yogi Bear is your pilot on this spaceship simulator, so it's understandable if your ride is a little bit bumpy. On your mission to rescue Elroy Jetson, you'll learn how cartoons are made, and afterward you can paint some cartoons of your own. Allow plenty of time for the children to interact with this favorite. Alas, the height restriction (40 inches) prevents all but the tallest 5-year-olds from enjoying a ride that appeals primarily to younger children.

Hercules & Xena: Wizards of the Screen

No, not that animated Hercules. This one is the live-action Hercules, whose TV program is syndicated all over the world. This interactive show dazzles audiences by mixing live performers, eye-popping costumes, and special effects, as well as a boffo sword fight between good and evil. Recommended for ages 8 and up.

Dollars & Sense

Orlando FlexTickets are a fabulous buy compared to single park admissions. You can leave the park, go back to your hotel for lunch and a nap, spend the hot afternoon at Wet 'n Wild, and then come back to Universal for the Dynamite Nights Stuntacular. A parking fee is paid at the first park you visit and it's good for all parks, all day.

Jaws

Just when you thought it was safe to go back in the water, here comes that menacing shark again. He wants to have *you* for breakfast, and we don't mean a sit-down character meal. You'll be jolted, bounced, and shocked almost to death. Go after dark for a truly frightening experience. Not recommended for kids under 8.

Kongfrontation

The fun starts while you're still standing in line at a dark, scary New York subway station and CBS News reports that King Kong is on a rampage. To flee the island, you board the tram—but not quite in time to escape the 32-foot-tall gorilla's noisy, terrifying attacks. Only the most jaded New Yorkers will fail to be exhilarated. Not for kids under 8, and riders have to be 40 inches tall.

Nickelodeon Studios Tour

See a beloved television show come alive (someone will even get slimed!) as you learn how things happen behind the scenes. Allow plenty of time to try the newest Sega video games.

Terminator 2: 3–D Battle Across Time

James Cameron, who directed the movie, is back to oversee production on this attraction, and so is the Terminator, who is beginning to have as many lives as Jason of *Friday the 13th* fame. The ride is violent, loud, and frightening, so it's not for everyone, but it's authentic to the movie and even stars the original cast. Three big screens come at you with 70mm and 3-D movies plus lots of fantastic special effects. Not for children under 8.

Twister

What's so exciting about right foot green, left hand blue? Oh, wait a minute. It's not that kind of Twister. It's the "Auntie Em, Auntie Em" variety. Universal pushes the edge of the envelope with this newest attraction, set to open in summer 1998, which puts you in the middle of a tornado even more realistically than the 1996 movie did. You'll be pounded by rain, punished by winds, and deafened by the "freight train" sound of a real tornado. It isn't however, for little kids under 8 or so and anyone who's physically frail.

Bet You Didn't Know

TV shows, including **Flamingo Fortune, America's Health, World Wrestling Championships**, and many Nickelodeon programs, are taped at Universal Studios, and admission is free to park guests. Watch for signage, or ask at Guest Services as you enter, to see if you can be a part of a studio audience.

Wild, Wild, Wild West Show

How do the stunt people fall off horses and throw saloon chairs without getting killed? You'll learn their secrets at this live-wire show. As you enter, note the Splash Zone and don't sit near it unless you want a shower.

The Parallel Universe: Other Attractions

The attractions listed above are our favorites, but there are tons of other things to see and do here—not to mention shopping and eating.

Fievel's Playland is a delightful playground themed to the wild West and packed with things for kids to try. It's a great place to go after lunch so that toddlers can nap in their strollers while big brother and sister run off excess energy.

The **Gory, Gruesome & Grotesque Horror Make-up Show** lets you behind the scenes to see how monsters and ghouls are made up.

I Love Lucy, **a Tribute** is a must for Lucy buffs. Angela Lansbury herself introduces you to the ***Murder She Wrote* Mystery Theater,** which lets you make some of the decisions about the plot.

In **Alfred Hitchcock: The Art of Making Movies** you'll be led by Tony Perkins through some memorable scenes from popular Hitchcock films such as *Psycho* and *Rear Window*.

The **Bone Yard** will please movie buffs. It's a storage space for old props.

In the **Animal Actors Show** you'll meet Benji, Mr. Ed, and Lassie look-alikes who do pet tricks for you.

Shopping

The shops at Universal Studios are a mecca for movie buffs who collect theme merchandise. Among them are shops themed to *Back to the Future,* the Bates Motel, *E.T., Jurassic Park,* and Hanna Barbera. Other shops sell all manner of serious and frivolous gifts, souvenirs, and collectibles. If you run out of time, go to the airport well before your flight and shop the Universal Studios shop there.

Time-Savers

Don't have lunch in the Hard Rock Cafe on days when you are paying to be in the park. Park admission isn't required to dine here, so the waits here are longer than at other park restaurants. Come on a different day and park in the cafe's own lot. Or have dinner here when you're totally pooped and don't mind sitting for a long time.

Dining

Universal Studios has no shortage of restaurants, as well as plenty of places where you can get candy or popcorn to complete the movie-theater experience. You can probably tell exactly the kind of food served at the dozen-plus restaurants just from the names. They include the Beverly Hills Boulangerie, Boardwalk Snacks, Cafe La Bamba Mexican Restaurant, Cartoon Cafe, Chez Alcatraz, Finnegan's Bar & Grill, The Fudge Shoppe, Haagen-Dazs Ice Cream, Hard Rock Cafe (which can be entered from the park or from outside), the International Food Bazaar, Lombard's Landing, Louie's Italian Restaurant, Mel's Drive-in, the Midway Grill, Richter's Burger Co., San Francisco Pastry Co., Schwab's Pharmacy, and the Studio Stars Restaurant.

None of these restaurants is worth a special trip (though some people just can't seem to leave any city without stopping in at the Hard Rock Cafe for a T-shirt and a burger) but the themes are nicely carried out and the variety is impressive.

Exploring the Universe: Some Suggested Itineraries

Universal Studios can provide hours of pleasure day after day. In addition to rides and shows that are worth seeing more than once, the streets are alive with entertainers and celebrity look-alikes. There are more than two dozen shops, 18 places to dine or snack, and three dozen street sets where you can imagine yourself on a shoot in the Psycho house, an industrial park, Coney Island, or the World's Fair. Bring your camera and loads of film. An entire day could be spent just taking pictures.

We've provided two itineraries here: one for young children and one for adults and older kids. If you plan to spend 2 days here, you'll have plenty of experiences you'll want to repeat, and assuredly, some you weren't able to get to on day 1.

Universal Studios in a Day with Kids

1. If you haven't already eaten, the **Beverly Hills Boulangerie** just inside the entrance is a good place to have a sweet roll and a drink.

2. Walk down Plaza of the Stars, turn right onto Rodeo Drive, and follow it into **Hollywood.** Head straight for the **Gory, Gruesome & Grotesque Horror Make-up Show** (though it may not be appropriate for children under age 7).

3. Continue along Exposition Boulevard to **Expo Center** and get in the line for the **Back to the Future ride.** It's not for preschoolers, but kids 8 or older won't want to leave without doing it at least once. Very young kids will delight in the **A Day in the Park with Barney,** just past the entrance to Hard Rock Cafe. Just about everybody in the family will love **E.T. Adventure,** which is well worth what may be a long wait. Shops in the area sell items having to do with E.T., Fievel, and other favorites.

4. Take the kids to **Fievel's Playland** and rest your feet while they roar around the playground. Then catch a show at the **Animal Actors Stage.** You'll meet Benji, Lassie, Mr. Ed, and other stars. If you're hungry, double back to Hollywood and have **lunch** at the **Cafe La Bamba** or **Mel's Drive-In.**

5. Proceed now around the lagoon to **Amity,** which quickly leads to **San Francisco** and then **New York.** Pose for a family picture with your heads in Jaws, and enjoy the comely scenery around the lagoon and the New England village. If you haven't eaten yet, have **lunch** in **Richter's Burger Co.** in San Francisco. This is a busy, popular part of the park because of the **Earthquake, Jaws,** and **Kongfrontation** attractions. Kids over 8 will want to spend all afternoon here, but if your kids are younger, you can minimize your time in this area. Young kids will want to stop at **Beetlejuice's Graveyard Revue** before leaving this area, however.

6. Turn left onto 57th Street and walk back toward the main gate. At the corner of Nickelodeon Way, don't miss **The Funtastic World of Hanna-Barbera,** a space ride with Yogi Bear. Children must be at least 40 inches tall, but any child tall enough to get in will love it.

7. Continue along Nickelodeon way to **Nickelodeon Studios,** where you'll see pilot shows, play all the games, and learn how slime is cooked up in the Universal Studios kitchen.

8. You're probably exhausted, but if you want to eat dinner before you fight traffic back to your hotel, **Studio Stars Restaurant** is not far

from the main entrance/exit. If dinner (or a nap in the stroller) rejuvenates you and your kids, stick around for the **Dynamite Nights Stuntacular.**

Universal Studios in a Day for Teenagers & Adults

1. Have breakfast in your hotel or on the way; you can have lunch at the park. If you arrive at the park hungry, have a sandwich or pastry at the **Beverly Hills Boulangerie** near the entry. Ask for a park map and today's show schedule and ask any uniformed staff what rides or shows are closed today. (Many of the top rides are closed more often than you'd hope.) Note chalkboards announcing special filmings that you can attend. Tickets are free, but if you have only 1 day here, you shouldn't waste time at filmings unless the star is someone you really want to see.

2. Head straight to **Expo Center** and get in line for the **Back to the Future ride.** Lines tend to build up quickly, but you still may want to ride it a second time. Then walk back toward **Hollywood** and try the **E.T. Adventure** ride.

3. Head back toward Back to the Future and cross the bridge to the New England village of **Amity.** Get in the **Jaws** line. When you leave, you'll be headed for San Francisco, but skip Earthquake for now and head for **New York** to ride **Kongfrontation** and **Twister.** Then go back to **San Francisco** to ride **Earthquake.**

4. If your stomach has stopped churning, check out possibilities for lunch. The biggest selection for families with different appetites is at the **International Food Bazaar,** near the Back to the Future ride. For quieter, sit-down dining, try **Studio Stars Restaurant** on **57th Street.** Or splurge on a meal at **Lombard's Landing** across from Earthquake. While lunching, check out the shows scheduled for the afternoon. If something special is going on, you'll have to tailor your itinerary to fit it in.

5. Head back down Hollywood Boulevard to Rodeo Drive, where you'll find **Terminator 2** on your left. Then continue along Rodeo Drive toward the park entrance, but instead of turning left to the main gate, turn right onto **Plaza of the Stars/57th Street** and check out the **Alfred Hitchcock** attraction.

6. If you have any energy left, you can try a return trip to some of the most popular rides. Or take a stroll back toward Amity and check out the **Wild West Stunt Show.**

7. If you want to stay on for the evening spectacular, have dinner at the **Hard Rock Cafe** and have your hand stamped for re-entry to the park. Lines here can be longer than those for the rides, but for hardcore rock fans it's an icon that must be visited. Lines at the gift shop aren't as long, so if you don't dine here, you can at least grab a T-shirt to add to your collection.

The Expanding Universe

Now that Universal has its foot squarely in Orlando's door, it plans to expand from a single theme park to a Universal City, with several parks, restaurant and shopping areas, and its own hotels.

City Walk, a 30-acre complex of shops and restaurants comparable to Disney's Pleasure Island, opened in summer 1998 in the area above Amity Avenue and the Wild West Stunt Show. The world's largest **Hard Rock Cafe** made its debut, too, thus guaranteeing crowds, but there are also several other theme restaurants, including re-creations of two New Orleans restaurants: **Pat O'Brien's** and **Emeril's of New Orleans,** featuring the cuisine of Food Network cult hero Emeril Lagasse.

Other venues include:

➤ A **Cineplex Odeon Megaplex** with 20 cinema screens

➤ The **E! Entertainment Television Production Center,** where guests can see network programs being staged

➤ The **NASCAR Cafe** with games, NASCAR artifacts, and eats

➤ **Marvel Mania,** a restaurant themed to Marvel comics characters including Spider-Man

➤ A replica of **Bob Marley's** home and garden

➤ The **Motown Cafe,** combining the Motown sound, comfort food, and memories

➤ A **Jazz Center** with a hall of fame and a venue for live performances

An entirely new park, **Universal's Islands of Adventure,** is scheduled to open in 1999. And Steven Spielberg is creative consultant for a park that will be the permanent home of **The Incredible Hulk, The Cat in the Hat,** the dinosaurs of **Jurassic Park, Spider-Man,** and dozens more American icons. Roller coasters will have the same thrust as an F-16 fighter jet. One roller coaster will leave passengers weightless before a 110-foot plunge under a bridge and into two underground trenches. For tots, the Sunday funnies will come alive in **Toon Lagoon,** and beloved **Dr. Seuss** characters will star in rides, restaurants, and shows. In Jurassic Park, dinosaurs will be so real that they blink and flinch.

Chapter 17

But Wait, There's More

In This Chapter

➤ Sea World

➤ The never-ending World of Disney

➤ Still more theme parks

➤ Other Orlando attractions

➤ Enjoying the outdoors

For most visitors to Central Florida, a theme park vacation begins and ends with Disney, with a trip to Universal Studios thrown in somewhere along the line. But for millions of people each year who just can't get enough of theme parks, the Orlando area has still more to whet their appetites. The most prominent of these is Sea World, home of Shamu the killer whale. But dozens of lesser-known parks also compete for tourist dollars. Orlando even boasts some attractions that kids *won't* like.

Sea World

Sea World (☎ **407/351-3600;** Web site www.seaworld.com) focuses on natural discovery more than on thrill rides (although it does have its share of exciting rides, including a major roller coaster, unveiled in 1997). More than 200 acres of splashy, educational fun beckon the family to learn about the sea and its creatures. Shamu the killer whale, and Klondike and Snow, the polar bears in the Wild Arctic section, are huge crowd pleasers. So are the many wading and feeding pools where you can get up close and personal with aquatic animals of all kinds.

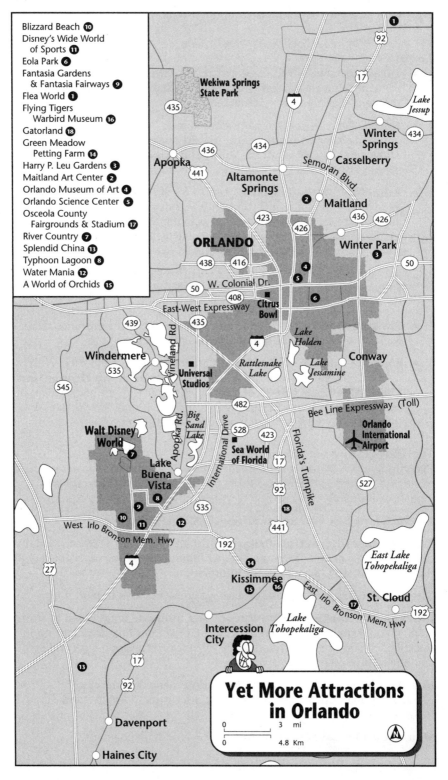

Blizzard Beach ⑩
Disney's Wide World
  of Sports ⑪
Eola Park ⑥
Fantasia Gardens
  & Fantasia Fairways ⑨
Flea World ❶
Flying Tigers
  Warbird Museum ⑯
Gatorland ⑱
Green Meadow
  Petting Farm ⑭
Harry P. Leu Gardens ❸
Maitland Art Center ❷
Orlando Museum of Art ❹
Orlando Science Center ❺
Osceola County
  Fairgrounds & Stadium ⑰
River Country ❼
Splendid China ⑬
Typhoon Lagoon ❽
Water Mania ⑫
A World of Orchids ⑮

Wekiwa Springs
State Park

Lake
Jessup

Winter
Springs

Casselberry

Semoran Blvd.

Apopka

Altamonte
Springs

Maitland

ORLANDO

Winter Park

Windermere

Universal
Studios

Lake
Holden

Conway

Rattlesnake
Lake

Lake
Jessamine

Citrus
Bowl

East-West Expressway

W. Colonial Dr.

Walt Disney
World

Vineland Rd

Apopka Rd.

Big
Sand
Lake

International Drive

Sea World
of Florida

Bee Line Expressway (Toll)

Orlando
International
Airport

Florida's Turnpike

Lake
Buena
Vista

West Irlo Bronson Mem. Hwy

East Lake
Tohopekaliga

Kissimmee

St. Cloud

East Irlo Bronson Mem. Hwy

Intercession
City

Lake
Tohopekaliga

Yet More Attractions
in Orlando

Davenport

0   3   mi

0   4.8 Km

Haines City

Logistics

➤ **Directions.** Sea World is located at 7007 Sea World Dr. Take I-4 to the Bee Line Expressway west (also known as State Road 528). Then follow the signs. The route is well marked.

➤ **Hours.** The park is open daily from 9am to 7pm, later in summer and on holidays, when nightly fireworks extravaganzas light up the sky. Allow a full day to see all the shows and exhibits; a 2-day pass is an excellent value and you won't run out of things to do.

➤ **Admission.** Park admission is $42.15 for everyone over age 10, and $33.95 for children ages 3 through 9. A 2-day pass costs $48.60 for adults and $41.95 for children. Tax is extra. Discover, MasterCard, and Visa are accepted. Discounts are available for AAA members, the disabled, seniors, and military personnel.

Sea World offers a pass valid for 2 years for $99.95 adults and $89.95 children. A 2-year pass that also includes unlimited admission to Busch Gardens is $149.95 adults and $139.95 children.

➤ **Parking** is $5 for cars, $7 for RVs. Take a tram to the entrance, or walk. *Make a note of the section where you left the car.*

➤ **Food.** Restaurants and food kiosks are found around the park. With reservations, you can see the **Aloha Polynesian Luau Dinner and Show** (☎ **407/351-3600** or 800/227-8048) at 6:15pm nightly. For adults over age 12 it's $29.95; ages 8 through 12 pay $19.95; ages 3 through 7 pay $9.95. Tax will be added to all prices.

Top Rides, Shows & Attractions

Everything in Sea World is suitable for children and adults of all ages except where indicated below. We have listed the best shows and attractions in alphabetical order.

Baywatch at Sea World is a roaring-good boat and stunt show.

The Dolphin Interaction Program. For an additional $125 each, adults can don a wet suit and get into a tank with dolphins. Admissions are very limited; call ☎ **407/363-2380** for information.

The Golden Dragon Acrobats stars sea lions that love to ham it up.

Journey to Atlantis is a new water-coaster thrill ride set to debut in spring 1998. It could frighten children under age 8 or 9. Your boat is caught up in unexplained currents and, in a final battle between the good guys and evil, you'll nose-dive 60 feet into a tidal wave.

Key West at Sea World is an entire section themed to the colorful, quirky island at Florida's tip. See the entertainers, sea turtles, dolphins, and stingrays.

Manatees: The Last Generation is heart-rendingly poignant.

The Mickey Finn Show features foot-stompin' ragtime.

The Penguin Encounter takes you into the chilly, silly world of strutting, swimming penguins in their best tuxedos.

The Polar Expedition Tour is a 1-hour tour behind the scenes to see the Sea World Penguin Research Facility and backstage at Wild Arctic. It's of primary interest to adults and older children.

Sharks! invites guests to get a behind-the-scenes view of sharks, their food, and their care.

Terrors of the Deep introduces visitors to sharks, eels, poisonous fish, and other ocean life that can kill you.

Dollars & Sense

The **Orlando FlexTicket** is a $94.95 pass good for 7 consecutive days at Universal Studios Florida, Sea World of Florida, and Wet 'n Wild. For $125.95, the FlexTicket buys 10 consecutive days and includes Busch Gardens Tampa. If these attractions figure heavily into your plans, this may be a good deal.

The Never-Ending World of Disney

In addition to the major theme parks described in chapters 11 through 15, Walt Disney World contains several smaller theme parks and attractions. In any city besides Orlando, these would all be top attractions for kids. But in the world's most fun place, they can get lost in the shuffle. Note than annual passes are available to the three Disney water parks, at a cost equivalent to about 3 days' admission.

Disney's Wide World of Sports™

This complex has a 7,500-seat baseball stadium and facilities for more than 30 sports including soccer, softball, basketball, and track and field. It's the spring training home of the Atlanta Braves and the training site of the Harlem Globetrotters. One world-class championship event or another will probably be going on during your visit.

If you're driving, take the Magic Kingdom (no. 25) exit off I-4 and follow signs to Disney's Wide World of Sports, which is between U.S. 192 and Osceola Parkway. If you're staying in WDW, take the bus to Blizzard Beach, and then transfer to Wide World of Sports.

General admission is $8 adults and $6.75 children ages 3 through 9. For special events, ticket prices will vary. Buy tickets from Ticketmaster at ☎ **407/839-3900.** Information is available at ☎ **407/363-6600.**

Blizzard Beach

This is one of three water parks in the Disney enterprise. Like the others, Blizzard Beach has plenty for the entire family, from ankle-deep waters for toddlers to the most shivery thrill rides for teenagers.

Of all the parks, this one has the most thrills and, because it's the newest, it fills up early in the day with people who have "done" the others. Arrive early to avoid long waits. When the park gets full, no new guests are admitted.

Beach towels and lockers are available at added cost.

Cross Country Creek is this park's lazy river, floating you on an inner tube around the park. The relaxing route takes a half hour or more through sunlight, shade, and a dark cave. **Mount Gushmore** is laced with speed slides and flumes including the Slush Gusher, Snow Stormer, and Summit Plummet. On the **Toboggan River,** guests race head first down an eight-lane water slide. **Run-Off Rapids** is an inner tube run that sends you down four flumes, sometimes through dark passages. **Ski-Patrol Training Camp** is aimed at preteens, who can swing on a rope, take the T-bar to drop into the water, and pick their way through the ice floes.

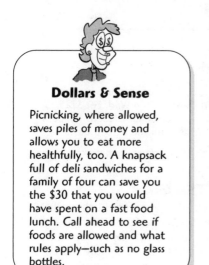

Dollars & Sense

Picnicking, where allowed, saves piles of money and allows you to eat more healthfully, too. A knapsack full of deli sandwiches for a family of four can save you the $30 that you would have spent on a fast food lunch. Call ahead to see if foods are allowed and what rules apply—such as no glass bottles.

Buses to Blizzard Beach are available throughout WDW. If you're driving, you'll find Blizzard Beach opposite Disney-MGM Studios. It's bounded by Osceola Parkway, World Drive, and the extension of Buena Vista Drive.

It's open daily from 10am to 5pm, later in summer. Admission is $26.45 for adults and $20.70 for ages 3 through 9.

River Country

This sweetly nostalgic, low-key attraction is themed after Tom Sawyer's ol' swimmin' hole. There's an Ol' Wadin' Hole for younger children. There's also a nature walk and playground. It's a lot more nostalgic and natural in appeal than Blizzard Beach, without all the razzle dazzle.

Light meals are available at Pop's Place. Towels and lockers are for rent at added cost. Take your own lunch and use the picnic tables.

Slippery Slide Falls are two 16-foot slides that send you crashing straight down into the **Up Stream Plunge. Whoop 'n Holler Hollow** consists of two water slides where people, not logs, speed down the flume to the lumber mill. **White Water Rapids** gives you a good dunking aboard rubber tubes that run the rapids and splash into the swimming hole.

From within WDW, take a bus from the Transportation and Ticket Center. Or take the boat from near the gates of the Magic Kingdom. By car, follow directions for Fort Wilderness and use its parking area.

Hours are daily from 10am to 7pm most of the year, and later in peak summer days. Admission for adults is $17.95; for children ages 3 through 9, it's $14.50. Prices include tax. Call ☎ **407/824-4321** for more information.

Typhoon Lagoon

Thrill-seekers will find it hard to choose between Typhoon Lagoon and Blizzard Beach, but that doesn't mean the whole family won't enjoy Typhoon Lagoon. There's plenty here for everybody, from heart-pumping speed slides to little rides for little squirts. Come here for one of the world's largest wave pools and for the floating Castaway Creek.

The gates here close when capacity is reached, so get here as early as 9am on peak days. You can't bring your own flotation devices, but you can bring your own food. Picnic tables are provided. Light meals are also available at two restaurants, and a beach bar sells beer and soda.

Castaway Creek is a cool and captivating float down a 2,100-foot river. **Ketchakiddie Creek** is for younger children under 4 feet tall. It's filled with waterfalls and wonderment designed for fun and happy squeals. **Shark Reef** is a 15-minute snorkel among real fish. Snorkel gear is provided, and you'll be told how to use it. **Typhoon Lagoon** is a huge lagoon complete with big waves for surfing. White-water rides come in three types: **Keelhaul Falls** is winding and spinning; **Mayday Falls** and the **Humungo Kowabunga** is the steepest and scariest. Families ride **Gangplank Falls** together on large tubes.

Direct transportation is available from some WDW resorts. From all other points, go to the Transportation and Ticket Center and transfer for Typhoon Lagoon. By car, take the Epcot/Downtown Disney exit. The park is bounded by Route 536 and Buena Vista Drive.

Hours are daily from 10am to 5pm, later in summer. Admission for adults is $27.51; for children ages 3 through 9, it's $21.73. Prices include tax. Call ☎ **407/824-4321** for more info.

Fantasia Gardens & Fantasia Fairways

These two 18-hole miniature golf courses are designed for riotous good times. Any family that likes miniature golf will be wowed by this little attraction with its Fantasia characters, sound effects, and surprises.

Both courses are on Epcot Resorts Boulevard (☎ **407/560-8760**), across from the Walt Disney World Swan. They're open Sunday through Thursday from 10am until 10pm, until 11pm on Friday and Saturday. It's $9 for adults, $8 for ages 3 through 9 for each course; you can play a second round for half price.

Extra! Extra!

If you like oddball stuff...Ripley's Believe It Or Not displays the weird, wonderful, and wickedly funny in a building that looks like it's falling into a Florida sinkhole. See dinosaurs, a piece of the Berlin Wall, shrunken heads, a Rolls Royce built from a million match sticks, and the world's largest tire. It's located at 8201 International Dr. (☎ **407/345-0501**). Hours are 9am to 11pm daily. (Allow 1 to 2 hours to see everything.) Ample parking is free. Admission is $9.55 for everyone over 13; $6.55 for children ages 4 through 12. American Express, Discover, MasterCard, and Visa are accepted.

Theme Parks, Theme Parks, Theme Parks & Theme Parks

Could there possibly be any more kinds of theme parks in Orlando? Well, now that you mention it, yes. Dozens of other companies seeking to capitalize on the Orlando audience are all lurking about town, hoping that you'll choose them as a change of pace from the big-name attractions. They are listed here in alphabetical order.

Gatorland

This is one of those cornball attractions that started with a pen of alligators just after World War II. Bring a picnic lunch, watch a show or two, ride the Gatorland Express Train around the grounds, and learn how gators and crocs live and breed. Gators are raised here for their meat and leather, both of which are available in the gift shop.

The park is located at 14501 S. Orange Blossom Trail (U.S. 441) between the Osceola Parkway and Hunter's Creek Boulevard (☎ **800/393-JAWS** or 407/855-5496). It's open daily from 9am to dusk. Admission is $13.95 for ages 13 and up, $9.95 for seniors over age 65, $8.95 for children ages 9 to 12, and $6.48 for children ages 3 through 9. However, one child is free for each paying adult. American Express, MasterCard, and Visa are accepted. Parking is free.

Water Mania

This is a smaller, quieter park than Wet 'n Wild (see below), just the place to spend a family day to beat the heat. While young adults may prefer wilder parks, this one offers plenty for everyone in the family including the small fry.

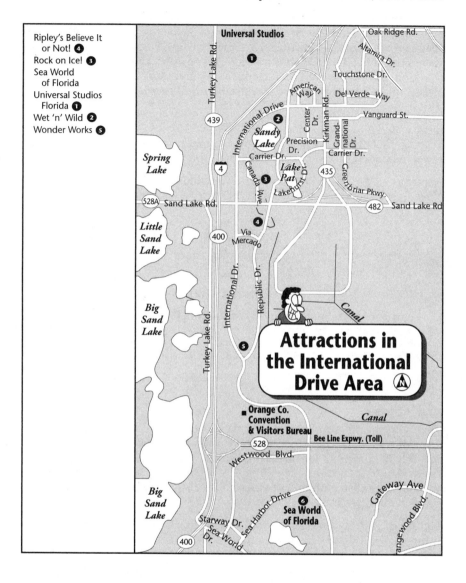

Universal Studios

Oak Ridge Rd.

Altamira Dr.

Touchstone Dr.

Del Verde Way

Vanguard St.

American Way

Turkey Lake Rd.

International Drive

Center Dr.

Kirkman Rd.

Grand national Dr.

439

2

Sandy Lake

Precision Dr.

Carrier Dr.

Carrier Dr.

Spring Lake

4

3

Lake Pat

435

Canada Ave.

Lakehurst Dr.

Greenbriar Pkwy.

528A Sand Lake Rd.

482 Sand Lake Rd

Little Sand Lake

400

Via Mercado

Big Sand Lake

Turkey Lake Rd.

International Dr.

Republic Dr.

5

Canal

Attractions in the International Drive Area

■ **Orange Co. Convention & Visitors Bureau**

Canal

Bee Line Expwy. (Toll)

528

Westwood Blvd.

Big Sand Lake

6
Sea World of Florida

Starway Dr.

Sea Harbor Drive

Gateway Ave

Orangewood Blvd.

400

Sea World Dr.

Light meals are available, or you can bring a picnic to eat on the tables in a shady grove. Float the lazy river, dare the speeding flumes, or take a white-water adventure. **The Abyss** sends you plummeting and spiraling through the darkness into the cold, wet deep. There's also miniature golf, a video arcade, and a rainforest-theme playground for little ones.

Water Mania is located at 6073 W. Irlo Bronson Memorial Hwy. (U.S. 192), just east of I-4, in Kissimmee (☎ **407/396-2626**). It's open from January to February daily from 11am to 5pm; other times it's open 9:30am to 7pm, with extended hours on some weekends during spring break.

Admission is $23.95 for adults, $17.95 for children 3 through 9. From November to February, admission is half price after 3pm. Parking is $4.

Extra! Extra!

If you want to take a romantic stroll...Eola Park surrounds a lovely little lake where people jog, picnic on the grass, attend concerts in the band shell, and watch the illuminated fountain at night. It's located between Rosalind and Robinson streets. Call ☎ **407/246-2287** for more info.

Wet 'n Wild

This is one of the world's best water parks, an Orlando fixture since 1977. There is endless fun here for families, thrill-seekers, and tiny tots, but be sure to study the brochure for ride ratings so that you don't get in over your head. Plan to spend a full day. (If you've followed our advice so far, your vacation is probably up to 35 full days.) It's also a great place to spend a warm summer evening.

Light meals are available in the park, and picnic tables are provided if you bring your own food. No glass containers are permitted (not even baby food jars); bag checks are made as you enter the park.

New for spring 1998 is the **Hydra Fighter** in which guests sit in swings equipped with water cannons that control how high and fast the swings go. **Fuji Flyer** is a pulse-pounding water toboggan; **Der Stuka** is for daredevils. **The Wild One,** in which two people are towed around the lake in big tubes, is another highlight.

The park is located at 6200 International Dr. (☎ **407/351-1800**; www.wetnwild.com). It's open daily, but hours vary widely throughout the year so call ahead. Admission is $25.95 for ages 10 and older, $20.95 for children ages 3 through 9, $13 for seniors. Note that Wet 'n Wild participates in the FlexTicket. Prices do not include tax. Parking is $4.

Wonder Works

You're lost on an "uncharted island in the Bermuda Triangle" where scientists study strange phenomena in an upside-down warehouse topped by a mysterious mansion. It's educational, but also loads of fun with its experiments, illusions, bubbles, earthquake, broadcast studio, and thundering displays. Have lunch in the Food Court.

It's located in Pointe Orlando, on International Drive (☎ **407/352-0411;** www.Wonderworks@totcon.com). It's open daily from 10am to 11pm; hours may be extended during peak periods. Admission for adults ages 13 through 54 is $12.95; seniors 55 and older and children ages 4 through 12 are charged $9.95; ages 4 and under enter free. Prices do not include tax. Parking is free and abundant.

Extra! Extra!

If you want to go ice skating...Rock on Ice! Ice Skating Arena is the coolest spot in town. Skate to music played by a DJ, and then rest while you snack in the restaurant or play the video arcade. It's located at 7500 Canada Ave. in Orlando (☎ **407/352-9878**); open daily, though hours vary seasonally. Admission is $6; skate rental is $2.

Rodeos, Science Centers & Other Attractions Kids Will Like

It's day 6 of your vacation and you're totally theme-parked out. The sight of another roller coaster is enough to make you barf, and the thought of negotiating all the crowds and traffic is already making you exhausted. Still, the kids won't be content with sitting by the pool with a good book, so you've got to do something with them. If you can't bear another theme park, here are some other ideas that the kids will like.

Green Meadows Petting Farm

Pack a picnic and make a day of it at a 40-acre farm where a pony ride, miniature train ride, and hayride are included in the admission. Make the rounds of the 200 animals to pet baby animals, feed friendly lambs and chickens, and see up close real llamas, turkeys, goats, pigs, donkeys, and many more farmyard friends. Everyone gets a chance to milk a cow. It's a joy for all ages and a must for children ages 8 and under.

It's located at 1368 S. Poinciana Blvd. (just off U.S. 192 between Polynesian Boulevard and FL 535; ☎ **407/846-0770**). Hours are daily from 9:30am to 4pm; last tour is at 4pm. Admission is $13 for everyone over age 2. Parking is free.

Flying Tigers Warbird Museum

This is a working restoration facility where onlookers are welcome. It's popular with current and ex-flyers and their kids or grandkids. See dozens of airplanes representing almost every era in aviation history in various states of repair and despair. One of the rarer planes displayed is a Paisacki Hup 1. Sometimes a 1930s-era biplane is here to offer airplane rides.

It's located at 231 N. Hoagland Blvd., off U.S. 192, the next traffic light west of Armstrong Boulevard and Yates Road (☎ **407/933-1942**). Hours vary seasonally but are generally 9am to 5pm daily. Admission is $6 for adults, $5 seniors and children ages 6 through 12; children under 6 enter free. Diners Club, MasterCard, and Visa are accepted. Parking is free.

Orlando Science Center

Local parents buy season passes because you can't drag the kids away from the 10 permanent exhibit areas, the planetarium, the ever-changing special exhibits, and the interactive displays for all ages. Let your kids build a bridge. Fire a laser. Touch an alligator. Play math games. Dig for dinosaur bones. Single-handedly lift a Volkswagen. Star in a movie. Afterward, you can all have lunch in the pleasant cafe overlooking Loch Haven Park.

The Science Center is located north of downtown at 777 E. Princeton St. (☎ **407/514-2000** or 888/OSC4FUN; www.osc.org). The Culture Quest shuttle (☎ **407/855-6434**) serves the museum and other cultural attractions from five hubs in the tourist corridor. Hours are Monday to Thursday from 9am to 5pm, Friday and Saturday from 9am to 9pm, and Sundays from noon to 5pm. Admission for adults is $8, seniors $7, children $6.50 ages 3 through 11. If you want to catch a CineDome film, the charge for adults is $6, seniors $5.50, children $4.50. Parking in the garage across the street is $3.50. Outdoor parking is free. MasterCard and Visa are accepted.

Extra! Extra!

If you love gardens… don't miss **A World of Orchids** at 2501 Old Lake Wilson Rd. (County Road 545) off U.S. 192 (☎ **407/396-1887**). Orchids bloom everywhere in this lavish attraction: under waterfalls, alongside ponds filled with flashing goldfish, in rare ferns, and tangled among rustling bamboo. Take a nature walk through the tropical beauty. Horticulturists give guided tours at 11am and 3pm. Hours are 9:30am to 5:30pm daily except New Year's Day, 4th of July, Thanksgiving, and Christmas. Admission is $8.95 for those over age 15; seniors $7.95; ages 15 and under enter free. Parking is free.

Rodeos at the Kissimmee Sports Arena

Historically, Florida has been one of the nation's major cattle centers, and its cowboys are among the best. The Silver Spurs Rodeo, held spring and fall, is one of the nation's oldest rodeos. Everything you want to see in a down-and-dirty western rodeo is here: bareback riding, bull riding, calf roping, and barrel racing. Serious competitors vie for prizes and glory.

The arena is at 1010 Sulls Lane in Kissimmee (☎ **407/933-0020**). Tickets for Silver Spurs spring and fall are available through your local Ticketmaster up to 2 months in advance, and they usually run $10 for adults and $5 for children under age 12. Parking is free.

Museums, Gardens & Other Attractions Kids Will Hate

If you're not traveling with kids and your stay in Orlando has made your ears hurt from all the screaming and whining, you might consider some of these attractions. They're not necessarily for adults only, but the only kids we know who like doing these kinds of things are weird.

Harry P. Leu Gardens

Fifty graciously groomed acres on Lake Rowena are the home of magnificent azaleas in spring, breathtaking camellias in winter, as well as orchids and century-old live oaks festooned with Spanish moss. Relax in the gazebo, walk the paths, and tour the restored Leu home. Allow at least 2 hours, less if you don't take the house tour and more if you are a flower fancier or photographer.

The gardens are located at 1920 N. Forest Ave., between Nebraska Street and Corrine Drive (☎ **407/246-2620**). Take I-4 east to Exit 43 (Princeton Street), and then east on Princeton, right on Mills Avenue, and left on Virginia Drive. Just after the road curves, be prepared to turn left into the gardens. Open daily except Christmas from 9am to 5pm. Admission is $4 for adults, $1 for children ages 6 through 16. MasterCard and Visa are accepted. Parking is free.

Maitland Art Center

Come here for the rather quirky arts, a placid parklike setting in a pleasant old neighborhood, and an excellent gift shop. Still a colony for resident artists, the Center began in 1937 as a research studio and gallery founded by American artist Jules André Smith. Unless you're an avid art fancier, the exhibits here won't take more than a half hour.

It's located at 231 W. Packwood Ave. in Maitland (☎ **407/539-2181**). Take U.S. 17–92 north. Just past Lee Road, turn left on Maitland, and then left on Packwood Avenue. It's open Monday to Friday from 10am to 4:30pm, Saturday and Sunday from noon to 4:30pm. Admission is free.

Orlando Museum of Art

The Orlando Museum of Art has improved a lot in recent years with an expansion that allows it to host traveling exhibits such as the blockbuster "Imperial Tombs of China." Permanent collections are American, pre-Columbian, and African art. Art Encounter has hands-on fun and learning for children. Give it at least 2 hours. The gift shop is one of the city's best places to find meaningful souvenirs.

The museum is at 2416 N. Mills Ave., in Loch Haven Park, off U.S. 17–92 (☎ **407/896-4231**). Take I-4 east to Princeton Street, Exit 43, and follow signs to Loch Haven Park. Hours are Tuesday to Saturday from 9am to 5pm, Sunday from noon to 5pm except major holidays. Admission is $4 for adults, $2 for children ages 4 through 11. Special exhibits may cost more and require advance ticketing. American Express, MasterCard, and Visa are accepted. Parking is free.

Bet You Didn't Know

If you've ever wanted to swim in the Fountain of Youth... well, it's in Florida. **DeLeon Springs State Recreation Area** may be the spot described by Ponce de Leon. Sprawling grounds graced with centuries-old live oaks draped in Spanish moss surround a natural spring where you can swim in water that stays 72° all year. Bring a picnic or eat in the Old Spanish Sugar Mill, where diners cook their own whole-grain pancakes on grills set into the tables. The entrance is at 600 Ponce de Leon Blvd., DeLeon Springs. It's open during daylight hours; admission is $3.25 per carload. Take I-4 east to the second DeLand exit (U.S. 44), and then follow U.S. 17 north to DeLeon Springs and watch for the turn-off to the park just past the bank. Call ☎ **904/985-4212** for more info.

Splendid China

Stroll through 5,000 years of Chinese history and culture along a 10,000-mile journey. See many of China's most famous landmarks in miniature: the Great Wall, Imperial Palace, Tombs of Sun Yat Sen and Ghengis Khan, and the Buddha of a Thousand Arms and a Thousand Eyes. Everybody loves the "The Magical Snow Tiger Adventure," which plays daily except Wednesday at 11:45am and 2:15pm. "The Mysterious Kingdom of the Orient," an acrobat spectacular that is the largest show of its kind outside China, plays daily except Monday.

It's located at 3000 Splendid China Blvd., off U.S. 192, 2 miles west of WDW's main entrance and 3 miles west of I-4 Exit 25-B (☎ **800/244-6226** or 407/397-8800). It opens daily at 9:30am; closings vary seasonally. Admission is $28.90 for ages 13 and older, $18.20 for children ages 5 through

12; ages 4 and under enter free. Prices include tax. American Express, MasterCard, and Visa are accepted.

Admission to "The Mysterious Kingdom of the Orient" only, Tuesday to Sunday evenings, is $16 per person. For dinner in the Golden Peacock Theater plus the show, the price is $34.95 per adult and $19.95 per child. Taxes are additional; gratuity is included. Dining is before or after the show.

Get Out! Enjoying the Outdoors

Within 1½ hours of Orlando are eight state parks, three national parks, and countless forests, natural springs, and gardens. Admission to state parks and state recreational areas (with a few exceptions) is $3.25 per car (up to eight people). Hours are generally dawn to dusk.

Also remember that only 6,000 acres of Walt Disney World are developed, leaving more than about 30,000 acres as wilderness, where you can fish, boat, ride horseback, bicycle, hike, or canoe. Call ☎ **407/824-4321** for more information.

Walt Disney World, with its many man-made lakes and lagoons, owns the nation's largest fleet of pleasure boats. At the **Walt Disney World Village Marina,** you can rent everything from Water Sprites to pontoon boats. For information, call ☎ **407/828-2204.**

A-Dora Day Trip (☎ 407/331-0991) is a 100-mile round trip by boat between Tavares and Silver Springs, through jungle-lined waters once used as background for the filming of Tarzan movies. Rates range from $10 to $100 per person.

Aquatic Wonders Tours (☎ 407/ 931-6247) can take you boating on Lake Tohopekeliga (Lake Toho for short) to see water birds, starlight wonders, fish, and historic sites. Trips are from $18.95 adults and from $12.95 children age 12 and under.

Bet You Didn't Know

Kissimmee is the spring training home of the **Houston Astros**, and if you're here in April, you can see the big leaguers play in an intimate setting. For information on their schedule and how to see an exhibition game, call ☎ **800/831-1844.**

Blue Springs State Park, on U.S. 17–92, about 45 minutes north of WDW (☎ **904/775-3663**), is a winter home for manatees. Here you can swim in a crystal spring that stays 72° all year, picnic overlooking the St. Johns River, and walk the boardwalk into the bush.

St. Johns River Cruises and Tours are narrated 2-hour wildlife tours of the river that was Central Florida's first highway. Before roads were built, paddlewheelers brought passengers deep into Florida on this deep, jungle-rimmed river. Captain Bob Hopkins is an area native who knows where to find nesting birds, wild boar, marshmallow in bloom, and other secrets of

215

nature. Boats leave from the Osteen Bridge on State Road 415, Sanford, about 45 minutes north of WDW. Reservations are required; call ☎ **407/330-1612.** Prices are $12 adults, $10 aged 60 and older, $6 age 12 and under.

The *Rivership Romance* (☎ **800/423-7401**) plies the St. Johns River on 3- and 4-hour luncheon or dinner-dance cruises. The shores of this river were also backdrops for Tarzan movies. Reservations are essential.

Canaveral National Seashore is located just 45 minutes east of Orlando and it's perfect for a day's outing. Adjoining the Kennedy Space Center is this 24-mile strand of golden beaches, creamy surf, and abundant bird life incorporating the Merritt Island National Wildlife Refuge and countless picnic areas, swimming spots, marked trails, and overlooks. Call ☎ **407/267-1110** for more info. Take the Bee Line Expressway east, and then head north on I-95 and east on FL 406. The entrance is 7 miles east of Titusville, about 1 hour from Orlando. Admission is $5 per carload, with discounts for seniors over age 62.

Captain Charlie's Sightseeing Boat Cruises (☎ **407/343-0200**) glide through the ancient cypress trees of the Dora Canal, a primeval jungle that a 1930s travel writer called the most beautiful mile of water in the world. Fare is $10.

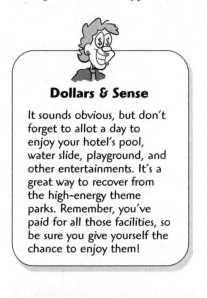

Dollars & Sense

It sounds obvious, but don't forget to allot a day to enjoy your hotel's pool, water slide, playground, and other entertainments. It's a great way to recover from the high-energy theme parks. Remember, you've paid for all those facilities, so be sure you give yourself the chance to enjoy them!

DeLeon Springs State Recreation Area (☎ **904/985-4212**), just off U.S. 17 north of DeLand, is thought to be the spring described by Ponce de Leon as the Fountain of Youth. Picnic under huge live oaks and swim in the sweetwater spring.

Winter Park Scenic Boat Tours (☎ **407/644-4056**) wind through tiny canals that join the sparkling lakes that lie just north of downtown Orlando. Trips and prices vary. Reservations are essential. Boats leave from the eastern foot of Morse Boulevard on Lake Osceola, Winter Park.

Hitting the Links

There are more than 100 golf courses within a 45-minute drive of downtown. Walt Disney World alone offers 99 holes of golf! (Their most famous hazard is a sand trap on Magnolia Course's 6th hole in the shape of Mickey Mouse.) All of the Disney courses are open to the general public and offer pro shops, equipment rentals, and instruction. For tee times and information, call ☎ **407/824-2270** up to 7 days in advance. (Disney resort guests can reserve up to 30 days in advance.) Call ☎ **407/W-DISNEY** for information about golf packages.

Out-of-This-World Attractions

After a few days in Orlando, you may start to think that this area has just about anything you could want to see and do. So if an attraction is going to convince somebody to drive 1 or 2 hours outside Orlando, it has to have something that Orlando doesn't. As the number of Worlds in the world continues to grow, that seems ever less likely. Still, there are a few places that might merit a special trip, even though they do require that you spend some portion of your day driving to and from them. They are listed alphabetically.

Busch Gardens Tampa Bay

Even though it's 1 hour west of Orlando's attractions area, Busch Gardens is a big part of the theme park bombast that makes up a Central Florida vacation—especially now that the 10-day version of the Orlando FlexTicket buys unlimited time here and in three Orlando theme parks.

A living zoo where animals appear to run free, this park is themed to the many areas of Africa: the Serengeti Plain, with its herds of animals; Nairobi, with its apes; The Congo, with its rare white Bengal tigers; Timbuktu, with its sandstorm ride and crafters; Stanleyville, with its crashing rides; Egypt, with the world's tallest inverted roller coaster; and Land of the Dragons, with a fairytale setting and rides just for tots.

Tanganyika Tidal Wave and **Stanley Falls** are splashy fun for the whole family—vigorous but not terrifying. For pure terror, ride **Montu,** the inverted roller coaster. For a calming ride and a good view of the animals, ride the **monorail, sky ride,** or **Trans-Veldt Railway.**

Extra! Extra!

If you want real adventure in the real Florida, but you'd rather leave the details up to someone else... Adventures in Florida will tailor a day, overnights, or a week in the outdoors: cookouts, camping, horseback rides, canoe trips, fishing, snorkeling, airboating, historic tours, you name it. Call them at ☎ **407/331-0991** or visit them on-line at www.discover-florida.com. The office is open daily 8:30am to 5:30pm. Prices vary according to the trip, but the average price is $75. American Express, Discover, MasterCard, and Visa are accepted. The staff is small and your calls may be answered by a machine. Start your planning before leaving home.

Disney's Animal Kingdom, which opens in mid-1998, is obviously seeking to take a bite out of the nature-loving theme-park audience. But since Disney has remained very hush-hush about what kind of attractions its new animal park will contain, we won't know whether Busch Gardens will continue to figure prominently in many people's itinerary.

Allot at least 1 full day for the rides, gardens, animal watching, dining, and shopping here. Dress for hot weather and expect to get soaked on some of the rides.

Busch Gardens is located at 3000 E. Busch Blvd. at McKinley Drive/North 40th Street, in Tampa (☎ **813/987-5283**). From Orlando, take I-4 west to the U.S. 41 exit, and then go right (north) on FL 583. The route to Busch Gardens is well marked. It's open daily from 9:30am to 6pm, later in peak periods and special events. Admission is $42.85 for adults, $36.60 for children ages 3 through 9, all plus tax. Discover, MasterCard, and Visa are accepted. Parking is $3.

Cypress Gardens

Allot at least 1 full day for browsing this wonderland of bedding plants, blooming shrubs, ancient cypress trees festooned with Spanish moss, and the hoop-skirted belles that have been a park fixture since the 1940s. It's been located in nearby Winter Haven since 1936 but it has grown with the years and it remains one of Florida's premier attractions.

You can bring your own lunch and picnic at one of the tables, or try the **Crossroads Restaurant** or **Lakeview Terrace.** The gift shops here are exceptionally nice.

Simply strolling the gardens is an enormous pleasure, but Cypress Gardens also offers a slow-moving ride, **Island in the Sky,** that lifts you high over the gardens. The water-ski spectaculars are funny, entertaining, and as stunning as an Olympics event. **Carousel Cove** is a charming little area of kiddy rides and games in a shady, parklike setting. **Cypress Junction** is an elaborate model railroad that will mesmerize train fanciers. Old-time Florida visitors will enjoy **Cypress Roots,** with its displays and photographs through the years at Cypress Gardens. **Electric boats** ghost through the park, passing one gorgeous vista after another. **Moscow on Ice Live!** and **Varieté International** are fast-paced shows starring world-class performers. **Wings of Wonder** is one of the nation's best butterfly conservatories.

Cypress Gardens is about 40 miles southwest of Walt Disney World, on FL 540 at Cypress Gardens Boulevard, in Winter Haven (☎ **800/282-2123** or 941/324-2111). Take I-4 west to U.S. 27, go south to FL 540, and then go west. If you don't have a car, ask at your hotel about excursions to Cypress Gardens. Hours are daily from 9:30am to 9pm, with later hours for special events. Adults are charged $29.95; children ages 6 through 17 pay $19.95; seniors pay $24.95. Ask about special promotions in which a paying adult may bring one child free. Discover, MasterCard, and Visa are accepted.

Daytona USA

Adjacent to the Daytona International Speedway is a state-of-the-art, interactive blockbuster that is a must for race fans. Allow at least half a day. You'll see winning cars, compete in a pit stop contest, see a spectacular IMAX film, and tour the speedway track, which is banked so steeply you'll be astounded. It's open daily except Christmas from 9am to 7pm (later during special events). Admission is $12 for adults, $10 for seniors, $6 for children ages 6 through 12, and free for kids under age 6. MasterCard and Visa are accepted. Parking is free.

Daytona is about 50 miles east of Orlando, so plan on an all-day outing, perhaps with a couple of hours on the famous hard-packed sands of **Daytona Beach.** To get there, take I-4 east to Daytona, and then east on U.S. 92 to the Speedway. For information on this and other Daytona attractions, call ☎ **904/255-0415** or check them on-line at www.travelfile.com/get?dbacvb.

Fantasy of Flight

If you're an aviation buff, head for **Fantasy of Flight,** which is part museum, part thrill ride (you can fly a simulator in a dogfight), and partly a nostalgic return to the airfields of World War II. Superbly designed, this is the largest private collection of vintage aircraft in the world. There's something here for everyone, even little planes for tots to "fly." Have lunch in the 1950s-style airport diner. It's located at Exit 21 on I-4, halfway between Orlando and Tampa. From the exit, turn north and go a half mile on FL 559. Call ☎ **941/984-3500,** ext. 221, for more info. Parking is free. It's open every day from 9am to 5pm, later in peak seasons. Admission for adults and ages 13 and older is $10.95; children ages 5 through 12 are charged $7.95; seniors pay $9.95; children age 4 and under are free. Ask about the annual pass and after-hours simulator flying. Add $7.95 to fly the simulators, which are available to ages 8 and older. MasterCard and Visa are accepted.

Extra! Extra!

If you like family fun at à la carte prices...Fun World at Flea World, on Highway 17–92 in nearby Sanford (☎ **407/330-1792**), is an old-fashioned amusement park with 50 rides and attractions plus 18 holes of miniature golf, batting cages, a video arcade, and three go-kart tracks. Live entertainment plays in the pavilion. It's all part of Flea World, which calls itself America's largest flea market, so one parent can shop while the other plays with the kids. It's open Friday to Sunday from 10am to midnight. Admission and parking are free.

Kennedy Space Center & Canaveral National Seashore

The Kennedy Space Center is about an hour's drive east of Orlando, in Cocoa Beach. There's always something going on here and it's always world news, as fresh and relevant as tomorrow's headlines.

Once you get here, take the motor coach tour and guided walking tour so that you don't miss a thing. Then wander around on your own. Catch the films in the back-to-back twin IMAX theaters and explore the new Launch

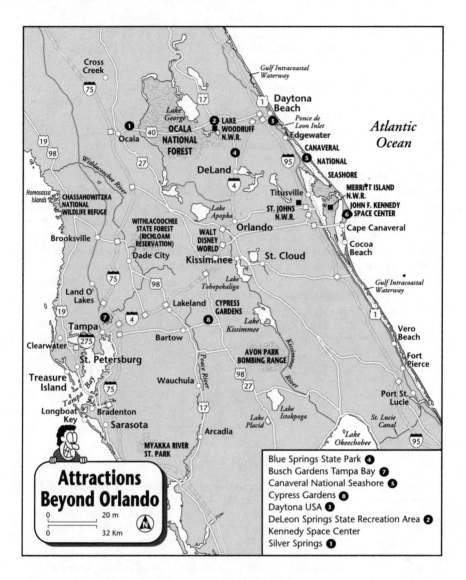

Cross
Creek

Gulf Intracoastal
Waterway

Daytona
Beach

Lake
George

*Ponce de
Leon Inlet*

❶ OCALA **❷ LAKE
WOODRUFF
N.W.R.**

Ocala **NATIONAL
FOREST**

Edgewater

*Atlantic
Ocean*

CANAVERAL

❺ NATIONAL

DeLand

SEASHORE

MERRITT ISLAND
N.W.R.

Titusville

*Lake
Apopka*

ST. JOHNS
N.W.R.

**JOHN F. KENNEDY
❻ SPACE CENTER**

WITHLACOOCHEE
STATE FOREST
(RICHLOAM
RESERVATION)

WALT
DISNEY
WORLD

Orlando

Cape Canaveral

Brooksville

Dade City

Kissimmee

St. Cloud

Cocoa
Beach

*Lake
Tohopekaliga*

Land O'
Lakes

Lakeland **CYPRESS
GARDENS**

Gulf Intracoastal
Waterway

Tampa

❽

*Lake
Kissimmee*

Vero
Beach

Clearwater

Bartow

St. Petersburg

**AVON PARK
BOMBING RANGE**

Fort
Pierce

Treasure
Island

Wauchula

Longboat
Key

Bradenton

Sarasota

Arcadia

*Lake
Placid*

*Lake
Istokpoga*

Port St.
Lucie

*St. Lucie
Canal*

**MYAKKA RIVER
ST. PARK**

*⁰Lake
Okeechobee*

Attractions
Beyond Orlando

| 0 | 20 m |
| 0 | 32 Km |

Blue Springs State Park **❹**
Busch Gardens Tampa Bay **❼**
Canaveral National Seashore **❺**
Cypress Gardens **❽**
Daytona USA **❸**
DeLeon Springs State Recreation Area **❷**
Kennedy Space Center
Silver Springs **❶**

Complex 39 Observation Gantry, a 45 foot–high observation deck overlooking the VAB, Launch Control, and the Crawlerway on which shuttles are
transported. A new exhibit focuses on the International Space Station, which
is scheduled to fly July 9, 1998.

To get here, take the Beeline Expressway east to FL 207, and then left and
turn right on FL 405. The entire route is well marked. Just follow the signs to
the Space Center. For more information, call ☎ **407/452-2121.** For information on upcoming launches, call ☎ **407/449-4343.** Admission to the Space
Center is free, but the highly recommended bus tour costs $8 for adults and

$3 for children ages 3 through 11. IMAX movies are $6 for adults and $4 for children. Parking is free. Launches can be viewed free from the surrounding area; tickets to the viewing area in the center are $10 to $15 and they must be picked up 2 days or more before the launch. American Express, MasterCard, and Discover are accepted.

For further information on sightseeing and accommodations in the area, get in touch with the **Cocoa Beach Chamber of Commerce,** 400 Fortenberry Rd., Merritt Island, FL 32952 (☎ **407/633-2100;** www.kscvisitor.com). They'll be happy to answer your questions daily from 9am to dusk (except on Christmas and some launch days).

As we mentioned earlier, **Canaveral National Seashore** (☎ **407/ 267-1110** for information) is also out this way, and perhaps you'd like to catch a couple hours' worth of sun after touring the Space Center. This 24-mile strand of golden beaches is right next door, and it offers spectacular bird watching in addition to the sun and sand. The entrance is 7 miles east of Titusville, about 1 hour from Orlando. Admission is $5 per carload, with discounts for seniors over age 62.

Also in this area is the **U.S. Astronaut Hall of Fame,** 6225 Vectorspace Blvd., in Titusville (☎ **407/269-6100**). Here simulators give you the feel of space flight and aerobatics while you view displays that honor the first 20 American astronauts. In one ride, you can pull 4 Gs. Sit in a full-size space shuttle to see a movie. Reopened in late 1997 as an interactive attraction, the hall of fame is educational as well as one of the best thrill-ride kicks in Florida. It's open daily from 9am to 5pm. Admission is $13.95 for adults and $9.95 for children. American Express, Discover, MasterCard, and Visa are accepted.

Silver Springs

An hour north of Orlando lies Florida's first tourist attraction, where a settler started taking people out in his glass-bottom canoe in 1878. The primeval beauty of the deep, clear spring is still here deep in a lush jungle, but the park also has boffo shows starring Nashville's biggest names. They're included in park admission, which is $29.95 for adults, $20.95 for children (ask about senior discounts). American Express, Discover, MasterCard, and Visa are accepted. The park's entrance is at 5656 E. Silver Springs Blvd., Silver Springs (☎ **352/236-2121**). Take I-75 north to Ocala, and then east on U.S. 40 to the park. It's open every day; hours vary seasonally.

Chapter 18

Charge It!
A Shopper's
Guide to
Orlando

In This Chapter

➤ The lowdown on Orlando's shopping scene

➤ Best buys and great places to browse

On your first trip to Orlando, you may not have thought to schedule time for shopping, but trust us, you'll have plenty of chances to put those credit cards to good use. Orlando has come a long way from the days when roadside vendors sold little more than orange wine, alligator teeth, and cypress knees.

Your kids will probably want T-shirts from each of the theme parks they visit, not to mention Planet Hollywood and the Hard Rock Cafe. Then you have to figure out how many mouse ears, baseball hats, pennants, and stickers you can possibly stuff into your suitcase. Oh, and did we mention what all these Goofy souvenirs are going to cost?

Compounding your dilemma is the multitude of T-shirt shops and other souvenir stores throughout the Orlando area. Shops within the theme parks themselves are sure to capture your fancy, especially the specialty shops from each "nation" at Epcot selling goods from around the world.

Much of what's for sale in the Disney theme parks is available at Disney stores in your home town, and a lot of it can be purchased at the airport, if you decide at the last minute that you just have to have a Donald Duck jacket. So don't feel you have to buy everything the moment you see it. Chances are, you'll see something just like it again later (and probably cheaper, too).

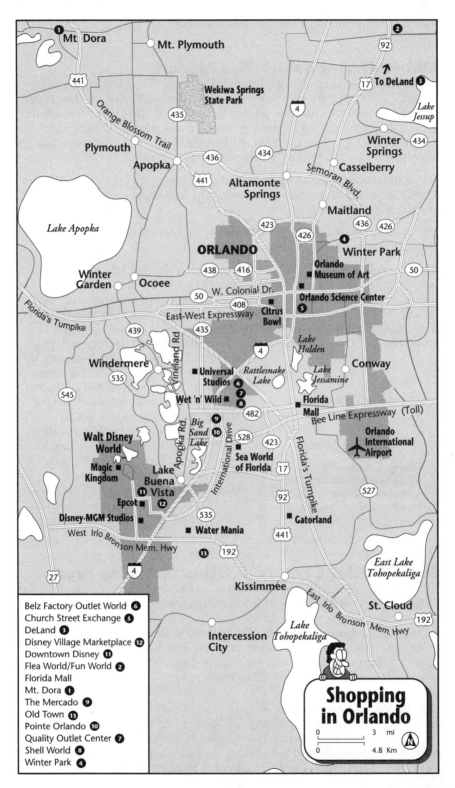

Shopping in Orlando

Belz Factory Outlet World **6**
Church Street Exchange **5**
DeLand **3**
Disney Village Marketplace **12**
Downtown Disney **11**
Flea World/Fun World **2**
Florida Mall
Mt. Dora **1**
The Mercado **9**
Old Town **13**
Pointe Orlando **10**
Quality Outlet Center **7**
Shell World **8**
Winter Park **4**

0   3   mi
0   4.8 Km

Old Stuff: Antiques & Flea Markets

The greatest concentration of antiques shops is downtown along **Orange Avenue,** between Princeton Street and New Hampshire Avenue. The 19th-century village of **Mount Dora,** with its authentic Main Street and rolling hills, is an artists' colony, a haven for retirees, and popular with antique hounds. Take I-4 to U.S. 441 West. Follow it to Route 44B into town. Take the signs that direct you to the "Business District."

For unusual boutiques, restaurants, and art galleries, spend a day in **Winter Park,** just north of downtown Orlando. The best concentration of shops there is along Fifth Avenue.

The main street of the town of **DeLand** is another good spot for antiquing, though it's a longer drive: about an hour north of WDW on U.S. 17–92.

Flea World, in Sanford (40 minutes north of Orlando), bills itself as the world's largest flea market and has more than 2,600 dealers to prove it. Most of the merchandise is new—everything from the outdated and outmoded to factory over-runs, factory seconds, claptrap, and treasures. Because it has its own amusement park, **Fun World,** it makes a great place for a family to spend the day. One parent can take the children to ride the race cars, play video games, and see what's playing at the Flea World stage, while the other stocks up on tools, toys, and bric-a-brac. Parking is unpaved, walks can be long, and most of the market is not air-conditioned. It's open only on Fridays, Saturdays, and Sundays, from 8am to 5pm. To get there, drive north from downtown on I-4 and take the Lake Mary exit; then drive east about 3 miles to U.S. 17–92, and go left for another mile. Call ☎ **407/321-1792** for more info.

Dollars & Sense

Orange County's sales tax is 6%; in Seminole County, tax is 7%. Don't forget to factor in sales tax when you're calculating your budget.

Malls, Outlet Centers, & Other Shopping Areas

In addition to nationally known chains like **FAO Schwarz** (Pointe Orlando), **Saks Fifth Avenue** (Florida Mall), and the **Virgin Megastore** (Disney West Side), the Orlando area is served by a few regional departmental stores: **Burdine's, Gayfer's,** and **Dillard's. Bealls** is a mid-price department store chain that carries family clothing and household accessories. There are **Target, Kmart,** and **Wal-Mart** stores throughout Greater Orlando in case you need something basic.

Disney Village Marketplace

Carrying everything from clothing and foods to gifts and collectibles, this big shopping center on the Buena Vista Lagoon is a fresh, colorful place to browse, people-watch, and have lunch. Shops include **Art of Disney,** a year-round **Christmas Chalet, Gourmet Pantry, Team Mickey's**

Athletic Club (selling athletic clothes with Disney logos), **2Rs Reading and Riding** for books, **World of Disney** for Disney collectibles, and clothing stores selling upscale resort and beach wear. Stores are open 9:30am to 11pm, and until midnight during peak periods. Call ☎ **407/824-4321** for more info.

Downtown Disney Marketplace & Downtown Disney Westside

Disney's newest shopping complex (it opened in 1997) includes a **Virgin Megastore, Bongos Cuban Cafe** (created by Gloria and Emilio Estefan), **House of Blues, Wolfgang Puck's Cafe,** an enormous **LEGO Imagination Center,** and a romantic **Rainforest Cafe.** Here you'll also find a huge **World of Disney Store,** a **Ghirardelli's Soda Fountain and Chocolate Shop, Fulton's Crab House,** and even a **McDonald's.**

The Florida Mall

This is the kind of mall you probably have at home, with 200 specialty shops, six department stores (including a **Saks Fifth Avenue**), a food court, and a 500-room Sheraton hotel. Come here for serious shopping at everyday mall prices. It's located at 8001 S. Orange Blossom Trail at Sand Lake Road, 4 miles east of International Drive (☎ **407/851-6255**). Hours are Monday to Saturday from 10am to 9:30pm, Sundays from 11am to 6pm.

Dollars & Sense

If you're headed for the Florida Mall, check the brochure racks for the Florida Mall brochure. Inside you'll find a coupon that can be exchanged at Guest Services in the mall for a booklet of discounts and freebies.

Old Town

This mall recreates Main Street of the 1950s. You can still get a bottle of cold Pepsi for a quarter, and kids can ride an old-style carnival Ferris wheel while parents shop the 75 stores. Every Saturday night, 300 classic cars cruise through the old brick streets. Admission and parking are free. It's located at 5770 W. Irlo Bronson Memorial Hwy., Kissimmee (☎ **407/396-4888**). Hours are daily from 10am to 11pm; rides are open later.

Belz Factory Outlet World & International Designer Outlets

Actually a succession of malls and shopping areas, this enormous complex in the International Drive Area has more than 160 stores, including dozens of shoe stores (**Capezio, Bally, Bass**), household goods outlets (**Fieldcrest-Cannon, Mikasa, Corning, Oneida**), clothing stores (**Van Heusen,**

225

Dollars & Sense

When you start your shopping spree at the Mercado, head for the mall's Guest Services booth and ask for a free Privilege Card, which gives you discounts at most of the stores.

Leslie Fay, Jordache, Calvin Klein), as well as bookstores, jewelry shops, lingerie boutiques, and toy stores. Factory closeouts, seconds, and over-runs are discounted, but selections are good and quality high. A drawback: The mall is so spread out that you have to drive from one end to the other.

It's located at 5401 W. Oak Ridge Rd., at the north end of International Drive. Call ☎ **407/354-0126** or 407/352-9600 for more info. It's open Monday to Saturday from 10am to 9pm, Sundays from 10am to 6pm.

The Mercado

Here's the place to go for a change of pace from the usual assortment of T-shirt shops and souvenir stands. It looks like a Mediterranean village, an attractive ramble of buildings and courtyards where you can drift from shop to shop to restaurant. Most evenings, there's live entertainment, giving the entire market a street festival ambience. Stop at the official Orlando/Orange County Visitor Information Center for discount tickets, reservations, maps, and any other Orlando information.

The Mercado is located at 8445 International Dr., just south of Sand Lake Road (☎ **407/851-6255**). Hours vary seasonally, but are usually 10am to 10pm.

Pointe Orlando

The newest (1997–98) of Orlando's hybrid "shop'ntainment" centers is this 70-venue center with its own IMAX 3D Theater. Restaurants include **Greg Norman's Down Under Grill,** the **NFL Players Grill,** a **Starbucks Coffee, Dan Marino's Town Tavern,** and the **Modern Art Café.** Stores include **Abercrombie & Fitch, Banana Republic, Foot Locker, Image Leather, Victoria's Secret, Everything But Water, Gap Kids,** book stores, a travel agency, and an **FAO Schwarz** toy store marked by a 32-foot-high Raggedy Ann. Open-air and indoor dining and 25 pushcart vendors add a dash of relaxed chic to the upscale scene.

Pointe Orlando is located at 9101 International Dr. at Republic Drive (☎ **407/248-2838**). It's open every day from 10am to 10pm, with later openings at clubs and restaurants.

Quality Outlet Center

Here you'll find 20 factory outlets including **American Tourister** luggage, **Arrow** shirts and blouses, **Laura Ashley, Le Creuset** cookware, **Great Western Boots, Florsheim** shoes, **Corning** glassware and **Revere** cookware, linens, and much more. It's located on International Drive, a block east of Kirkman Road (☎ **407/423-5885**). Stores are open Monday to Saturday from 10am to 10pm, Sundays from 11am to 6pm.

Shell World
Orlando institutions for a quarter of a century, these family-run stores display more than 50,000 seashells and shell novelties from all over the world. Buy unique ornaments in the "Christmas in the Caribbean" section or pick your own pearl fresh from the oyster.

There's a branch at 5684 International Dr. on the corner of Kirkman Road, in the Shoppes of International Plaza (☎ **407/370-3344**). Another location is at 4727 W. Irlo Bronson Memorial Hwy. (U.S. 192) at Marker 13, in Kissimmee (☎ **407/396-9000**). Hours are Monday to Saturday from 10am to 9pm, Sunday from 11am to 5pm.

Time-Savers
If you shop inside the theme parks, you can have packages delivered to the gates so that you can pick them up as you leave; you don't have to carry all your purchases around with you all day. Allow 3 hours for your delivery to arrive.

Church Street Exchange Shopping Emporium & Church Street Market
Here's a place downtown that keeps your kids entertained while you shop (and for no admission charge). You can peruse the more than 50 fascinating stores in the Exchange for lingerie, stones and gems, snacks and treats, and many other goodies and gifts while the children enjoy **Commander Ragtime's Midway of Fun.**

The Market, which is across the street, has another 30 shops selling confections, unusual clothing, and more gifts. It also has a **Brookstone** and a **Sharper Image.** The many eateries include **Pizzeria Uno** and an **Olive Garden.**

To get there, take I-4 to downtown Orlando and exit at Anderson Street, Exit 38. Turn left on Boone Avenue, left on South Street, and then right on Garland Avenue, where you'll find a city parking lot. Most shops are open Monday to Saturday from 10am to 10pm, Sundays from noon to 6pm. Restaurants stay open later.

Chapter 19

Designing Your Own Itinerary

If you've been religiously following our advice on how to budget your time, you should have about a 45-day vacation planned by now. (And if you have 45 days of vacation coming to you, you can't be a complete idiot.) However, we'll assume that you have significantly less vacation time and you're starting to worry about how you're going to fit in all the fun stuff without running yourself ragged. The worksheets and hints that follow will help you start to figure it out.

How to Design Your Own Itinerary

Now comes the hard part. You can't possibly do it all. So now you have to go back through the attractions and shopping chapters in this section and choose the ones you can't leave Orlando without doing. Write them down in the chart below. Have other members of your family do the same. When you're all done, total up the time you expect these attractions will take and compare it with the total time you have in Orlando. If you have planned too many activities, figure out which ones you can skip. If you've got too few...never mind. Nobody ever plans too few activities.

We Can't Leave Orlando Before We...

Use this chart to enter the attractions you most would like to visit to see how they'll fit into your schedule. Then use the date book at the end of this chapter to plan your itinerary.

Your Must-See Attractions

Enter the attractions you most would like to visit to see how they'll fit into your schedule. Then use the date book to plan your itinerary.

Attraction and location	Amount of time you expect to spend there	Best day and time to go

Some Helpful Hints

Now, before you start deciding which day you're going to undertake each activity, here are some pointers.

➤ Only an idiot would venture onto I-4 at rush hour (between 7 and 9am or 5 and 6pm). The traffic on this road is pretty heavy at all times. Come to think of it, traffic is pretty heavy on *all* the roads. It always takes longer than you think to get almost everywhere. Traffic gets worse every day and still new residents pour in. WDW transportation is superb, but during peak times and at park closing, two or three filled transports may pull out before you reach the head of the line. When you have appointments, a tee time, or reservations, plan ahead and don't schedule activities too close together.

➤ Don't go to a theme park the first day of your vacation. Unpack at a leisurely pace, take a nap by the pool, read up on all the things there are to see and do before you go plunking down $40 per person on a park that will wipe you out. And don't try to breeze through the parks. Lines can be long, especially on the one ride that you want to ride a second and third time.

➤ Spend a little time figuring out meals ahead of time so that you don't pay through the nose for sub-par lunches, dinners, and snacks. You'd be surprised how much money you save by doing a little planning.

➤ Orlando's heat and humidity take a greater toll than most northerners expect. If you can reserve 2 or 3 midday hours for a nap or swim, your energy wattage will get a boost.

➤ Cut yourself some slack. Don't try to fill in every line on the work-sheet. If you want to extend your half day at the Orlando Science Center into a full day, or if the Magic Kingdom isn't your cup of java, give yourself permission to change plans, bail out, or linger on.

➤ Consider your travel mates. Thanks to shuttles and other public transportation, everyone doesn't have to go everywhere in lock-step together. Plan mother-daughter, father-daughter, sister-brother, and mom-and-dad activities. Or a grandfather-grandson canoe trip, shopping just for the girls, a romantic romp to the beach just for him and her. Then everyone can get back together for dinner with lots to talk about.

➤ We are mere book authors, so what do we know about how long you need to see an art museum or how many times you'll stand in line to ride Space Mountain? We've given average times, but if you know your 4-year-old is going to want to spend 4 hours at Mickey's Toontown Fair, by all means budget the entire morning there. Tailor your schedule to your own interests.

➤ This is your vacation, for heaven's sake! You don't have to keep a schedule, put on a tie, or check your voice mail. Break habits. Dare to wear yourself out, sleep until noon, buy a watermelon at the roadside and eat nothing else for lunch, or hop on a city bus and ride to the end of the line just to see what's there.

Worksheet: If This Is Tuesday, We Must Be at Epcot

Now you can start matching attractions with vacation days. Enter the most complicated and lengthiest attractions first (for example, an all-day excursion to Epcot on Sunday), and then fit shorter, easier activities (such as lunch at King Stefan's) around them.

DAY 1

Morning:

Lunch:

Afternoon:

Dinner:

Evening:

DAY 2

Morning:

Lunch:

Afternoon:

Dinner:

Evening:

DAY 3

Morning:

Lunch:

Afternoon:

Dinner:

Evening:

DAY 4

Morning:

Lunch:

Afternoon:

Dinner:

Evening:

DAY 5

Morning:

Lunch:

Afternoon:

Dinner:

Evening:

Part 6

On The Town:
Nightlife & Entertainment

Orlando may be all mouse ears by day, but at night the sidewalks stream with street parties and fun-seekers hurrying from one club to the next. If you've got the energy for a night on the town after a day at the parks, Orlando and Walt Disney World won't disappoint you. The same people responsible for entertaining you during the day have not forgotten that people like to party at night, too.

Orlando's nightlife was planned wisely and is very geared toward visitors. That means the most fashionable clubs, lounges, bars, and nightspots are usually pretty close to the major clusters of hotels—maybe even in your hotel itself. And if you have to drive somewhere, parking is almost always abundant.

Chapter 20

Hitting the Bars & Clubs

Orlando's reputation is so dominated by its theme parks that many visitors never discover that the city also has a variety of hip nightspots offering everything from folk music to jazz, country to grunge. The dress code depends on the place, but jeans are permitted in most places, and they enjoy even more widespread acceptance when dressed up with a jacket. Chic resort wear is seen everywhere; the only people who wear ties are young businesspeople who stop in for a drink after work or suited professionals out for a working dinner meeting. You'll need a jacket or sweater in winter for the cool evenings outdoors and in summer for overeager air-conditioning indoors. The drinking age is 21 and is rigidly enforced in bars and package stores.

If you want to escape the tourists and mingle with the locals, try heading downtown or to Winter Park. Both are very *in* right now, and are untouristy places to go for an evening out.

The "Calendar" section of the Friday ***Orlando Sentinel*** provides the most current listings of who's playing where. Look under Nightspots, where clubs are divided into Comedy, Country Music, Dancing/Live Music, and Disco, with a special sidebar on current gigs. You can also check out the *Sentinel* online: www.orlandosentinel.com.

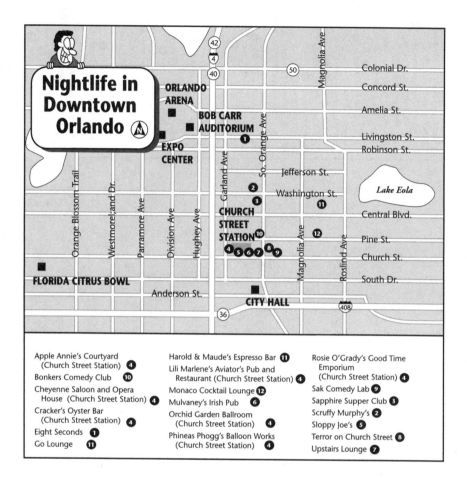

Nightlife in Downtown Orlando

Apple Annie's Courtyard
  (Church Street Station) **4**
Bonkers Comedy Club **10**
Cheyenne Saloon and Opera
  House (Church Street Station) **4**
Cracker's Oyster Bar
  (Church Street Station) **4**
Eight Seconds **1**
Go Lounge **11**

Harold & Maude's Espresso Bar **11**
Lili Marlene's Aviator's Pub and
  Restaurant (Church Street Station) **4**
Monaco Cocktail Lounge **12**
Mulvaney's Irish Pub **6**
Orchid Garden Ballroom
  (Church Street Station) **4**
Phineas Phogg's Balloon Works
  (Church Street Station) **4**

Rosie O'Grady's Good Time
  Emporium
  (Church Street Station) **4**
Sak Comedy Lab **9**
Sapphire Supper Club **3**
Scruffy Murphy's **2**
Sloppy Joe's **5**
Terror on Church Street **8**
Upstairs Lounge **7**

Extra! Extra!

For a sparkling view after dark...Top of the Palace in the Buena Vista Palace or **Topper's** in the Travelodge Hotel, 2000 Hotel Plaza Blvd., between Buena Vista Drive and FL 535 in Lake Buena Vista. Both have a truly buena vista. You can see Epcot's IllumiNations (☎ **407/828-2424** for info) from either spot.

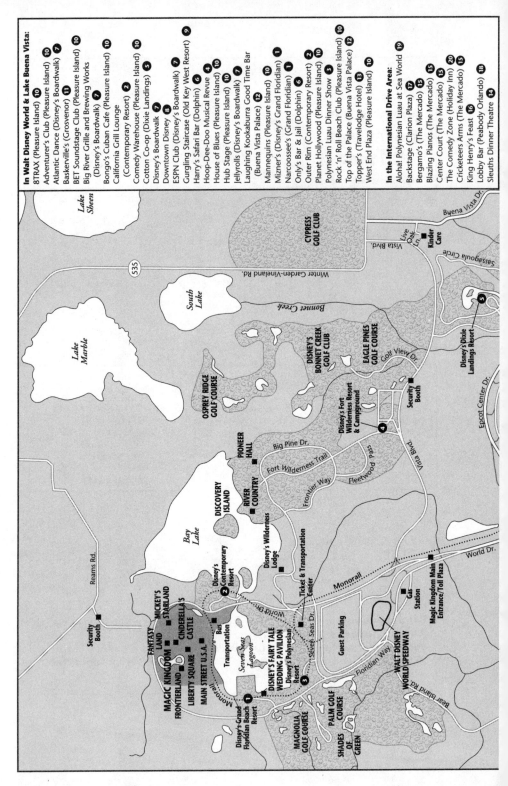

In Walt Disney World & Lake Buena Vista:

8TRAX (Pleasure Island) ⑩
Adventurer's Club (Pleasure Island) ⑩
Atlantic Dance (Disney's Boardwalk) ⑦
Baskerville's (Grosvenor) ⑪
BET Soundstage Club (Pleasure Island) ⑩
Big River Grille and Brewing Works
  (Disney's Boardwalk) ⑦
Bongo's Cuban Cafe (Pleasure Island) ⑩
California Grill Lounge
  (Contemporary Resort) ②
Comedy Warehouse (Pleasure Island) ⑩
Cotton Co-op (Dixie Landings) ⑤
Disney's Boardwalk ⑦
Downtown Disney ⑧
ESPN Club (Disney's Boardwalk) ⑦
Gurgling Staircase (Old Key West Resort) ⑨
Harry's Safari Bar (Dolphin) ⑥
Hoop-Dee-Doo Musical Revue ④
House of Blues (Pleasure Island) ⑩
Hub Stage (Pleasure Island) ⑩
Jellyrolls (Disney's Boardwalk) ⑦
Laughing Kookaburra Good Time Bar
  (Buena Vista Palace) ⑫
Mannequins (Pleasure Island) ⑩
Mizner's (Disney's Grand Floridian) ①
Narcoossee's (Grand Floridian) ①
Only's Bar & Jail (Dolphin) ⑥
Outer Rim (Contemporary Resort) ②
Planet Hollywood (Pleasure Island) ⑩
Polynesian Luau Dinner Show ③
Rock 'n' Roll Beach Club (Pleasure Island) ⑩
Top of the Palace (Buena Vista Palace) ⑫
Topper's (Travelodge Hotel) ⑬
West End Plaza (Pleasure Island) ⑩

In the International Drive Area:

Aloha! Polynesian Luau at Sea World ⑲
Backstage (Clarion Plaza) ⑰
Bergamo's (The Mercado) ⑮
Blazing Pianos (The Mercado) ⑮
Center Court (The Mercado) ⑮
The Comedy Zone (Holiday Inn) ⑳
Cricketeers Arms (The Mercado) ⑮
King Henry's Feast ⑯
Lobby Bar (Peabody Orlando) ⑱
Sleuths Dinner Theatre ⑭

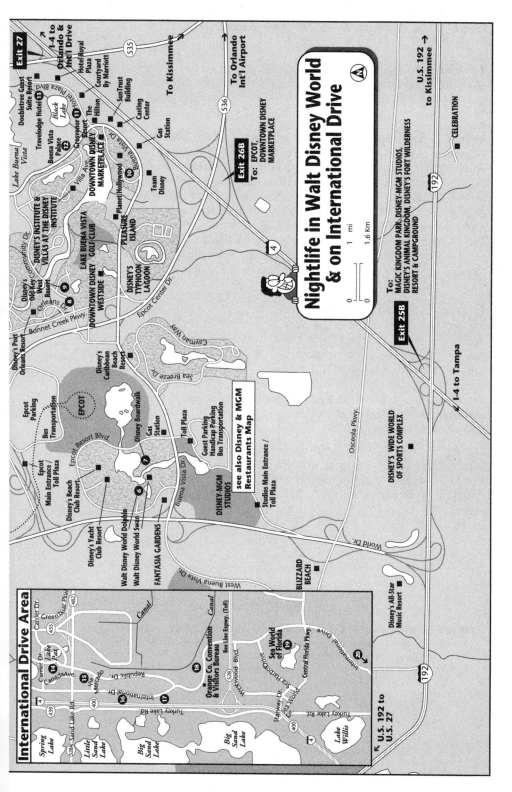

Nightlife in Walt Disney World & on International Drive

1 mi

1.6 Km

To:
MAGIC KINGDOM PARK, DISNEY-MGM STUDIOS,
DISNEY'S ANIMAL KINGDOM, DISNEY'S FORT WILDERNESS
RESORT & CAMPGROUND

Exit 25B

I-4 to Tampa

Exit 26B

To: EPCOT, DOWNTOWN DISNEY
MARKETPLACE

To Orlando Int'l Airport

To Kissimmee

U.S. 192 →
to Kissimmee

CELEBRATION

Exit 27

I-4 to Orlando & Int'l Drive

see also Disney & MGM
Restaurants Map

International Drive Area

Spring Lake

Little Sand Lake

Big Sand Lake

Big Sand Lake

Big Sand Lake

Lake Willis

Sea World of Florida

Orange Co. Convention & Visitors Bureau

DISNEY'S WIDE WORLD OF SPORTS COMPLEX

Disney's All-Star Music Resort

BLIZZARD BEACH

DISNEY-MGM STUDIOS

FANTASIA GARDENS

Walt Disney World Dolphin

Walt Disney World Swan

Disney's Yacht Club Resort

Disney's Beach Club Resort

Disney's Caribbean Beach Resort

EPCOT

Epcot Parking

Bus Transportation

Epcot Main Entrance / Toll Plaza

Disney Boardwalk

Gas Station

Toll Plaza

Guest Parking Handicap Parking Bus Transportation

Studios Main Entrance / Toll Plaza

Disney's Port Orleans Resort

Disney's Old Port Royal West Resort

Orleans

Bonnet Creek Pkwy.

DOWNTOWN DISNEY WESTSIDE

DISNEY'S TYPHOON LAGOON

LAKE BUENA VISTA GOLF/CLUB

PLEASURE ISLAND

DISNEY'S INSTITUTE & VILLAS AT THE DISNEY INSTITUTE

Planet Hollywood

DOWNTOWN DISNEY MARKETPLACE

Team Disney

Villa Ave.

Buena Vista Palace

Grosvenor Resort

The Hilton

Black Lake

Casting Center

Gas Station

SunTrust Building

Courtyard By Marriott

Hotel Royal Plaza

Doubletree Guest Suite Resort

Travelodge Hotel

Lake Buena Vista

To Kissimmee

U.S. 192 to U.S. 27

The Orlando Weekly is a free magazine that often has better listings for alternative and offbeat nightlife. Look for their boxes anywhere throughout the area and pick up a copy.

What's Going on in the Parks After Dark?

Of course, the parks themselves are a source of nighttime entertainment, either with or without the kids, especially when something special is going on. The fireworks that go on nightly are eye-popping and should not be missed. Holidays such as Halloween, New Year's Eve, Christmas tree lighting or caroling, and 4th of July call for extra hours and extravaganzas. Keep in mind, however, that only the hardiest of souls can hack a theme park all day and all night. If you're on a 1-day visit, take a break for lunch, a swim, and a nap before returning for the evening. Or watch local papers for news of reduced admissions after 4pm during special evening events.

Disney's BoardWalk

One of the newest complexes at Walt Disney World is this "seaside" village built to resemble Atlantic City in the 1930s, complete with boardwalk, cotton candy vendors, clubs, restaurants, and shops. Some of the rooms and suites of Disney's BoardWalk hotel almost hang out over the boardwalk, which ends at the shores of Lake Crescent. Some of our favorite nights have been spent simply strolling the boardwalk while enjoying the night sounds and water views. But if you want more excitement, you can choose from a variety of nightspots.

The **ESPN Club** here is a razzle-dazzle sports bar with big-screen TVs and smaller TVs in the bathrooms so you don't miss a moment of the big game. Play video games, nosh on Buffalo wings and big burgers, and enjoy the sports memorabilia, decor, and trivia games.

Extra! Extra!

If you want to dance the night away... Atlantic Dance in Disney's BoardWalk, **Backstage** in the Clarion Plaza, **Cricketeers Arms** in the Mercado, **Laughing Kookaburra** in the Buena Vista Plaza, **Mizners** in Disney's Grand Floridian, or the **Orchid Garden Ballroom** in Church Street Station are all good choices.

The **Big River Grille and Brewing Works** is a restaurant and microbrewery offering dozens of "boutique" beers and ales.

A 10-piece orchestra is the attraction at **Atlantic Dance,** where music ranges from big-band sounds to top 40. At **Jellyrolls,** you can sing along or just listen to the dueling pianos.

Disney's BoardWalk is located at 2101 N. Epcot Resorts Blvd., off Buena Vista Drive (☎ **407/939-5100**). Admission and parking are free. After 5pm, valet parking is available for $5. If you're staying at WDW, ride the free transportation system. Hours are daily from 7am to 2am.

Pleasure Island & Downtown Disney

Formerly a simple shopping village, Pleasure Island has been transformed into a vast complex now housing some of Orlando's most sizzling nightspots. Many of the restaurants here, including **Planet Hollywood, House of Blues,** and **Bongos Cuban Cafe,** are an evening's worth of entertainment in themselves. But there is also no shortage of places better known for their nightlife than their food.

Have a drink or two before dinner at the safari-themed **Adventurer's Club,** which opens at 7pm, with comfy seating, no smoking, and tall tales told by a "professional hunter."

The **Rock 'n' Roll Beach Club** has bars on three levels, a dance floor on the ground floor, and air hockey and pool tables on the second and third levels. The bands here play classic rock from the 1960s and 1970s, including a lot of surfer music.

Time-Savers

Parking at Pleasure Island is tight. Take WDW transportation or a taxi and you won't have to worry about parking or driving home after drinking.

The first of four nightly shows in the **Comedy Warehouse** is at 7:30pm. The resident troupe takes suggestions from the audience and does improvs.

Mannequins is the most energetic dance club, with a revolving dance floor, mind-blowing technical effects, and speakers that could wake the dead. You must be 21 to get in.

8TRAX remembers the 1970s; the old Neon Armadillo is now the **BET SoundStage Club** playing R&B. For jazz, including occasional national acts, try the **Pleasure Island Jazz Company.**

In addition to the clubs, music groups play outdoors, usually at the **West End Plaza** or the **Hub Stage.** Check your schedule for show times or just listen for the beat and follow it to the music.

Dollars & Sense

Admission to Pleasure Island and Church Street Station is free during the day, when shops and some restaurants are open but when there is no entertainment. Beat the cover charge by arriving in the late afternoon. If you stay in the same place all evening, you can save the admission fee, but once you leave one restaurant or club, you'll have to pay the full freight to get into another.

The complex is located at Walt Disney World Village (☎ **407/934-7781**). Admission is free before 7pm and to holders of the World Hopper Pass. After 7pm, admission is $19.05 except for the restaurants and movies. Admission buys a plastic bracelet that pays your way into all the clubs. Shops open at 11am, clubs at 7pm; both stay open to 2am. Self-parking is free; valet parking is $5.

The Mercado

By day, this is a mild-mannered shopping complex; by night, it's the scene of frequent free entertainment in the **Center Court** as well as a host of restaurants and other nightspots.

Blazing Pianos, with its three grand pianos all painted candy apple red, is one of our favorite nightspots. Admission is $5 and nobody under 21 is admitted on weekend nights. It's open earlier for great burgers, sandwiches, and light meals, but the fun begins about 9pm when three piano players start pounding the ivories with lively rock and roll. Smoke rises from the stage when they get to "Great Balls of Fire." The scene includes requests, audience participation, and mayhem so intense that four players are needed to rotate among the three pianos. Don't miss the piano-shaped chocolate dessert.

In **Bergamo's,** servers burst into operatic arias or Broadway classics while waiting on tables. You can also dance to live music after 9:30pm nightly at **Cricketeers Arms.**

The Mercado is located at 8445 International Dr., just south of Sand Lake Road (☎ **407/345-9337**). Parking and admission are free. It's open daily from 8am; restaurants and clubs are hopping till as late as 2am.

Lounges Without the Lizards: The Best Hotel Nightlife

Some of Orlando's best nightlife is located right in the hotels—perhaps one you're staying in. Even the locals come out to the resort areas for fun after dark. If you're staying at one of the places listed here, you can do an evening on the town without ever getting behind the wheel.

In WDW hotels, **Cotton Co-Op** at Dixie Landings has music and Cajun food until midnight. **Mizner's** in the Grand Floridian has orchestra music until 1am and an elegant library look. **Narcoossee's** has Victorian decor and beer by the yard or half yard. **Outer Rim** in the Contemporary Resort is trendy and close to the monorail. **Harry's Safari Bar** in the Dolphin has an African jungle theme, generous appetizers, draft beers, and cocktails with or without alcohol.

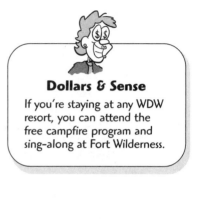

Dollars & Sense

If you're staying at any WDW resort, you can attend the free campfire program and sing-along at Fort Wilderness.

Among the best hotel nightspots is **The Comedy Zone** in the Holiday Inn, 6515 International Dr. (☎ **407/934-7781**). Five shows nightly start at 7:30pm.

Backstage, in the Clarion Plaza Hotel, 9700 International Dr. (☎ **407/354-1719**), features live music and jam nights.

The **Laughing Kookaburra Good Time Bar** in the Buena Vista Palace, Lake Buena Vista (☎ **407/827-3722**), is open until 2am with great music, yarns, dining, noshing, people-watching, and its own waterfall.

Jazz plays at **Baskerville's Restaurant** in the Grosvenor Resort Hotel, 1850 Hotel Plaza Blvd., Lake Buena Vista, (☎ **407/827-6500**).

The **Lobby Bar** at the Peabody Orlando, 9801 International Dr. (☎ **407/352-4000**), is a popular gathering spot with good piano music, drinks, and conversation.

Extra! Extra!

For easy listening and quiet conversation… the **Lobby Bar** in the Orlando Peabody is quite the scene these days. **Only's Bar & Jail** in Disney's Dolphin closes at 11:30pm; open later are the tiny **Gurgling Staircase** in Disney's Old Key West and the **California Grill Lounge** in Disney's Contemporary Resort.

Church Street Station

This block of mammoth warehouses along the railroad tracks downtown was transformed into a glittering night-time fun station where you can wander from club to club to enjoy easy listening, ragtime, comedy, Dixieland, and country and western music. **Rosie O'Grady's Good Time Emporium** is dressed up to look like a gay-nineties gambling hall/saloon and has honky-tonk piano and a Dixieland band to go along with the decor. **Apple Annie's Courtyard,** with the appearance of a New Orleans garden, plays folk and bluegrass while listeners sip fruit drinks.

For more formal dining, try **Lili Marlene's Aviator's Pub and Restaurant.** The decor is 1850s Paris; the menu features steaks and seafood in the expensive range. Pickin' and stompin' reign at the **Cheyenne Saloon and Opera House.** Free lessons in country dance are offered Friday through Sunday from 2pm to 5:30pm. Order barbecue and watch the clogging, strumming, and singing. **The Orchid Garden Ballroom** is a regal setting for dancing to tunes from big-band to rock, bop, and boogie. **Phineas Phogg's Balloon Works** has dancing nightly and, on Wednesday from 6:30pm to 7:30pm, beer for a nickel. You must be 21 to get in. **Crackers Oyster Bar,** mellow and woody, serves oysters and other seafood, as well as more than 50 imported beers. In addition to its venues, Church Street Station ropes off entire blocks for its special events. Street parties, held during the Lynx Jazz Festival, Halloween, New Year's Eve, and Mardi Gras, are some of the best in the city.

Extra! Extra!

If you want to hear some cool jazz... try **House of Blues** and the **Pleasure Island Jazz Company** (both at Pleasure Island), or **Baskerville's Restaurant,** in the Grosvenor Resort Hotel, Lake Buena Vista. For Dixieland, **Rosie O'Grady's** downtown at Church Street Station is your best bet.

Church Street Station is located downtown at 129 W. Church St., between Garland and Orange avenues. Take the Anderson Street Exit off I-4 and follow the signs. Parking lots and garages have sprung up in the area; watch for signs.

Better still, take the shuttles that operate between major hotels and downtown and you'll have a designated driver. The round-trip shuttle service runs 4 nights a week between eight International Drive hotels and downtown. Prices and times vary; call ☎ **407/422-2434** for info.

The hours vary, but most shops and many restaurants are open at 11am. Shops close at 11pm; restaurants and bars stay open as late as 2am.

There's no admission charge before 5pm. After 5pm, $16.95 buys admission to clubs and entertainment, though you're on your own for food and drinks.

Admission to **Church Street Exchange** is always free. Its shops and arcades are fun for browsing and people-watching.

Call ☎ **407/422-2434** for more info.

Extra! Extra!

If you like to get scared silly...Terror on Church Street, 100 S. Orange Ave., downtown (☎ **407/649-3327**), is a permanent haunted house filled with ghouls, spine-chilling noises, near-misses, and blood-curdling shocks. It's not for young children or the faint-hearted. It's open Sunday through Thursday from 7pm to midnight, Friday and Saturday from 7pm to 1am. Admission is $12 for adults and $10 for ages 17 and under. American Express, MasterCard, and Visa are accepted.

Too Hip for the Mall: Other Downtown Nightspots

Eight Seconds, 100 W. Livingston St. (☎ **407/839-4800**), is named for the length of time you have to stay atop a bucking bull to score in nightly contests. This is a down-and-dirty club with live music, free line-dancing lessons, monster truck wars, mud runs, country dancing, beer, and snacks.

Sloppy Joe's, 41 W. Church St. (☎ **407/843-5825**), has dancing to live groups nightly. It's touristy but fun and remotely patterned after the Key West bar where Ernest Hemingway did his drinking.

Go Lounge, in Wall Street Plaza, off Orange Avenue (☎ **407/422-3322**), may have jazz, an open mike night, readings, or a DJ.

Also in Wall Street Plaza is **Harold & Maude's Espresso Bar** with easy listening music nightly for ages 21 and over (☎ **407/422-3322**).

Everyone loves **Mulvaney's Irish Pub,** at 27 W. Church St. (☎ **407/872-3296**), for Irish folk music and pub grub.

Scruffy Murphy's, 9 W. Washington St. (☎ **407/648-5460**), is less scruffy than it sounds. People come for the wide selection of Irish beers, good conversation, and easy-listening music. There is never a cover charge.

Extra! Extra!

If you want to catch the big game... the best sports bar in town is the **ESPN Club** at Disney's BoardWalk. **Toppers,** in the Travelodge Hotel, 2000 Hotel Plaza Blvd., between Buena Vista Dr. and FL 535 in Lake Buena Vista, has a great sports bar, too (☎ **407/828-2424**).

Upstairs Lounge, 23 W. Church St. (☎ 407/426-9100), is open for drinks and easy-listening music nightly except Sundays.

The **Sapphire Supper Club,** 54 N. Orange Ave. (☎ 407/246-1419), features nationally known jazz and blues acts.

Monaco Cocktail Lounge in Le Provence, 50 E. Pine St. (☎ 407/843-4410), features French singers every night except Thursday, which is jazz night, and an intimate atmosphere.

Bonkers Comedy Club, Sunset Strip, 25 S. Orange Ave. (☎ 407/649-8829), features stand-up comics. **Sak Comedy Lab** at 45 E. Church St. (☎ 407/648-0001) has improvisational gigs two and three times nightly. Admission is $6 to $13.

Gay & Lesbian Nightlife

Favorite local restaurants for gay men include the **Dug Out Diner** at the somewhat seedy **Parliament House Motor Inn,** 410 N. Orange Blossom Trail (☎ 407/425-7571), and the **Thornton Park Café** at 900 E. Washington St. (☎ 407/425-0033), which specializes in seafood and Italian dishes and is in the heart of the city's most prominent gay residential neighborhood.

For nightlife, try **Uncle Walt's** at 5454 International Dr. (☎ 407/351-4866). There's also **The Complex,** 3400 S. Orange Blossom Trail (☎ 407/629-4779).

The city's leading gay gym is **New Image Fitness Center,** 3400 S. Orange Ave. (☎ 407/420-9890). Several of the **Bally's** are said to attract a gay crowd. If you're a member, call around the local Bally's and inquire.

Lesbians like to dance at **Southern Nights** at 375 S. Bumby Ave. (☎ 407/898-0424) and drink at **Faces,** 4910 Edgewater Dr. (☎ 407/291-7571). Southern Nights is also an in spot for gay men; on Friday nights, female impersonators are featured. Theme nights are especially for women on Saturdays and for men on Sundays.

Chapter 21

HELP ME
BECOME PRESIDENT

Dinner Shows & Orlando's Cultural Scene

In This Chapter

➤ How to find out what's going on and get tickets

➤ Dinner show for the whole family

➤ The performing arts

Orlando has raised the dinner show to something of an art form. Aimed primarily at kids, the dinner show is a little like dining in front of the television, only the entertainment is live, and in many cases you're asked—even required—to participate.

And yes, folks, one of the hidden secrets about Orlando is that it has a rich cultural scene.

Seriously!

You may find spending a night in Orlando at the opera akin to going to England for its fine wines, but there is first-rate culture here. The city's Shakespeare Company is outstanding (and outdoors, often under a starlit midsummer night's sky). Orlando also has a sizeable number of professional actors whose costumes include neither a giant animal head nor a long tail.

Dinner *and* a Show, at the Same Time

At Orlando's dinner shows there's usually a choice of two or three mediocre main dishes, all the beer, wine, or soda you want, and the diversion of a raucous show. It's hard to say which is more pedestrian, the dinner or the theater, but kids love it and it's sure to be an evening of fun for the whole family.

Shows are listed here alphabetically. Prices listed include food and drinks but not tax or tips.

Aloha! Polynesian Luau at Sea World

Not to be confused with Disney's Polynesian Luau Dinner Show (or maybe it is!), Sea World's version serves barbecue food accompanied by torchlights, lilting South Seas dances, and music for a memorable family evening with audience participation and plenty to eat.

*Sea World is located at 7007 Sea World Dr. (☎ **800/227-8048** or 407/351-3600 for information). Admission is $29.95 adults, $19.95 youths ages 8–12, and $9.95 children ages 3 through 7. AE, MC, V accepted. Parking is free if you have a confirmed reservation, and we do recommend reservations. Nightly seatings are at 6:30pm.*

Extra! Extra!

Dinner shows that offer a senior discount include Arabian Nights, Capone's, King Henry's Feast, Medieval Times, Pirate's Dinner Adventure, Sleuths Mystery Dinner Theater, Wild Bill's Wild West Dinner Extravaganza, and Mark Two Dinner Theater. Age limits and rules vary. Call and ask—you can save big time!

American Gladiators Orlando Live!

If you've seen American Gladiators on TV, you have an idea of how this goes. Dinner shows include a full chicken dinner; snacks are served at other shows. While you eat, gladiators battle the set and each other.

*Shows are held at 5515 W. Irlo Bronson Memorial Hwy. (U.S. 192) between I-4 and FL 535 (☎ **800/BATTLE-4** or 407/390-0000). The charge for a snack and the show is $19.95 adults and $14.95 children ages 3–12. Dinner shows are $39.95 adults and $21.50 children ages 3–12. AE, DC, MC, V accepted. Hours vary seasonally. Reservations are strongly recommended. Parking is free.*

Arabian Nights

The horses are the stars of this show, which features Royal Lipizzaner Stallions and herds of other horses that perform, race, preen, and prance. The menu features prime rib with all the trimmings.

*Head for 6225 W. Irlo Bronson Memorial Hwy. (U.S. 192), just east of Exit 25A off I-4 (☎ **800/553-6116** or 407/239-9223). Admission is $39.54 for adults and $25.63 for children ages 3–11. AE, DC, MC, V accepted. Shows are held nightly at 7:30pm. Reservations are recommended. Parking is free.*

Hoop-Dee-Doo Musical Revue

Feast on down-home barbecue and all the fixin's while you sing, stomp, and laugh at jokes you haven't heard since second grade. The show is well animated, with good sound. Book the 7:15pm show, and then stay for the Electric Water Pageant, which can be viewed at 9:45pm from the Fort Wilderness Beach. The menu includes unlimited soft drinks, beer, or sangria.

The fun happens at Disney's Fort Wilderness Resort and Campground, 3520 N. Fort Wilderness Trail (☎ 407/WDW-DINE). Admission is $37 for adults and $19.50 for children ages 3–11. AE, MC, V accepted. Reservations are required. Parking is free. Shows begin at 5, 7:15, and 9:30pm nightly.

Dollars & Sense

Look through the free magazines and newspapers distributed at all Orlando hotels and most shopping areas. Many of them include discount coupons to be used at dinner shows.

King Henry's Feast Banquet & Show

King Henry himself presides over a banquet hall where royal entertainers duel, tumble, joust, and jest. It has more jesters and fewer horses than Medieval Times (see below), but both of these Middle Ages restaurants have plenty of hijinks, audience interaction, lusty food, swaggering knaves, and swooning ladies. Both are rated PG and are fun for the entire family.

Henry holds court at 8984 International Dr. (☎ 800/883-8181 or 407/ 351-5151). Prices are $36.95 for adults, $22.95 for children ages 3–11. AE, CB, DC, DISC, MC, V accepted. Shows are nightly at 7pm, sometimes also at 9:30pm. Parking is free.

Medieval Times

This is the Orlando branch of the restaurant Jim Carrey went to in *The Cable Guy*. Here you'll pig out on soup, barbecued ribs, or a whole chicken with all the trimmings while knights pound around the arena on horses, jousting and clanging to please their fair ladies. Arrive early for free admission to Medieval Village, which is patterned after a Middle Ages settlement.

It's at 4510 W. Irlo Bronson Hwy. (U.S. 192), 11 miles east of the main entrance to WDW; look for the Super Wal-Mart (☎ 800/229-8300 or 407/239-0214; www.medivaltimes.com). Admission is $36.95 for adults, $22.95 for children ages 3–12. AE, DC, MC, V accepted. Reservations are highly recommended. Shows are daily at 8pm; come earlier for cocktails and milling around the great baronial hall. Parking is free.

Time-Savers

If you absolutely, positively have to be to an evening event on time, call ahead and get detailed directions from your hotel—or you might even want to scope out the route by daylight. Signage throughout the area, including that inside WDW, leaves much to be desired. At the very least, leave yourself plenty of time to get lost so that you find your way before the show starts.

Pirates Dinner Adventure

Feast on a three-course meal and all the beer, wine, and soft drinks you like while hijinks and dazzling special effects (including a full-size ship in a 300,000-gallon lagoon) keep you on the edge of your seat.

*It's at 6400 Carrier Dr. (☎ **800/866-2469** or 407/248-0590). Dinner is $35.95 for adults and $21.15 for children ages 3–9. AE, MC, V accepted. Shows start nightly at 7:45pm, but get here at 6:30pm for the preshow. Parking is free.*

Polynesian Luau Dinner Show

Authentic South Seas dances are a delight to watch, and kids don't get restless during the 2-hour show because they get to participate. Most other dinner shows are air-conditioned. This one is outdoors, so it can be chilly or steamy—you decide if you don't mind the weather. The tropical menu features fruit, barbecued chicken, and cinnamon monkey bread. The same venue serves Mickey's Tropical Luau at 4:30pm daily.

*It's all at Disney's Polynesian Resort, 1600 Seven Seas Dr. (☎ **407/ WDW-DINE**). Reservations are required. Dinner and the show cost $37 for adults, $19.50 for children ages 3–11. Shows are nightly at 6:45 and 9:30pm; arrive early for preshow fun. Parking is free.*

Extra! Extra!

Almost all dinner theaters offer a vegetarian alternative. Just ask when you make your reservation. If you're averse to eating meat, you don't want to find yourself seated in front of a prime rib platter.

Sleuths Dinner Theater

The gimmick here is a crime that the audience must solve together. That makes for a different experience each night, depending on how many budding Sherlock Holmeses are present.

It's at 7508 Republic Dr., off International Drive in Republic Square, ¼ mile behind Wet 'n Wild (☎ 800/393-1985 or 407/363-1985; www.he.net/sleuths). Reservations are required. Admission for adults is $35.95; for children ages 3–11, it's $22.95. Prime rib is $3 extra. Show times vary. Parking is free.

Kids Wild Bill's Wild West Dinner Extravaganza

Fort Liberty is a 22-acre ranch where the chuck wagon serves barbecued ribs, fried chicken, biscuits, beans, baked potatoes, corn on the cob, and a slab of hot apple pie with all the beer, wine, or Coca-Cola you want. The show is hokier than a spaghetti western, but everyone from old grumps to young kids loves it. There's 10 gallons of audience participation, so be prepared to make a fool of yourself.

Round up at 5260 U.S. 192, just east of I-4 (☎ 800/883-8181 or 407/ 351-5151). Reservations are recommended. Admission is $35.95 adults and $22.50 children ages 3–11. Dinner is at 7pm nightly, with additional 9:30pm shows some nights. Parking is free.

The Arts

It ain't Broadway, and it ain't the London Symphony, but Orlando's performing arts are nothing to sneer at, either. Here's a sampling of some of the more popular venues, performers, and events.

The **Bob Carr Performing Arts Centre,** 401 W. Livingston St., Orlando (☎ 407/849-2577), plays host to touring Broadway shows, symphony, opera, and more. Its box office sells tickets only to its own events and only in the 3 hours before show times. At other times, tickets for Bob Carr events are available at the Orlando Arena, 600 W. Amelia St. Phone purchases must be made through Ticketmaster.

Festival of Orchestras productions, featuring internationally known conductors, play in the Performing Arts Theater in the Orange County Convention Center and in the Bob Carr Performing Arts Centre. For schedules and ticket information, call ☎ 407/896-2451.

The **Orlando Broadway Series** brings

Time-Savers

The Orlando Peabody, a major player in the local arts scene, offers packages that include accommodations and admissions to many of the city's hottest, hard-to-get tickets. Call ☎ 800/ **PEABODY** or 407/ 352-4000 for details.

in international stars and shows for week-long runs at the Bob Carr Performing Arts Centre. For information, call ☎ **800/448-6322** from within Florida, or 407/423-9999.

The **Orlando Opera Company** presents several major operas each year at the Bob Carr Performing Arts Centre. For information on presentations and tickets, call ☎ **800/336-7372** or 407/426-1700.

The **Orlando Philharmonic Orchestra** performs classics and light classics throughout the year at various venues. For ticket information, call ☎ **407/647-8525.**

Orlando-UCF (University of Central Florida) Shakespeare Festival performs at various times and places indoors and under the stars. Call ☎ **407/245-0985** for details.

The **Southern Ballet Theater** usually performs at the Bob Carr Performing Arts Centre. Tickets are available from Ticketmaster or through the SBT box office at ☎ **407/426-1728.**

What's Going On & How to Get In

If you're already in town, your hotel's concierge will have the latest theater listings and ticket information. Or check the ***Orlando Sentinel,*** especially the Friday edition with its extensive Calendar section.

If you want to get tickets before you arrive, check the *Sentinel's* web site at www.orlandosentinel.com.

Many of the tourist bureaus and information centers listed in chapter 1 will also have information about upcoming performances during the week you plan to come to Orlando. Give them a call, too. National acts and other popular cultural events often sell out long in advance. If you're planning to see something for which you'll need advance tickets, check the section on "Making Reservations & Getting Tickets Ahead of Time" in chapter 4.

Ticketmaster (☎ 407/839-3900) is the best source of tickets for almost all performances, including the blockbuster stars that fill the city's largest stadiums. American Express, MasterCard, and Visa are accepted, and you can call Monday to Friday from 9am to 9pm and on Saturdays and Sundays from 9am to 7pm. Tickets can also be purchased online at www.ticketmaster.com, or you may be able to call a local Ticketmaster number where you live (to avoid the long-distance charges). Ticketmaster outlets are also found at **Gayfers** stores in the Altamonte Mall, Orlando Fashion Square, Florida Mall, and the Volusia Mall in Daytona Beach, as well as at **Blockbuster Music,** 4900 E. Colonial Dr. in Orlando, and 303 E. Altamonte Dr. in Altamonte Springs.

Orlando A to Z:
Facts at Your Fingertips

AAA For emergency road service, call ☎ **800/222-4357;** for other services, call ☎ **800/926-4222.**

American Express There's an office providing travel services in the Sun Bank Center, downtown at 2 Church St. (☎ **407/843-0004;** www. americanexpress.com/travel). If you lose American Express traveler's checks, call ☎ **800/221-7282.**

Baby-sitters Check with your hotel or **American Childcare Services** (☎ 407/354-0082), **Anny's Nannys** (☎ 407/370-4577), **Kid's Konvention** (☎ 407/897-5437), **KinderCare** (☎ 407/827-5444), or **Super Sitters, Inc.** (☎ 407/944-1557). The going rate is $9 per hour for the first child, $10 per hour for two children, $11 for three, and $14 hourly for four. Usually a minimum of 4 hours, including the sitter's travel time, is required. Advance notice of at least 24 hours is recommended. For baby equipment rental, try **All About Kids** (☎ 407/812-9300).

Camera Repair Try **Colonial Photo & Hobby,** 634 N. Mills Ave. (☎ **407/841-1485**), or **Leonard Chapman Studio Equipment,** 9460 Delegates Dr. (☎ **407/856-8252**).

Doctors For non-emergencies, try **Orlando Regional Walk-In Medical Care** (☎ 407/841-5111), **Housemed/Mediclinic** (☎ 407/396-1195), **Mainstreet Physicians** (☎ 407/238-1009), or **Buena Vista Walk-In Center–Centra Care** (☎ 407/239-7777). Your hotel may also have a list of recommended local doctors on call.

Emergencies Dial ☎ **911** for police, fire, and medical emergencies.

Information   See chapter 1 for numbers and addresses to contact when making plans and reservations from home. Once you're in Orlando, get visitor information from the **Orlando/Orange County Convention & Visitor Bureau** (☎ 407/363-5871), the **Walt Disney World Company** (☎ 407/934-7639), or the **Kissimmee–St. Cloud Convention & Visitors Bureau** (☎ 407/847-5000).

Liquor Laws   The drinking age in Florida is 21 and if you look even remotely under 30, you'll be carded everywhere, including supermarkets. Liquor laws vary slightly among counties and the city of Orlando. No alcohol is served in the Magic Kingdom, but drinks are available in most restaurants in Epcot and Disney-MGM Studios. Liquor can be served until 2 or 3am, although some clubs stay open later. It's illegal to consume alcohol on the street or in a vehicle. Alcohol is generally available from room service until 3am.

Newspapers   The *Orlando Sentinel* is published every day and is found throughout the city in coin-operated machines and hotel newsstands. It's available online at www.orlandosentinel.com. Its Calendar section, published Fridays, is the visitor's best guide to restaurants, attractions, and events. Also pick up free publications, guides, and coupon books found at hotel desks, fuel stations, and supermarkets. Titles include *See*, *TV & Visitor's Guide*, and *On the Go*.

Rest Rooms   Clean, safe public toilets are found in all the theme parks, supermarkets, large stand-alone stores (Target, Kmart), and shopping malls. Along the interstates, rest areas are clearly marked according to whether they have rest rooms and 24-hour security. Each interstate and turnpike exit has signs pointing to fuel and food stops, which have rest rooms.

Safety   Orlando visitors, surrounded by good times and magic, too often let down their guard. Maintain all the same precautions you would in any large city. Lock your hotel room door, even if you'll be gone only a minute to get ice. Check the peephole before opening the door. Use the security lock. Don't invite strangers to your room, or admit people you met at the pool or playground. Keep the key handy at your bedside in case you have to leave the room for a fire alarm. If you're driven back by the fire, your room may be your only safe haven. Park in safe, lighted areas and check the back seat and under the car before getting in. Keep car doors locked. A cell phone is always a safety plus when you're on the road; keep track of where you are in case you need to summon help.

Taxes   Sales taxes of 6 to 7%, depending on the county, apply to all purchases except food and prescriptions. They are also charged on restaurant meals. Hotels rooms are taxed at 11 to 12% in most counties.

Taxis   Cabs are readily available at the airports, train stations, and bus stations, and at major hotels, but cannot be hailed on the street. Call **Yellow Cab** at ☎ **407/699-9999** or **Luxury Cab** at ☎ **407/855-1111.** Cab fare is $2.75 for the first mile and $1.50 each additional mile.

Transit Info   To arrange a trip to outlying attractions including Kennedy Space Center, Cypress Gardens, or Busch Gardens Tampa, call **Mears Transportation Group** at ☎ **407/423-5566.** For local bus information, call **Lynx** at ☎ **407/841-2279.**

Video Camera Rental   Camcorders can be rented by the day at Epcot and Disney-MGM Studios. Or try **Videotourist** at ☎ **407/363-7062**.

Wheelchair and Scooter Rentals   These are available from Care Medical Equipment (☎ **800/741-2282** or 407/856-2273).

Handy Toll-Free Numbers for Airlines, Car Rental Agencies & Hotel Chains

Airlines

Air Canada
☎ 800/776-3000
www.aircanada.ca

Airtran Airways
☎ 800/247-8726
or 407/859-1579

Alaska Airlines
☎ 800/426-0333
www.alaskaair.com

America West Airlines
☎ 800/235-9292
www.americawest.com

American Airlines
☎ 800/433-7300
www.americanair.com

British Airways
☎ 800/247-9297
☎ 0345/222-111 in Britain
www.british-airways.com

Canadian Airlines International
☎ 800/426-7000
www.cdair.ca

Carnival Airlines
☎ 800/824-7386
www.carnivalair.com

Continental Airlines
☎ 800/525-0280
www.flycontinental.com

Delta Air Lines
☎ 800/221-1212
www.delta-air.com

Kiwi International Air Lines
☎ 800/538-5494
www.jetkiwi.com

Martinair Holland
☎ 800/627-8462
or 407/977-0408

Northwest Airlines
☎ 800/225-2525
www.nwa.com

Southwest Airlines
☎ 800/435-9792
www.iflyswa.com

Tower Air
☎ 800/34-TOWER (800/348-6937) outside New York, or
☎ 718/553-8500 in New York
www.towerair.com

Trans World Airlines (TWA)
☎ 800/221-2000
www2.twa.com

United Airlines
☎ 800/241-6522
www.ual.com

US Airways
☎ 800/428-4322
www.usairways.com

Virgin Atlantic Airways
☎ 800/862-8621 in the Continental U.S.
☎ 0293/747-747 in Britain
www.fly.virgin.com

Car-Rental Agencies
Advantage
☎ 800/777-5500
www.arac.com

Alamo
☎ 800/327-9633
www.goalamo.com

Avis
☎ 800/331-1212 in the Continental U.S.
☎ 800/TRY-AVIS in Canada
www.avis.com

Budget
☎ 800/527-0700
www.budgetrentacar.com

Dollar
☎ 800/800-4000

Enterprise
☎ 800/325-8007

Hertz
☎ 800/654-3131
www.hertz.com

National
☎ 800/CAR-RENT
www.nationalcar.com

Payless
☎ 800/PAYLESS
www.paylesscar.com

Rent-A-Wreck
☎ 800/535-1391
rent-a-wreck.com

Thrifty
☎ 800/367-2277
www.thrifty.com

Value
☎ 800/327-2501
www.go-value.com

Major Hotel & Motel Chains
Best Western International
☎ 800/528-1234
www.bestwestern.com

Clarion Hotels
☎ 800/CLARION
www.hotelchoice.com/
cgi-bin/res/webres?clarion.html

Comfort Inns
☎ 800/228-5150
www.hotelchoice.com/
cgi-bin/res/webres?comfort.html

Courtyard by Marriott
☎ 800/321-2211
www.courtyard.com

Days Inn
☎ 800/325-2525
www.daysinn.com

Doubletree Hotels
☎ 800/222-TREE
www.doubletreehotels.com

Econo Lodges
☎ 800/55-ECONO
www.hotelchoice.com/
cgi-bin/res/webres?econo.html

259

Fairfield Inn by Marriott
☎ 800/228-2800
www.fairfieldinn.com

Hampton Inn
☎ 800/HAMPTON
www.hampton-inn.com

Hilton Hotels
☎ 800/HILTONS
www.hilton.com

Holiday Inn
☎ 800/HOLIDAY
www.holiday-inn.com

Howard Johnson
☎ 800/654-2000
www.hojo.com/hojo.html

Hyatt Hotels & Resorts
☎ 800/228-9000
www.hyatt.com

ITT Sheraton
☎ 800/325-3535
www.sheraton.com

Marriott Hotels
☎ 800/228-9290
www.marriott.com

Motel 6
☎ 800/4-MOTEL6 (800/466-8536)

Quality Inns
☎ 800/228-5151
www.hotelchoice.com/
cgi-bin/res/webres?quality.html

Radisson Hotels International
☎ 800/333-3333
www.radisson.com

Ramada Inns
☎ 800/2-RAMADA
www.ramada.com

Red Roof Inns
☎ 800/843-7663
www.redroof.com

Residence Inn by Marriott
☎ 800/331-3131
www.residenceinn.com

Rodeway Inns
☎ 800/228-2000
www.hotelchoice.com/
cgi-bin/res/webres?rodeway.html

Super 8 Motels
☎ 800/800-8000
www.super8motels.com

Travelodge
☎ 800/255-3050

Index

265

269

X-Y-Z